Dave Muller

Comparing the Gospels

A Study Guide

David G. Muller, Jr.

Editor

Rockbridge Books

Lexington, Virginia

All rights reserved. No part of this book may be used or reproduced by any means, graphic, electronic, or mechanical, including photocopying, recording, taping, or by any information storage and retrieval system without the written permission of the editor except in the case of brief quotations embodied in books, articles, and reviews.

Scriptures taken from the Holy Bible, New International Version®, NIV®
Copyright © 1973, 1978, 1984, 2011 by Biblica, Inc.®
Used by permission. All rights reserved worldwide.

Copyright © 2016 by David G. Muller, Jr.

Published in 2016 by Rockbridge Books, Lexington, Virginia (rockbridgebooks0@gmail.com)

Printed by CreateSpace, An Amazon.com Company

Muller, David G., Jr., 1948 –

Comparing the Gospels: A Study Guide

ISBN 978-1537046433

EAN 1537046438

Also by David G. Muller, Jr.

Testing the Apocalypse: A History of the Book of Revelation

China as a Maritime Power

China as a Maritime Power: The Early Years, 1945-1983

COMPARING THE GOSPELS

A guide for students of the Bible

that places parallel passages of the Gospels

side by side for comparison, study, and understanding

Scriptural passages are from the

New International Version®

COMPARING THE GOSPELS
A STUDY GUIDE

CONTENTS

INTRODUCTION   Page xiii

1. INTRODUCTORY MATERIALS   Page 1
     a. Gospel Prologues
     b. Genealogies of Jesus

2. BIRTH AND CHILDHOOD   Page 5
     a. Announcements to Mary and Joseph
     b. The Nativity
     c. The Boyhood of Jesus

3. JOHN THE BAPTIST   Page 10
     a. Introduction of John the Baptist
     b. Jesus as Related to John the Baptist
     c. The Death of John the Baptist

4. BEGINNINGS OF MINISTRY   Page 16
     a. The Baptism of Jesus
     b. Jesus Begins His Ministry
     c. Jesus Tempted in the Wilderness

5. THE DISCIPLES   Page 22
     a. Jesus Gathers His First Disciples
     b. Jesus Calls Matthew (Levi)
     c. Named and Unnamed Disciples
     d. Jesus Sends Out His Disciples
     e. Expect to Be Persecuted
     f. The Costs of Discipleship
     g. Who Is the Greatest Disciple?
     h. The Death of Judas

6. Healings and Resuscitations — Page 36
    a. Various Healings
    b. Healing a Leper
    c. A Centurion's Faith
    d. Pick Up Your Mat and Walk
    e. Resuscitations
    f. Jesus Heals the Blind
    g. Jesus Heals a Shriveled Hand
    h. Healings at Gennesaret

7. Exorcisms — Page 48
    a. Jesus Casts Out a Demon
    b. The Gerasene Swine
    c. Driving Out Demons
    d. Jesus Heals a Demon-Possessed Girl
    e. Jesus Drives Out a Boy's Demon
    f. Others Driving Out Demons

8. Supernatural Actions — Page 57
    a. Jesus Calms the Storm
    b. A Prodigious Catch of Fish
    c. Feeding the 5,000
    d. Jesus Walks on Water
    e. Feeding the 4,000

9. Parables — Page 64
    a. About Parables
    b. Parable of the Sower
    c. Parable of the Mustard Seed
    d. Parable of the Yeast
    e. Parable of the Lost Sheep
    f. Parable of the Two Sons
    g. Parable of the Banquet
    h. Parable of the Talents

10. PROPER ACTIONS AND ATTITUDES   Page 76
    a. The Beatitudes
    b. The Salt of the Earth
    c. Resolving Grievances
    d. Avoiding Temptation
    e. Divorce
    f. Love Your Enemies
    g. The Lord's Prayer
    h. Forgiveness
    i. Treasure in Heaven
    j. Serving Two Masters
    k. Do Not Worry
    l. Do Not Judge
    m. Prayer
    n. Do Unto Others
    o. The Narrow Gate
    p. Building on Rock
    q. Fasting
    r. That Which Defiles
    s. Dealing with Sin
    t. Let the Children Come
    u. The Eye of the Needle
    v. Render unto Caesar
    w. Marriage at the Resurrection
    x. The Greatest Commandments
    y. The Widow's Mite

11. CURSES AND IMPRECATIONS   Page 104
    a. Known by Their Fruit
    b. The Sign of Jonah
    c. Yeast of the Pharisees
    d. Cleansing the Temple
    e. Jesus Curses the Fig Tree
    f. Woe to Pharisees and Teachers of the Law

12. THE END TIMES   Page 113
    a. End Times: Only the Father Knows When
    b. End Times: the Temple
    c. End Times: Deception

    d. End Times: Persecution
    e. End Times: Hurry!
    f. End Times: False Messiahs
    g. End Times: Keep Watch
    h. End Times: Son of Man Comes
    i. End Times: the Fig Tree
    j. End Times: As in the Days of Noah

13. THE NATURE OF CHRIST   Page 123
    a. The Fulfillment of the Law and Prophets
    b. The Light
    c. Teaching with Authority
    d. Did Jesus Consider Himself the Messiah?
    e. Father and Son
    f. The Lord of the Sabbath
    g. Jesus Fulfills Isaiah's Prophecy
    h. The Unforgiveable Sin
    i. Giving Signs
    j. Who Are My Mother and Brothers?
    k. A Prophet Not Honored in His Home Town
    l. Who Do You Say I Am?
    m. The Transfiguration
    n. The Son of Man Came to Serve
    o. Priests Question the Authority of Jesus
    p. Jesus as David's Son

14. TRIAL, CRUCIFIXION, RESURRECTION   Page 145
    a. Jesus Predicts His Death
    b. Jesus Enters Jerusalem
    c. A Lament for Jerusalem
    d. Plotting Against Jesus
    e. Jesus Is Anointed
    f. Judas Betrays Jesus
    g. On What Day Was the Crucifixion?
    h. The Last Supper
    i. Jesus Predicts the Apostles' Denials
    j. Jesus Prays in Gethsemane
    k. Jesus Is Arrested

    l. Jesus Before the Sanhedrin
    m. Peter Denies Jesus
    n. Jesus Before Pilate
    o. Jesus Is Crucified
    p. The Death of Jesus
    q. The Burial of Jesus
    r. The Empty Tomb
    s. Post-Resurrection Appearances

INDEXES   **Page 182**

ABOUT THE EDITOR   **Page 191**

INTRODUCTION

Imagine a serious traffic accident has occurred at an intersection in town. While ambulances and tow trucks do their jobs, an investigating officer approaches the bystanders on the street corners. To her satisfaction, she finds four witnesses who saw the event and are ready to give their statements. Interviewing them separately, the investigator finds – as usual – that the four accounts differ from one another. One remembers a detail the others did not mention; one makes a mistake the others do not; one is sure of something that another confidently states happened in a different way. But it's far from hopeless: often two witnesses, three, or even all four agree on a certain aspect of the account. The experienced investigator is able to weave the four witnesses' accounts into a coherent story that is probably true – or as close to the truth as it will be possible to get. She is not frustrated by the inconsistencies in the witnesses' accounts; in fact, if all four witnesses agreed on every detail, she would suspect collusion among them.

This is where the Bible reader stands when considering the Gospels. There are four witnesses to the life, words, and works of Jesus of Nazareth: we know them as Matthew, Mark, Luke, and John. Few if any of the four were *eye*witnesses, but their accounts are plausible, credible, and largely – not entirely – consistent. This means, of course, that they tell many of the same stories about Jesus, but from different perspectives, and perhaps using different sources of information.

The reader of the Gospels knows this. Having finished Matthew's Gospel, the reader goes into Mark and before long begins to recognize accounts of episodes that he remembers from Matthew. He goes on into Luke, and finds many more familiar stories; the reader then gets to John's Gospel and the echoes are less frequent but still numerous. The reader realizes there is a four-fold story in the Gospels, but which details agree? Which differ? What Gospel adds details the others omit? It is tedious to make exact comparisons, so few people bother doing so.

In this book, we will take on the role of the investigator in the word-picture above. We have our four plausible witnesses to Jesus, we recognize they tell many of the same stories, but that there are differences among them. We will identify these parallel passages and lay them side by side so we can compare them in detail. Relieved of the burden of finding all the passages, then flipping Bible pages back and forth among two, three, or all four of the

Gospels, we can focus on what each witness has to report. As a rule, we will end up with a more complete picture of each episode, as details from each can often be added together. We will also find some sources of perplexity, however, where two or more of the Gospel witnesses tell inconsistent stories, even some where it appears that not all the accounts of a particular episode can possibly be true. Just as the investigator has to decide to discount one witness's detail, or just "live with" an unresolved inconsistency, the reader of this book will find it necessary to decide what to make of conflicting pieces of evidence.

Bible study leaders and students should find this approach intellectually challenging and a welcome variation from classic book-of-the-Bible studies. Pastors developing a sermon on a particular theme, or seminary students, should also find it useful to have at their fingertips all the Gospel passages that report on an episode in Christ's ministry.

How Extensive and Significant are the Gospel Comparisons?

Granted it may be instructive to compare parallel passages of the Gospels, but how many such comparisons are there? A few words of definition are in order before considering the numbers and proportions. In this book, comparisons, or types of comparability, fall into two categories:

- *Literary derivation.* It is evident when studying certain passages in different Gospels that one is derived from another. In some cases, a passage has been copied nearly verbatim from one Gospel into another. Passages from Mark copied into Matthew are the most common appearance of this case. In other cases, two or more passages are so similar to each other that it is clear that one is an edited version of another.
- *Same topic.* In these cases, two or more Gospel passages discuss the same subject or episode, but in words that are quite different.

This book identifies 122 comparisons for study. That is, close reading of the Gospels revealed *122 sets of parallel passages that were either literarily derived from one another or addressed the same subject or episode*. (The sets are listed as the table of contents; citations of passages in each set appear in the indexes.) These comparative sets consist of passages from two, three, or all four Gospels. A small number of other comparisons among the Gospels are possible, but they were omitted from this volume as being too brief or inconsequential for study – often just transitional bridges from one episode to another.

One might expect that comparative sets drawn from just two Gospels would be the most common, sets drawn from all four relatively rare. This is not the case, however. Of the 122 comparative sets of passages, 59 (or 48 percent) drew from all four Gospels; 41 sets (34 percent) drew from three Gospels, and only 22 sets (18 percent) drew from just two of the Gospels. It will not surprise experienced Bible readers that by far most of the two-Gospel sets drew from Matthew and Luke (18 of the 22 sets). These statistics are interesting in a way, but their *significance is that comparative study of parallel Gospel passages has a rich collection of material to work with.*

Are these comparative sets of passages an important part of the Gospel texts, or just some minor curiosities? In fact, it is no exaggeration to say that *most* of the volume of the Gospels falls into one or another of the 122 comparative sets, even including the Gospel of John, an outlier in so many other respects.

As the earliest of the Gospels, and a primary source for Matthew and Luke, it is no surprise that 95 percent of the text of Mark (by English-language word count) appears in one comparative set or another. Not far behind are the other Synoptic Gospels: Matthew with 88 percent and Luke with 82 percent of their texts appearing in one or more comparative sets. Most surprising to readers familiar with the Gospels will be the fact that fully 70 percent of the text of the Gospel of John appears in the 122 comparative sets of parallel passages. Granted, few passages in John are *literary derivations* of passages in the Synoptics; most, however, do address the *same subjects* or episodes that are reported in the Synoptic Gospels.

Considered from another perspective, only 5 percent of Mark is *not* reflected one way or another in one or more of the other Gospels. Only 12 percent of Matthew and 18 percent of Luke are *not* reflected elsewhere. And even in the outlier Gospel of John, only 30 percent of its text is *not* reflected in one or more of the Synoptic Gospels.

Again, these statistics themselves may be interesting to those of a quantitative bent, but their *significance for all Bible readers is this: comparative analysis of parallel passages is an approach that can yield a valid new perspective on these core books of the New Testament.*

What Kind of Writings Are the Gospels?

In seeking to better understand the Gospels by comparing parallel passages in them, it is useful to consider just what kind of literature they are. This will help us grapple with the differences we will find as we examine each set of passages. Some thoughts about what the Gospels are, and what they are not:
- The Gospels contain historical information, but they are not histories.
- The Gospels contain statements of theological significance, but they are not theological treatises.

- The Gospels contain quotations plausibly attributable to Jesus, the disciples, Pilate, and others, but they are not verbatim transcripts.
- The Gospels contain accounts of some events on which no one who was present reported, but they are not works of fiction.
- The Gospels most resemble biographies as written in Greco-Roman antiquity, but they are not quite the same and certainly differ from biographies as written today.

The reader must avoid forcing the Gospels into any of these five molds: history, theology, transcripts, fiction, or biography. The Gospels should be approached on their own terms, and evaluated with an open mind.

Is Any Particular Gospel More Credible Than Others?

All four Gospels are established in the New Testament canon, but as we compare passages in one with those of another, should we bear in mind that one might be more credible than others when we find differences between them? Entire books have been written on topics related to this question, and this is not the place to reconstruct their research, analysis, and theories. Here are some key points for consideration, however.

The first step in answering the question is to consider who wrote the Gospels. We may think we know the answer: Matthew, Mark, Luke, and John. Consider, however, that none of the Gospels tells us who its author is; they are all anonymous. When each was originally written, copied, and passed along, no doubt the early recipients knew who its author was; but this knowledge has long been lost. Our present author attributions were first put into writing – as far as we know – by the early Church father Irenaeus … but not until nearly 200 A.D.! Perhaps Irenaeus had impeccable sources for his attributions of Gospel authorship, but if so, he did not mention them and they have been lost.

We are compelled to look at indirect evidence, then, and to make what judgments we can. As we have no better names to assign to the Gospels, we will continue to refer to them by their traditional author attributions.

- Scholars find a number of factors in Mark that lend some credence to the traditional idea that Peter's associate John Mark is in fact the book's author. We can have only low to medium confidence in this assessment, but no better information is available.
- There is no credible evidence that the disciple Matthew was, or was not, the author of the Gospel that bears his name. Scholars have long asked why – if the Gospel was in fact written by the apostle Matthew – it depends so heavily on Mark's text and the "Q" source (see below) and is relatively meager in original material. So Matthew may have been the author, but we have no persuasive reason to say so.

- As with Mark, there is inconclusive but plausible evidence that the traditional identification of the physician Luke as the author of that Gospel (as well as the book of Acts) is valid. As Luke's preface says, he did not know Jesus personally but rather sought and evaluated a variety of historical sources about him to write his Gospel. This preface lends credence to the identity of Luke as the book's author, but we can have only low to medium confidence in that conclusion.
- It is most *unlikely* that the apostle John son of Zebedee wrote the Gospel according to John. John would have been quite elderly in 90 A.D., when life expectancy was about 50, not to mention the persistent but inconclusive reports of his martyrdom decades earlier. There is a plausible case that the Gospel was written by another man named John, known locally in Ephesus as John the Elder, who probably wrote the letters 1, 2, and 3 John (note how the author of those letters identifies himself – as the "Elder," not as the apostle). There is even a tantalizing theory that the Gospel of John was written by the risen Lazarus, whom some scholars have identified as the "disciple whom Jesus loved." So we conclude with low confidence that John the Elder was the author of this Gospel, while allowing for the possibility it was Lazarus.
- An important factor standing against Matthew, Mark, and John as being the actual authors of the Gospels attributed to them is the fact that they were all poorly educated speakers of Aramaic, while "their" gospels are written in competent Greek. Luke, a Gentile physician, no doubt was proficient in Greek.

These may be fascinating lines of inquiry, but it is enough for present purposes to re-state that *we simply do not have a firm grip on who actually wrote any of the Gospels.*

We do have a good idea of *when* each Gospel was written, however. Mark was written about the year 65, Matthew and Luke about 75, and John in about 90. Each date may be off by five years, perhaps even by ten. (Note that Paul wrote most or all of his letters before any of the Gospels appeared.)

- So if Mark was written closest to Jesus' lifetime, should we place the greatest confidence in it? Its early date does stand in Mark's favor, but without knowing what source material the author of Mark worked from, a definitive judgment is not possible.
- Matthew and Luke made use of some 95 percent of the text of Mark in their Gospels, though as you will note in this volume they often edited or expanded Mark's text, presumably in light of other source material. Matthew and Luke also both had access to an early collection of Jesus' sayings (now lost, but known to scholars as "Q"). Both Matthew and Luke separately discovered and included in their Gospels this additional Q material that appears nowhere else. It must also be admitted as logically possible that one or both enhanced their source material by creating text that made a

point better than what their sources provided; this is particularly plausible in passages that reflect upon Jesus' divinity, where neither Mark nor Q has a great deal to say on the subject.

- Together, Matthew, Mark, and Luke constitute the Synoptic triad of Gospels and as becomes clear by comparing their parallel passages they share a great deal of material. The Gospel of John is different. Because it omits so much Synoptic material but includes material of which the Synoptics seem to be ignorant, many scholars discount John as a useful source of historically valid information. Their rationales are not convincing, however. A plausible, traditional explanation for the Gospel's uniqueness is that John probably read the Synoptics, did not repeat information he thought they had reported accurately, and concentrated on information and insights he alone had. Another line of analysis suggests that the content of John is quite different from that of the Synoptics because the author of the Gospel was not a witness to most of the events described in the Synoptics (and thus was not one of the Twelve). The theory that the author of John's Gospel was Lazarus, the beloved disciple, provides grist for *speculation* about unique things the author knew because of his special relationship with Jesus.

In assessing which variant of a Gospel episode is more likely to be true, it may be tempting to "take a vote" among the four: Matthew, Mark, and Luke say X, while John says Y, therefore it is more likely that X is true. As will become apparent in this study, however, when Matthew, Mark, and Luke agree on an account, it is usually because Matthew and Luke read Mark's account and used it. Thus, instead of a three-to-one majority, we have a one-to-one tie in any such "vote." The lesson here is to consider the parallel passages in each set on their own merits and avoid simplistic analysis.

Readers of the Gospels have long noted that the later a Gospel was written, the more exalted a view of the divinity of Jesus it contains. In Mark, for example, the disciples often seem to have little clue about the full nature of Jesus, and the narrative itself is sparing: no virgin birth is mentioned and in the original there are no post-Resurrection appearances reported. Matthew and Luke, in contrast, make the divinity of Jesus abundantly clear, while John goes so far as to identify Jesus with God himself. Some scholars say that Mark had the Gospel story fairly straight, while the others embellished it with pious fabrications and therefore their accounts should be considered more questionable.

This interpretation is plausible, but at least three important factors weigh against it. Recall that Paul wrote his letters before any of the Gospels were composed, and yet he takes a very high view of Christ's divinity; so a high view goes back to early times. Second, the three later Gospels probably had access to considerably more source information than Mark did. Third, Christians in the decades after the Resurrection engaged in intensive consideration of just what the role and significance of Jesus was. Thus as the first century proceeded, the relevance and meaning of some of Jesus' words and actions were seen in an ever-clearer light, accounting for the greater theological richness of the later Gospels.

It is commonly held that the books of the Bible are divinely inspired. What might that mean in talking about the Gospels? There is no question that each of the Gospel writers was a believer in Jesus as the Messiah, God's son. Thus it is self-evident that each was thereby inspired to research and write his Gospel. The differences among the Gospels – including some outright contradictions – tell us that divine inspiration does not mean that the authors simply wrote down what God told them; God does not contradict himself. (By contrast, in the Islamic tradition, the angel Gabriel ostensibly dictated God's words to Muhammad, who repeated them verbatim to his followers.) The evidence of the texts themselves, made clearer by comparisons as found in this book, shows that divine inspiration of Scripture does not – necessarily, at least – entail the writers transcribing God's actual words.

Much as it may go against the grain, we cannot logically exclude the possibility that the Gospel writers embellished their accounts here and there with details they believed "must have happened," "probably happened," or that better conveyed what they believed to be an accurate understanding of Christ. This filling-in of gaps was not rare in ancient Greek writings, nor are such embellishments, if they occurred, necessarily false. Recall that the Gospels are not histories, journalism, or transcripts written to modern standards; we must accept them on their own terms.

On Contradictions in the Gospels

One could go through this book with a red pen and mark the many differences in parallel Gospel accounts as "contradictions," then toss the Gospels aside as an untenable basis for trust and faith. Indeed, atheists often cite contradictions within the Bible as one of their primary reasons for disbelief. But this is a juvenile and obtuse position to take, lacking in logical or intellectual depth. Let us return to our original example of the traffic accident with four witnesses. When the investigating officer finds that the accounts differ from each other, in some respects even directly contradicting each other, does she abandon her investigation? Of course not.

When we encounter the differences between parallel Gospel accounts – and there are many – we simply have to keep in mind that the Gospel writers did not all have the same information to work with. As Luke says in his preface, they interviewed numerous and different sources – not all of them first-hand witnesses to begin with; they used numerous and different written source documents; they chose what to write about and what to omit; they worked at different times and in different places; and they interpreted all this evidence through the lens of their own understanding. If there *were* no contradictions among the Gospels, then perhaps the atheists might have grounds for doubt about their reliability.

The reader is invited to join the many Bible scholars who wrestle with these questions, in the course of comparing the parallel Gospel passages that follow. This is not the first time anyone has thought to lay down the parallel passages for comparison – some books from the earliest centuries do so – but surprisingly this approach is rare in Bible study today. This volume is meant to fill the gap.

Final Points

Two things this book is *not*. It is not a commentary on the content and meaning of the Gospels. There are many excellent commentaries already available. Nor is this book a Gospel harmony. Harmonies weave the four Gospels together into a single composite document. Perhaps there is value in a Gospel harmony, but they obscure the unique perspectives of each witness and preclude comparison of varying accounts of the same episode. This is not to mention their presumption in editing Scripture, retaining some bits while discarding others.

The discussion questions posed at the end of each set pertain to comparative aspects of the passages, not to their full meaning. It remains for the Bible study leader, the preacher, or the seminary student to do any necessary research in commentaries or other references.

As in all Bible study, context is always important for sound interpretation. Readers will often find it useful to go to the passages in their Bibles and consider the full contexts in which they appear.

David G. Muller, Jr.
Lexington, Virginia
dgmullerjr@gmail.com
October 2016

Chapter 1: Introductory Materials

1.a Gospel Prologues

MATTHEW
1:1 This is the genealogy of Jesus the Messiah the son of David, the son of Abraham:
MARK
1:1 The beginning of the good news about Jesus the Messiah, the Son of God, ² as it is written in Isaiah the prophet: "I will send my messenger ahead of you, who will prepare your way"— ³ "a voice of one calling in the wilderness, 'Prepare the way for the Lord, make straight paths for him.'" ⁴ And so John the Baptist appeared in the wilderness, preaching a baptism of repentance for the forgiveness of sins. ⁵ The whole Judean countryside and all the people of Jerusalem went out to him. Confessing their sins, they were baptized by him in the Jordan River. ⁶ John wore clothing made of camel's hair, with a leather belt around his waist, and he ate locusts and wild honey. ⁷ And this was his message: "After me comes the one more powerful than I, the straps of whose sandals I am not worthy to stoop down and untie. ⁸ I baptize you with water, but he will baptize you with the Holy Spirit."
LUKE
1:1 Many have undertaken to draw up an account of the things that have been fulfilled among us, ² just as they were handed down to us by those who from the first were eyewitnesses and servants of the word. ³ With this in mind, since I myself have carefully investigated everything from the beginning, I too decided to write an orderly account for you, most excellent Theophilus, ⁴ so that you may know the certainty of the things you have been taught.
JOHN
1:1 In the beginning was the Word, and the Word was with God, and the Word was God. ² He was with God in the beginning. ³ Through him all things were made; without him nothing was made that has been made. ⁴ In him was life, and that life was the light of all mankind. ⁵ The light shines in the darkness, and the darkness has not overcome it. ⁶ There was a man sent from God whose name was John. ⁷ He came as a witness to testify concerning that light, so that through him all might believe. ⁸ He himself was not the light; he came only as a witness to the light. ⁹ The true light that gives light to everyone was coming into the world. ¹⁰ He was in the world, and though the world was made through him, the world did not recognize him. ¹¹ He came to that which was his own, but his own did not receive him. ¹² Yet to all who did receive him, to those who believed in his name, he gave the right to become children of God— ¹³ children born not of natural descent, nor of human decision or a husband's will, but born of God. ¹⁴ The Word became flesh and made his dwelling among us. We have seen his glory, the glory of the one and only Son, who came from the Father, full of grace and truth.

1. We see major differences in the four Gospel witnesses starting from the first words in each. Imagine you were about to read the Gospels seriously for the first time. What impression do you get from each prologue? What expectation does each prologue create?
2. Mark and John – the earliest Gospel and the latest – both evidently consider John the Baptist important enough to introduce him in their first few verses. Why do they feature John so prominently?

3. Are there differences in Mark's and John's introductory words about John the Baptist? What do you make of these differences? Are the descriptions similar in any way?
4. Matthew and Mark explicitly identify Jesus as the Messiah. Is there wording in Luke or John that can be read as making a similar statement?

1.b Genealogies of Jesus

MATTHEW

1:1 This is the genealogy of Jesus the Messiah the son of David, the son of Abraham:
² Abraham was the father of Isaac, Isaac the father of Jacob, Jacob the father of Judah and his brothers, ³ Judah the father of Perez and Zerah, whose mother was Tamar, Perez the father of Hezron, Hezron the father of Ram, ⁴ Ram the father of Amminadab, Amminadab the father of Nahshon, Nahshon the father of Salmon, ⁵ Salmon the father of Boaz, whose mother was Rahab, Boaz the father of Obed, whose mother was Ruth, Obed the father of Jesse, ⁶ and Jesse the father of King David. David was the father of Solomon, whose mother had been Uriah's wife, ⁷ Solomon the father of Rehoboam, Rehoboam the father of Abijah, Abijah the father of Asa, ⁸ Asa the father of Jehoshaphat, Jehoshaphat the father of Jehoram, Jehoram the father of Uzziah, ⁹ Uzziah the father of Jotham, Jotham the father of Ahaz, Ahaz the father of Hezekiah, ¹⁰ Hezekiah the father of Manasseh, Manasseh the father of Amon, Amon the father of Josiah, ¹¹ and Josiah the father of Jeconiah and his brothers at the time of the exile to Babylon.
¹² After the exile to Babylon: Jeconiah was the father of Shealtiel, Shealtiel the father of Zerubbabel, ¹³ Zerubbabel the father of Abihud, Abihud the father of Eliakim, Eliakim the father of Azor, ¹⁴ Azor the father of Zadok, Zadok the father of Akim, Akim the father of Elihud, ¹⁵ Elihud the father of Eleazar, Eleazar the father of Matthan, Matthan the father of Jacob, ¹⁶ and Jacob the father of Joseph, the husband of Mary, and Mary was the mother of Jesus who is called the Messiah.
¹⁷ Thus there were fourteen generations in all from Abraham to David, fourteen from David to the exile to Babylon, and fourteen from the exile to the Messiah.

MARK

LUKE

3:23 Now Jesus himself was about thirty years old when he began his ministry. He was the son, so it was thought, of Joseph, the son of Heli, ²⁴ the son of Matthat, the son of Levi, the son of Melki, the son of Jannai, the son of Joseph, ²⁵ the son of Mattathias, the son of Amos, the son of Nahum, the son of Esli, the son of Naggai, ²⁶ the son of Maath, the son of Mattathias, the son of Semein, the son of Josek, the son of Joda, ²⁷ the son of Joanan, the son of Rhesa, the son of Zerubbabel, the son of Shealtiel, the son of Neri, ²⁸ the son of Melki, the son of Addi, the son of Cosam, the son of Elmadam, the son of Er, ²⁹ the son of Joshua, the son of Eliezer, the son of Jorim, the son of Matthat, the son of Levi, ³⁰ the son of Simeon, the son of Judah, the son of Joseph, the son of Jonam, the son of Eliakim, ³¹ the son of Melea, the son of Menna, the son of Mattatha, the son of Nathan, the son of David, ³² the son of Jesse, the son of Obed, the son of Boaz, the son of Salmon, the son of Nahshon, ³³ the son of Amminadab, the son of Ram, the son of Hezron, the son of Perez, the son of Judah, ³⁴ the son of Jacob, the son of Isaac, the son of Abraham, the son of Terah, the son of Nahor, ³⁵ the son of Serug, the son of Reu, the son of Peleg, the son of Eber, the son of Shelah, ³⁶ the son of Cainan, the son of Arphaxad, the son of Shem, the son of Noah, the son of Lamech, ³⁷ the son of Methuselah, the son of Enoch, the son of Jared, the son of Mahalalel, the son of Kenan, ³⁸ the son of Enosh, the son of Seth, the son of Adam, the son of God.

JOHN

1. As both genealogies indicate, Jesus was not the biological son of Joseph. Why, then, did Matthew and Luke bother tracing Joseph's ancestry? What might their objective have been?

2. Matthew's genealogy begins with Abraham, the father of the Jews, while Luke's goes all the way back to Adam, the first human. Does this difference suggest something about the audience each writer was trying to reach?
3. Despite differences between the genealogies, both clearly note that King David was in the line of ancestry. What would Matthew's and Luke's early readers find significant about this?
4. Both Matthew's and Luke's genealogies contain far fewer generations than that found in 1 Chronicles. Surely this was not an error, but rather an editorial choice that each author made. What explanations for this editorial choice suggest themselves?
5. Mark omits genealogies altogether, simply referring to Jesus as "Mary's son." What might this suggest about Mark's knowledge of Jesus' background?

Chapter 2: Birth and Childhood

2.a Announcements to Mary and Joseph

MATTHEW
1:18 This is how the birth of Jesus the Messiah came about: His mother Mary was pledged to be married to Joseph, but before they came together, she was found to be pregnant through the Holy Spirit. [19] Because Joseph her husband was faithful to the law, and yet did not want to expose her to public disgrace, he had in mind to divorce her quietly. [20] But after he had considered this, an angel of the Lord appeared to him in a dream and said, "Joseph son of David, do not be afraid to take Mary home as your wife, because what is conceived in her is from the Holy Spirit. [21] She will give birth to a son, and you are to give him the name Jesus, because he will save his people from their sins." [22] All this took place to fulfill what the Lord had said through the prophet: [23] "The virgin will conceive and give birth to a son, and they will call him Immanuel" (which means "God with us"). [24] When Joseph woke up, he did what the angel of the Lord had commanded him and took Mary home as his wife. [25] But he did not consummate their marriage until she gave birth to a son. And he gave him the name Jesus.

MARK

LUKE
1:26 In the sixth month of Elizabeth's pregnancy, God sent the angel Gabriel to Nazareth, a town in Galilee, [27] to a virgin pledged to be married to a man named Joseph, a descendant of David. The virgin's name was Mary. [28] The angel went to her and said, "Greetings, you who are highly favored! The Lord is with you." [29] Mary was greatly troubled at his words and wondered what kind of greeting this might be. [30] But the angel said to her, "Do not be afraid, Mary; you have found favor with God. [31] You will conceive and give birth to a son, and you are to call him Jesus. [32] He will be great and will be called the Son of the Most High. The Lord God will give him the throne of his father David, [33] and he will reign over Jacob's descendants forever; his kingdom will never end." [34] "How will this be," Mary asked the angel, "since I am a virgin?" [35] The angel answered, "The Holy Spirit will come on you, and the power of the Most High will overshadow you. So the holy one to be born will be called the Son of God. [36] Even Elizabeth your relative is going to have a child in her old age, and she who was said to be unable to conceive is in her sixth month. [37] For no word from God will ever fail." [38] "I am the Lord's servant," Mary answered. "May your word to me be fulfilled." Then the angel left her. [39] At that time Mary got ready and hurried to a town in the hill country of Judea, [40] where she entered Zechariah's home and greeted Elizabeth. [41] When Elizabeth heard Mary's greeting, the baby leaped in her womb, and Elizabeth was filled with the Holy Spirit. [42] In a loud voice she exclaimed: "Blessed are you among women, and blessed is the child you will bear! [43] But why am I so favored, that the mother of my Lord should come to me? [44] As soon as the sound of your greeting reached my ears, the baby in my womb leaped for joy. [45] Blessed is she who has believed that the Lord would fulfill his promises to her!" [46] And Mary said: "My soul glorifies the Lord [47] and my spirit rejoices in God my Savior, [48] for he has been mindful of the humble state of his servant. From now on all generations will call me blessed, [49] for the Mighty One has done great things for me—holy is his name. [50] His mercy extends to those who fear him, from generation to generation. [51] He has performed mighty deeds with his arm; he has scattered those who are proud in their inmost thoughts. [52] He has brought down rulers from their thrones but has lifted up the humble. [53] He has filled the hungry with good things but has sent the rich away empty. [54] He has helped his servant Israel, remembering to be merciful [55] to Abraham and his descendants forever, just as he promised our ancestors."

> [56] Mary stayed with Elizabeth for about three months and then returned home.

JOHN

1. Matthew's shorter account describes the news about Jesus' birth as given to Joseph, while Mary is mentioned only in passing. Luke's account, in contrast, barely mentions Joseph and focuses instead on Mary. What do we make of this difference?
2. Does Joseph's reaction seem realistic to you? Does Mary's? Do Matthew, and especially Luke, have points to make beyond historical reporting?
3. The fathering of Jesus by the Holy Spirit, rather than by Joseph, is commonly accepted among Christians as an important aspect of Christ's identity. Where else in the New Testament is the virgin birth discussed, or referred to? What do we make of Paul's statement at Romans 1:3-4?
4. Matthew refers to Isaiah 7:14 as prophesying the Messiah's virgin birth. Read the verse in Isaiah in context, in more than one translation, if available.

2.b The Nativity

MATTHEW
1:24 When Joseph woke up, he did what the angel of the Lord had commanded him and took Mary home as his wife. [25] But he did not consummate their marriage until she gave birth to a son. And he gave him the name Jesus. 2:1 After Jesus was born in Bethlehem in Judea, during the time of King Herod, Magi from the east came to Jerusalem [2] and asked, "Where is the one who has been born king of the Jews? We saw his star when it rose and have come to worship him." [3] When King Herod heard this he was disturbed, and all Jerusalem with him. [4] When he had called together all the people's chief priests and teachers of the law, he asked them where the Messiah was to be born. [5] "In Bethlehem in Judea," they replied, "for this is what the prophet has written: [6] "'But you, Bethlehem, in the land of Judah, are by no means least among the rulers of Judah; for out of you will come a ruler who will shepherd my people Israel.'" [7] Then Herod called the Magi secretly and found out from them the exact time the star had appeared. [8] He sent them to Bethlehem and said, "Go and search carefully for the child. As soon as you find him, report to me, so that I too may go and worship him." [9] After they had heard the king, they went on their way, and the star they had seen when it rose went ahead of them until it stopped over the place where the child was. [10] When they saw the star, they were overjoyed. [11] On coming to the house, they saw the child with his mother Mary, and they bowed down and worshiped him. Then they opened their treasures and presented him with gifts of gold, frankincense and myrrh. [12] And having been warned in a dream not to go back to Herod, they returned to their country by another route.

MARK

LUKE
2:1 In those days Caesar Augustus issued a decree that a census should be taken of the entire Roman world. [2] (This was the first census that took place while Quirinius was governor of Syria.) [3] And everyone went to their own town to register. [4] So Joseph also went up from the town of Nazareth in Galilee to Judea, to Bethlehem the town of David, because he belonged to the house and line of David. [5] He went there to register with Mary, who was pledged to be married to him and was expecting a child. [6] While they were there, the time came for the baby to be born, [7] and she gave birth to her firstborn, a son. She wrapped him in cloths and placed him in a manger, because there was no guest room available for them. 2:8 And there were shepherds living out in the fields nearby, keeping watch over their flocks at night. [9] An angel of the Lord appeared to them, and the glory of the Lord shone around them, and they were terrified. [10] But the angel said to them, "Do not be afraid. I bring you good news that will cause great joy for all the people. [11] Today in the town of David a Savior has been born to you; he is the Messiah, the Lord. [12] This will be a sign to you: You will find a baby wrapped in cloths and lying in a manger." [13] Suddenly a great company of the heavenly host appeared with the angel, praising God and saying, [14] "Glory to God in the highest heaven, and on earth peace to those on whom his favor rests." [15] When the angels had left them and gone into heaven, the shepherds said to one another, "Let's go to Bethlehem and see this thing that has happened, which the Lord has told us about." [16] So they hurried off and found Mary and Joseph, and the baby, who was lying in the manger. [17] When they had seen him, they spread the word concerning what had been told them about this child, [18] and all who heard it were amazed at what the shepherds said to them. [19] But Mary treasured up all these things and pondered them in her heart. [20] The shepherds returned, glorifying and praising God for all the things they had heard and seen, which were just as they had been told. [21] On the eighth day, when it was time to circumcise the child, he was named Jesus, the name the angel had given

him before he was conceived.
JOHN

1. What facts about the nativity are reported in both Matthew and Luke?
2. Typical modern Christmas scenes of the Nativity show both local shepherds and wise men (magi) from the East gathered around Jesus in the manger. What picture of that first night do you draw based on the accounts in Matthew and Luke?
3. Luke tells of the appearance of singing angels overhead during the nativity, while Matthew is silent on the subject. What do you make of this difference in reporting?
4. As we have seen, there are differences in the nativity accounts of Matthew and Luke, but are there any actual contradictions between them? Could both accounts be completely true?
5. By starting their Gospel accounts with Jesus' baptism as an adult, did Mark and John leave out any key facts necessary for our understanding of Jesus?

2.c. The Boyhood of Jesus

MATTHEW
2:13 When they had gone, an angel of the Lord appeared to Joseph in a dream. "Get up," he said, "take the child and his mother and escape to Egypt. Stay there until I tell you, for Herod is going to search for the child to kill him." [14] So he got up, took the child and his mother during the night and left for Egypt, [15] where he stayed until the death of Herod. And so was fulfilled what the Lord had said through the prophet: "Out of Egypt I called my son." [16] When Herod realized that he had been outwitted by the Magi, he was furious, and he gave orders to kill all the boys in Bethlehem and its vicinity who were two years old and under, in accordance with the time he had learned from the Magi. [17] Then what was said through the prophet Jeremiah was fulfilled: [18] "A voice is heard in Ramah, weeping and great mourning, Rachel weeping for her children and refusing to be comforted, because they are no more." [19] After Herod died, an angel of the Lord appeared in a dream to Joseph in Egypt [20] and said, "Get up, take the child and his mother and go to the land of Israel, for those who were trying to take the child's life are dead." [21] So he got up, took the child and his mother and went to the land of Israel. [22] But when he heard that Archelaus was reigning in Judea in place of his father Herod, he was afraid to go there. Having been warned in a dream, he withdrew to the district of Galilee, [23] and he went and lived in a town called Nazareth. So was fulfilled what was said through the prophets, that he would be called a Nazarene.

MARK

LUKE
2:39 When Joseph and Mary had done everything required by the Law of the Lord, they returned to Galilee to their own town of Nazareth. [40] And the child grew and became strong; he was filled with wisdom, and the grace of God was on him. [41] Every year Jesus' parents went to Jerusalem for the Festival of the Passover. [42] When he was twelve years old, they went up to the festival, according to the custom. [43] After the festival was over, while his parents were returning home, the boy Jesus stayed behind in Jerusalem, but they were unaware of it. [44] Thinking he was in their company, they traveled on for a day. Then they began looking for him among their relatives and friends. [45] When they did not find him, they went back to Jerusalem to look for him. [46] After three days they found him in the temple courts, sitting among the teachers, listening to them and asking them questions. [47] Everyone who heard him was amazed at his understanding and his answers. [48] When his parents saw him, they were astonished. His mother said to him, "Son, why have you treated us like this? Your father and I have been anxiously searching for you." [49] "Why were you searching for me?" he asked. "Didn't you know I had to be in my Father's house?" [50] But they did not understand what he was saying to them. [51] Then he went down to Nazareth with them and was obedient to them. But his mother treasured all these things in her heart. [52] And Jesus grew in wisdom and stature, and in favor with God and man.

JOHN

1. Matthew, alone among the Gospel writers, tells of a flight to Egypt when Jesus was very young. What do you make of Luke and all other New Testament writers omitting this fact from his story?
2. It is interesting to speculate on the sources from which Matthew and Luke learned about the birth and childhood of Jesus. What are your ideas?

Chapter 3: John the Baptist

3.a. The Introduction of John the Baptist

MATTHEW
3:1 In those days John the Baptist came, preaching in the wilderness of Judea ²and saying, "Repent, for the kingdom of heaven has come near." ³ This is he who was spoken of through the prophet Isaiah: "A voice of one calling in the wilderness, 'Prepare the way for the Lord, make straight paths for him.'" ⁴ John's clothes were made of camel's hair, and he had a leather belt around his waist. His food was locusts and wild honey. ⁵ People went out to him from Jerusalem and all Judea and the whole region of the Jordan. ⁶ Confessing their sins, they were baptized by him in the Jordan River. ⁷ But when he saw many of the Pharisees and Sadducees coming to where he was baptizing, he said to them: "You brood of vipers! Who warned you to flee from the coming wrath? ⁸ Produce fruit in keeping with repentance. ⁹ And do not think you can say to yourselves, 'We have Abraham as our father.' I tell you that out of these stones God can raise up children for Abraham. ¹⁰ The ax is already at the root of the trees, and every tree that does not produce good fruit will be cut down and thrown into the fire. ¹¹ "I baptize you with water for repentance. But after me comes one who is more powerful than I, whose sandals I am not worthy to carry. He will baptize you with the Holy Spirit and fire. ¹² His winnowing fork is in his hand, and he will clear his threshing floor, gathering his wheat into the barn and burning up the chaff with unquenchable fire."

MARK
1:1 The beginning of the good news about Jesus the Messiah, the Son of God, ² as it is written in Isaiah the prophet: "I will send my messenger ahead of you, who will prepare your way"—³ "a voice of one calling in the wilderness, 'Prepare the way for the Lord, make straight paths for him.'" ⁴ And so John the Baptist appeared in the wilderness, preaching a baptism of repentance for the forgiveness of sins. ⁵ The whole Judean countryside and all the people of Jerusalem went out to him. Confessing their sins, they were baptized by him in the Jordan River. ⁶ John wore clothing made of camel's hair, with a leather belt around his waist, and he ate locusts and wild honey. ⁷ And this was his message: "After me comes the one more powerful than I, the straps of whose sandals I am not worthy to stoop down and untie. ⁸ I baptize you with water, but he will baptize you with the Holy Spirit."

LUKE
1:57 When it was time for Elizabeth to have her baby, she gave birth to a son. ⁵⁸ Her neighbors and relatives heard that the Lord had shown her great mercy, and they shared her joy. ⁵⁹ On the eighth day they came to circumcise the child, and they were going to name him after his father Zechariah, ⁶⁰ but his mother spoke up and said, "No! He is to be called John." ⁶¹ They said to her, "There is no one among your relatives who has that name." ⁶² Then they made signs to his father, to find out what he would like to name the child. ⁶³ He asked for a writing tablet, and to everyone's astonishment he wrote, "His name is John." ⁶⁴ Immediately his mouth was opened and his tongue set free, and he began to speak, praising God. ⁶⁵ All the neighbors were filled with awe, and throughout the hill country of Judea people were talking about all these things. ⁶⁶ Everyone who heard this wondered about it, asking, "What then is this child going to be?" For the Lord's hand was with him. ⁶⁷ His father Zechariah was filled with the Holy Spirit and prophesied: ⁶⁸ "Praise be to the Lord, the God of Israel, because he has come to his people and redeemed them. ⁶⁹ He has raised up a horn of salvation for us in the house of his servant David ⁷⁰ (as he said through his holy prophets of long ago), ⁷¹ salvation from our enemies and from the hand of all who hate us— ⁷² to show mercy to our

ancestors and to remember his holy covenant, ⁷³ the oath he swore to our father Abraham: ⁷⁴ to rescue us from the hand of our enemies, and to enable us to serve him without fear ⁷⁵ in holiness and righteousness before him all our days.

⁷⁶ And you, my child, will be called a prophet of the Most High; for you will go on before the Lord to prepare the way for him, ⁷⁷ to give his people the knowledge of salvation through the forgiveness of their sins, ⁷⁸ because of the tender mercy of our God, by which the rising sun will come to us from heaven ⁷⁹ to shine on those living in darkness and in the shadow of death, to guide our feet into the path of peace." ⁸⁰ And the child grew and became strong in spirit; and he lived in the wilderness until he appeared publicly to Israel.

* * *

3:1 In the fifteenth year of the reign of Tiberius Caesar—when Pontius Pilate was governor of Judea, Herod tetrarch of Galilee, his brother Philip tetrarch of Iturea and Traconitis, and Lysanias tetrarch of Abilene— ² during the high-priesthood of Annas and Caiaphas, the word of God came to John son of Zechariah in the wilderness. ³ He went into all the country around the Jordan, preaching a baptism of repentance for the forgiveness of sins. ⁴ As it is written in the book of the words of Isaiah the prophet: "A voice of one calling in the wilderness, 'Prepare the way for the Lord, make straight paths for him. ⁵ Every valley shall be filled in, every mountain and hill made low. The crooked roads shall become straight, the rough ways smooth. ⁶ And all people will see God's salvation.'"

⁷ John said to the crowds coming out to be baptized by him, "You brood of vipers! Who warned you to flee from the coming wrath? ⁸ Produce fruit in keeping with repentance. And do not begin to say to yourselves, 'We have Abraham as our father.' For I tell you that out of these stones God can raise up children for Abraham. ⁹ The ax is already at the root of the trees, and every tree that does not produce good fruit will be cut down and thrown into the fire."

¹⁰ "What should we do then?" the crowd asked. ¹¹ John answered, "Anyone who has two shirts should share with the one who has none, and anyone who has food should do the same."

¹² Even tax collectors came to be baptized. "Teacher," they asked, "what should we do?" ¹³ "Don't collect any more than you are required to," he told them. ¹⁴ Then some soldiers asked him, "And what should we do?" He replied, "Don't extort money and don't accuse people falsely—be content with your pay."

¹⁵ The people were waiting expectantly and were all wondering in their hearts if John might possibly be the Messiah. ¹⁶ John answered them all, "I baptize you with water. But one who is more powerful than I will come, the straps of whose sandals I am not worthy to untie. He will baptize you with the Holy Spirit and fire. ¹⁷ His winnowing fork is in his hand to clear his threshing floor and to gather the wheat into his barn, but he will burn up the chaff with unquenchable fire." ¹⁸ And with many other words John exhorted the people and proclaimed the good news to them.

¹⁹ But when John rebuked Herod the tetrarch because of his marriage to Herodias, his brother's wife, and all the other evil things he had done, ²⁰ Herod added this to them all: He locked John up in prison.

JOHN

1:6 There was a man sent from God whose name was John. ⁷ He came as a witness to testify concerning that light, so that through him all might believe. ⁸ He himself was not the light; he came only as a witness to the light.

* * *

1:19 Now this was John's testimony when the Jewish leaders in Jerusalem sent priests and Levites to ask him who he was. ²⁰ He did not fail to confess, but confessed freely, "I am not the Messiah."

²¹ They asked him, "Then who are you? Are you Elijah?" He said, "I am not." "Are you the Prophet?" He answered, "No." ²² Finally they said, "Who are you? Give us an answer to take back to those who sent us. What do you say about yourself?"

²³ John replied in the words of Isaiah the prophet, "I am the voice of one calling in the wilderness, 'Make straight the way for the Lord.'"

²⁴ Now the Pharisees who had been sent ²⁵ questioned him, "Why then do you baptize if you are not the Messiah, nor Elijah, nor the Prophet?" ²⁶ "I baptize with water," John replied, "but among you stands one you do not know. ²⁷ He is the one who comes after me, the straps of whose sandals I am not worthy to untie."

²⁸ This all happened at Bethany on the other side of the Jordan, where John was baptizing.

1. Do you suppose John the Baptist was unique in these times, or were there probably other similar prophets or preachers?
2. Did John the Baptist know (or know of) Jesus during this phase of his ministry? What do the Gospels suggest?
3. All four Gospels report John the Baptist's heralding the Messiah's imminent appearance. What Scripture did they cite as prophesying the event?
4. How do the accounts differ in describing the baptism that the Messiah will perform? What do the differing terms mean?
5. How did John the Baptist characterize the religious establishment in the several Gospel accounts?

3.b Jesus as Related to John the Baptist

MATTHEW
11:2 When John, who was in prison, heard about the deeds of the Messiah, he sent his disciples [3] to ask him, "Are you the one who is to come, or should we expect someone else?" [4] Jesus replied, "Go back and report to John what you hear and see: [5] The blind receive sight, the lame walk, those who have leprosy are cleansed, the deaf hear, the dead are raised, and the good news is proclaimed to the poor. [6] Blessed is anyone who does not stumble on account of me." [7] As John's disciples were leaving, Jesus began to speak to the crowd about John: "What did you go out into the wilderness to see? A reed swayed by the wind? [8] If not, what did you go out to see? A man dressed in fine clothes? No, those who wear fine clothes are in kings' palaces. [9] Then what did you go out to see? A prophet? Yes, I tell you, and more than a prophet. [10] This is the one about whom it is written: "'I will send my messenger ahead of you, who will prepare your way before you.' [11] Truly I tell you, among those born of women there has not risen anyone greater than John the Baptist; yet whoever is least in the kingdom of heaven is greater than he. [12] From the days of John the Baptist until now, the kingdom of heaven has been subjected to violence, and violent people have been raiding it. [13] For all the Prophets and the Law prophesied until John. [14] And if you are willing to accept it, he is the Elijah who was to come. [15] Whoever has ears, let them hear. [16] "To what can I compare this generation? They are like children sitting in the marketplaces and calling out to others: [17] "'We played the pipe for you, and you did not dance; we sang a dirge, and you did not mourn.' [18] For John came neither eating nor drinking, and they say, 'He has a demon.' [19] The Son of Man came eating and drinking, and they say, 'Here is a glutton and a drunkard, a friend of tax collectors and sinners.' But wisdom is proved right by her deeds."

MARK
1:6 John wore clothing made of camel's hair, with a leather belt around his waist, and he ate locusts and wild honey. [7] And this was his message: "After me comes the one more powerful than I, the straps of whose sandals I am not worthy to stoop down and untie.

LUKE
7:18 John's disciples told him about all these things. Calling two of them, [19] he sent them to the Lord to ask, "Are you the one who is to come, or should we expect someone else?" [20] When the men came to Jesus, they said, "John the Baptist sent us to you to ask, 'Are you the one who is to come, or should we expect someone else?'" [21] At that very time Jesus cured many who had diseases, sicknesses and evil spirits, and gave sight to many who were blind. [22] So he replied to the messengers, "Go back and report to John what you have seen and heard: The blind receive sight, the lame walk, those who have leprosy are cleansed, the deaf hear, the dead are raised, and the good news is proclaimed to the poor. [23] Blessed is anyone who does not stumble on account of me." [24] After John's messengers left, Jesus began to speak to the crowd about John: "What did you go out into the wilderness to see? A reed swayed by the wind? [25] If not, what did you go out to see? A man dressed in fine clothes? No, those who wear expensive clothes and indulge in luxury are in palaces. [26] But what did you go out to see? A prophet? Yes, I tell you, and more than a prophet. [27] This is the one about whom it is written: "'I will send my messenger ahead of you, who will prepare your way before you.' [28] I tell you, among those born of women there is no one greater than John; yet the one who is least in the kingdom of God is greater than he." [29] (All the people, even the tax collectors, when they heard Jesus' words, acknowledged that God's way was right, because they had been baptized by John. [30] But the Pharisees and the experts in the law rejected God's purpose for themselves, because they had not been baptized by John.) [31] Jesus went on to say, "To what, then, can I compare the people of this generation? What are they like? [32] They are like children sitting in the marketplace and calling out to each other: "'We played the pipe for you, and you did not dance; we sang a dirge, and you did not cry.'

³³ For John the Baptist came neither eating bread nor drinking wine, and you say, 'He has a demon.' ³⁴ The Son of Man came eating and drinking, and you say, 'Here is a glutton and a drunkard, a friend of tax collectors and sinners.' ³⁵ But wisdom is proved right by all her children."

* * *

16:16 "The Law and the Prophets were proclaimed until John. Since that time, the good news of the kingdom of God is being preached, and everyone is forcing their way into it.

JOHN

3:22 After this, Jesus and his disciples went out into the Judean countryside, where he spent some time with them, and baptized. ²³ Now John also was baptizing at Aenon near Salim, because there was plenty of water, and people were coming and being baptized. ²⁴ (This was before John was put in prison.) ²⁵ An argument developed between some of John's disciples and a certain Jew over the matter of ceremonial washing. ²⁶ They came to John and said to him, "Rabbi, that man who was with you on the other side of the Jordan—the one you testified about—look, he is baptizing, and everyone is going to him."
²⁷ To this John replied, "A person can receive only what is given them from heaven. ²⁸ You yourselves can testify that I said, 'I am not the Messiah but am sent ahead of him.' ²⁹ The bride belongs to the bridegroom. The friend who attends the bridegroom waits and listens for him, and is full of joy when he hears the bridegroom's voice. That joy is mine, and it is now complete. ³⁰ He must become greater; I must become less."
³¹ The one who comes from above is above all; the one who is from the earth belongs to the earth, and speaks as one from the earth. The one who comes from heaven is above all. ³² He testifies to what he has seen and heard, but no one accepts his testimony. ³³ Whoever has accepted it has certified that God is truthful.

1. Only Matthew and Luke report John the Baptist's question to Jesus and Jesus' response and subsequent public statement. What does this passage add to our knowledge of how Jesus understood his role, that is absent from Mark and John?
2. Was there rivalry between John the Baptist and Jesus? Or between the two groups of disciples?
3. How does John's account of John the Baptist differ from those of the other Gospels?

3.c The Death of John the Baptist

MATTHEW
14:6 On Herod's birthday the daughter of Herodias danced for the guests and pleased Herod so much [7] that he promised with an oath to give her whatever she asked. [8] Prompted by her mother, she said, "Give me here on a platter the head of John the Baptist." [9] The king was distressed, but because of his oaths and his dinner guests, he ordered that her request be granted [10] and had John beheaded in the prison. [11] His head was brought in on a platter and given to the girl, who carried it to her mother. [12] John's disciples came and took his body and buried it. Then they went and told Jesus.

MARK
6:17 For Herod himself had given orders to have John arrested, and he had him bound and put in prison. He did this because of Herodias, his brother Philip's wife, whom he had married. [18] For John had been saying to Herod, "It is not lawful for you to have your brother's wife." [19] So Herodias nursed a grudge against John and wanted to kill him. But she was not able to, [20] because Herod feared John and protected him, knowing him to be a righteous and holy man. When Herod heard John, he was greatly puzzled; yet he liked to listen to him. [21] Finally the opportune time came. On his birthday Herod gave a banquet for his high officials and military commanders and the leading men of Galilee. [22] When the daughter of Herodias came in and danced, she pleased Herod and his dinner guests. The king said to the girl, "Ask me for anything you want, and I'll give it to you." [23] And he promised her with an oath, "Whatever you ask I will give you, up to half my kingdom." [24] She went out and said to her mother, "What shall I ask for?" "The head of John the Baptist," she answered. [25] At once the girl hurried in to the king with the request: "I want you to give me right now the head of John the Baptist on a platter." [26] The king was greatly distressed, but because of his oaths and his dinner guests, he did not want to refuse her. [27] So he immediately sent an executioner with orders to bring John's head. The man went, beheaded John in the prison, [28] and brought back his head on a platter. He presented it to the girl, and she gave it to her mother. [29] On hearing of this, John's disciples came and took his body and laid it in a tomb.

LUKE
3:19 But when John rebuked Herod the tetrarch because of his marriage to Herodias, his brother's wife, and all the other evil things he had done, [20] Herod added this to them all: He locked John up in prison.

JOHN

1. Note that only Mark and Matthew report on John's execution, though in Luke Herod later refers to having had John killed.

CHAPTER 4: BEGINNINGS OF MINISTRY

4.a The Baptism of Jesus

MATTHEW
3:13 Then Jesus came from Galilee to the Jordan to be baptized by John. [14] But John tried to deter him, saying, "I need to be baptized by you, and do you come to me?" [15] Jesus replied, "Let it be so now; it is proper for us to do this to fulfill all righteousness." Then John consented. [16] As soon as Jesus was baptized, he went up out of the water. At that moment heaven was opened, and he saw the Spirit of God descending like a dove and alighting on him. [17] And a voice from heaven said, "This is my Son, whom I love; with him I am well pleased."

MARK
1:9 At that time Jesus came from Nazareth in Galilee and was baptized by John in the Jordan. [10] Just as Jesus was coming up out of the water, he saw heaven being torn open and the Spirit descending on him like a dove. [11] And a voice came from heaven: "You are my Son, whom I love; with you I am well pleased."

LUKE
3:21 When all the people were being baptized, Jesus was baptized too. And as he was praying, heaven was opened [22] and the Holy Spirit descended on him in bodily form like a dove. And a voice came from heaven: "You are my Son, whom I love; with you I am well pleased."

JOHN
1:29 The next day John saw Jesus coming toward him and said, "Look, the Lamb of God, who takes away the sin of the world! [30] This is the one I meant when I said, 'A man who comes after me has surpassed me because he was before me.' [31] I myself did not know him, but the reason I came baptizing with water was that he might be revealed to Israel." [32] Then John gave this testimony: "I saw the Spirit come down from heaven as a dove and remain on him. [33] And I myself did not know him, but the one who sent me to baptize with water told me, 'The man on whom you see the Spirit come down and remain is the one who will baptize with the Holy Spirit.' [34] I have seen and I testify that this is God's Chosen One."

1. What are the elements of the baptism account that appear in all four of the Gospel witnesses? What does the appearance of these details in all four Gospels tell us?
2. In the accounts of Mark and Luke, God is quoted as speaking to Jesus when He says, "You are my Son, whom I love; with you I am well pleased." Matthew, however, renders the statement in the third person, "This is my Son, whom I love; with him I am well pleased." What might explain this difference? To whom is God speaking in Matthew's version? Did bystanders hear God's announcement in Mark and Luke, or did only Jesus hear it?
3. A school of thought developed in early Christianity – later rejected – that held Jesus was only a mortal human being until the dove imparted God's divinity to him at his baptism. Reread carefully the passages describing

the descent of the dove. How might this theory have developed or been opposed, based on the wording of the accounts?
4. Identify other differences between the four accounts of Jesus' baptism. What, if any, significance might be attached to them?

4.b Jesus Begins His Ministry

MATTHEW
3:12 When Jesus heard that John had been put in prison, he withdrew to Galilee. [13] Leaving Nazareth, he went and lived in Capernaum, which was by the lake in the area of Zebulun and Naphtali— [14] to fulfill what was said through the prophet Isaiah: [15] "Land of Zebulun and land of Naphtali, the Way of the Sea, beyond the Jordan, Galilee of the Gentiles— [16] the people living in darkness have seen a great light; on those living in the land of the shadow of death a light has dawned."   [17] From that time on Jesus began to preach, "Repent, for the kingdom of heaven has come near."

MARK
1:14 After John was put in prison, Jesus went into Galilee, proclaiming the good news of God. [15] "The time has come," he said. "The kingdom of God has come near. Repent and believe the good news!"

LUKE
4:14 Jesus returned to Galilee in the power of the Spirit, and news about him spread through the whole countryside. [15] He was teaching in their synagogues, and everyone praised him.   [16] He went to Nazareth, where he had been brought up, and on the Sabbath day he went into the synagogue, as was his custom. He stood up to read, [17] and the scroll of the prophet Isaiah was handed to him. Unrolling it, he found the place where it is written: [18] "The Spirit of the Lord is on me, because he has anointed me to proclaim good news to the poor. He has sent me to proclaim freedom for the prisoners and recovery of sight for the blind, to set the oppressed free, [19] to proclaim the year of the Lord's favor." [20] Then he rolled up the scroll, gave it back to the attendant and sat down. The eyes of everyone in the synagogue were fastened on him. [21] He began by saying to them, "Today this scripture is fulfilled in your hearing."   [22] All spoke well of him and were amazed at the gracious words that came from his lips. "Isn't this Joseph's son?" they asked.   [23] Jesus said to them, "Surely you will quote this proverb to me: 'Physician, heal yourself!' And you will tell me, 'Do here in your hometown what we have heard that you did in Capernaum.'" [24] "Truly I tell you," he continued, "no prophet is accepted in his hometown. [25] I assure you that there were many widows in Israel in Elijah's time, when the sky was shut for three and a half years and there was a severe famine throughout the land. [26] Yet Elijah was not sent to any of them, but to a widow in Zarephath in the region of Sidon. [27] And there were many in Israel with leprosy in the time of Elisha the prophet, yet not one of them was cleansed—only Naaman the Syrian."   [28] All the people in the synagogue were furious when they heard this. [29] They got up, drove him out of the town, and took him to the brow of the hill on which the town was built, in order to throw him off the cliff. [30] But he walked right through the crowd and went on his way.

JOHN
4:1 Now Jesus learned that the Pharisees had heard that he was gaining and baptizing more disciples than John— [2] although in fact it was not Jesus who baptized, but his disciples. [3] So he left Judea and went back once more to Galilee.   ***   4:43 After the two days he left for Galilee. [44] (Now Jesus himself had pointed out that a prophet has no honor in his own country.) [45] When he arrived in Galilee, the Galileans welcomed him. They had seen all that he had done in Jerusalem at the Passover Festival, for they also had been there.

1. In this set of passages, only Matthew cites verses from the Old Testament as predicting Jesus' ministry. What was Matthew's objective? Whom was he trying to reach?
2. How is Jesus' interaction with demons depicted in Mark and Matthew?

3. Mark 3:12 reports that Jesus told them (presumably the disciples or those healed, not the demons) not to tell others about him. This admonition appears elsewhere in Mark, but not at all in the other Gospels. What do we make of this?
4. Matthew and Mark both report an apocalyptic announcement of Jesus, calling on Jews to repent, for the kingdom of God/heaven has come near. Luke and John omit this, yet Luke does report Jesus as saying the Spirit had called him to proclaim good news to the poor. Can Jesus be considered an apocalyptic prophet? Is this idea reflected as clearly in John as in the Synoptics?

4.c Jesus Is Tempted in the Wilderness

MATTHEW
4:1 Then Jesus was led by the Spirit into the wilderness to be tempted by the devil. ² After fasting forty days and forty nights, he was hungry. ³ The tempter came to him and said, "If you are the Son of God, tell these stones to become bread." ⁴ Jesus answered, "It is written: 'Man shall not live on bread alone, but on every word that comes from the mouth of God.'" ⁵ Then the devil took him to the holy city and had him stand on the highest point of the temple. ⁶ "If you are the Son of God," he said, "throw yourself down. For it is written: "'He will command his angels concerning you, and they will lift you up in their hands, so that you will not strike your foot against a stone.'" ⁷ Jesus answered him, "It is also written: 'Do not put the Lord your God to the test.'" ⁸ Again, the devil took him to a very high mountain and showed him all the kingdoms of the world and their splendor. ⁹ "All this I will give you," he said, "if you will bow down and worship me." ¹⁰ Jesus said to him, "Away from me, Satan! For it is written: 'Worship the Lord your God, and serve him only.'" ¹¹ Then the devil left him, and angels came and attended him.
MARK
1:12 At once the Spirit sent him out into the wilderness, ¹³ and he was in the wilderness forty days, being tempted by Satan. He was with the wild animals, and angels attended him.
LUKE
4:1 Jesus, full of the Holy Spirit, left the Jordan and was led by the Spirit into the wilderness, ² where for forty days he was tempted by the devil. He ate nothing during those days, and at the end of them he was hungry. ³ The devil said to him, "If you are the Son of God, tell this stone to become bread." ⁴ Jesus answered, "It is written: 'Man shall not live on bread alone.'" ⁵ The devil led him up to a high place and showed him in an instant all the kingdoms of the world. ⁶ And he said to him, "I will give you all their authority and splendor; it has been given to me, and I can give it to anyone I want to. ⁷ If you worship me, it will all be yours." ⁸ Jesus answered, "It is written: 'Worship the Lord your God and serve him only.'" ⁹ The devil led him to Jerusalem and had him stand on the highest point of the temple. "If you are the Son of God," he said, "throw yourself down from here. ¹⁰ For it is written: "'He will command his angels concerning you to guard you carefully; ¹¹ they will lift you up in their hands, so that you will not strike your foot against a stone.'" ¹² Jesus answered, "It is said: 'Do not put the Lord your God to the test.'" ¹³ When the devil had finished all this tempting, he left him until an opportune time.
JOHN

1. What do you think accounts for the fact that Mark's account of the temptations in the wilderness is so brief? Are there any *essential* facts that Matthew and Luke include in their accounts that Mark misses by writing such a brief account?

2. According to Matthew, at the end of the temptations, Satan simply "left" Jesus. Luke, however, gives a more suggestive account, saying that Satan "left him until an opportune time." What may Luke have had in mind in closing the account in this way?

3. Although the accounts of Matthew and Luke are closely parallel, they differ on the sequence of the three temptations. Is there any significance in this difference? Does one account contain an error, or might another factor be in play?

4. Reading the three accounts carefully, what other differences do you find among them – particularly between the more detailed accounts of Matthew and Luke?

5. These passages bring up a question about the sourcing of some of the stories in the Gospels: since Jesus was alone in the wilderness, how did the Gospel authors learn about what happened there? What possible explanations can you identify?

6. The wording of all three Gospels seems to say Jesus was led into temptation by the Holy Spirit. Is this an accurate reading?

Chapter 5: The Disciples

5.a. Jesus Gathers His First Disciples

MATTHEW
4:18 As Jesus was walking beside the Sea of Galilee, he saw two brothers, Simon called Peter and his brother Andrew. They were casting a net into the lake, for they were fishermen. [19] "Come, follow me," Jesus said, "and I will send you out to fish for people." [20] At once they left their nets and followed him. [21] Going on from there, he saw two other brothers, James son of Zebedee and his brother John. They were in a boat with their father Zebedee, preparing their nets. Jesus called them, [22] and immediately they left the boat and their father and followed him.

MARK
1:16 As Jesus walked beside the Sea of Galilee, he saw Simon and his brother Andrew casting a net into the lake, for they were fishermen. [17] "Come, follow me," Jesus said, "and I will send you out to fish for people." [18] At once they left their nets and followed him. [19] When he had gone a little farther, he saw James son of Zebedee and his brother John in a boat, preparing their nets. [20] Without delay he called them, and they left their father Zebedee in the boat with the hired men and followed him.

LUKE
5:1 One day as Jesus was standing by the Lake of Gennesaret, the people were crowding around him and listening to the word of God. [2] He saw at the water's edge two boats, left there by the fishermen, who were washing their nets. [3] He got into one of the boats, the one belonging to Simon, and asked him to put out a little from shore. Then he sat down and taught the people from the boat. [4] When he had finished speaking, he said to Simon, "Put out into deep water, and let down the nets for a catch." [5] Simon answered, "Master, we've worked hard all night and haven't caught anything. But because you say so, I will let down the nets." [6] When they had done so, they caught such a large number of fish that their nets began to break. [7] So they signaled their partners in the other boat to come and help them, and they came and filled both boats so full that they began to sink. [8] When Simon Peter saw this, he fell at Jesus' knees and said, "Go away from me, Lord; I am a sinful man!" [9] For he and all his companions were astonished at the catch of fish they had taken, [10] and so were James and John, the sons of Zebedee, Simon's partners. Then Jesus said to Simon, "Don't be afraid; from now on you will fish for people." [11] So they pulled their boats up on shore, left everything and followed him.

JOHN
1:35 The next day John was there again with two of his disciples. [36] When he saw Jesus passing by, he said, "Look, the Lamb of God!" [37] When the two disciples heard him say this, they followed Jesus. [38] Turning around, Jesus saw them following and asked, "What do you want?" They said, "Rabbi" (which means "Teacher"), "where are you staying?" [39] "Come," he replied, "and you will see." So they went and saw where he was staying, and they spent that day with him. It was about four in the afternoon. [40] Andrew, Simon Peter's brother, was one of the two who heard what John had said and who had followed Jesus. [41] The first thing Andrew did was to find his brother Simon and tell him, "We have found the Messiah" (that is, the Christ). [42] And he brought him to Jesus. Jesus looked at him and said, "You are Simon son of John. You will be

> called Cephas" (which, when translated, is Peter).
> ⁴³ The next day Jesus decided to leave for Galilee. Finding Philip, he said to him, "Follow me." ⁴⁴ Philip, like Andrew and Peter, was from the town of Bethsaida. ⁴⁵ Philip found Nathanael and told him, "We have found the one Moses wrote about in the Law, and about whom the prophets also wrote—Jesus of Nazareth, the son of Joseph."
> ⁴⁶ "Nazareth! Can anything good come from there?" Nathanael asked. "Come and see," said Philip.
> ⁴⁷ When Jesus saw Nathanael approaching, he said of him, "Here truly is an Israelite in whom there is no deceit."
> ⁴⁸ "How do you know me?" Nathanael asked. Jesus answered, "I saw you while you were still under the fig tree before Philip called you."
> ⁴⁹ Then Nathanael declared, "Rabbi, you are the Son of God; you are the king of Israel."
> ⁵⁰ Jesus said, "You believe because I told you I saw you under the fig tree. You will see greater things than that."
> ⁵¹ He then added, "Very truly I tell you, you will see 'heaven open, and the angels of God ascending and descending on' the Son of Man."

1. Matthew's account of Jesus' call to Simon Peter and Andrew, and to the sons of Zebedee James and John, is clearly taken from Mark's Gospel. In contrast, what does John tell us about Andrew's previous activities and about how Simon Peter came to join Jesus?

2. John omits the account of Jesus' call to James and John, yet he does account for them in John 21:2, referring to them only as "the sons of Zebedee" and not anywhere in his Gospel by name. Can you speculate on an explanation for this difference in treatment?

3. Is the Sea of Galilee (mentioned in Matthew and Mark) the same as the Lake of Gennesaret (in Luke)?

4. Mark, the earliest Gospel, has a short and simple account of how Peter, Andrew, James, and John found Jesus. Matthew essentially repeats Mark. But the later Gospels, Luke and John, include much more detail, and differ from each other. How do we account for the greater and divergent detail found in Luke and John?

5.b. Jesus Calls Matthew (Levi)

MATTHEW
9:9 As Jesus went on from there, he saw a man named Matthew sitting at the tax collector's booth. "Follow me," he told him, and Matthew got up and followed him. ¹⁰ While Jesus was having dinner at Matthew's house, many tax collectors and sinners came and ate with him and his disciples. ¹¹ When the Pharisees saw this, they asked his disciples, "Why does your teacher eat with tax collectors and sinners?" ¹² On hearing this, Jesus said, "It is not the healthy who need a doctor, but the sick. ¹³ But go and learn what this means: 'I desire mercy, not sacrifice.' For I have not come to call the righteous, but sinners."
MARK
2:13 Once again Jesus went out beside the lake. A large crowd came to him, and he began to teach them. ¹⁴ As he walked along, he saw Levi son of Alphaeus sitting at the tax collector's booth. "Follow me," Jesus told him, and Levi got up and followed him. ¹⁵ While Jesus was having dinner at Levi's house, many tax collectors and sinners were eating with him and his disciples, for there were many who followed him. ¹⁶ When the teachers of the law who were Pharisees saw him eating with the sinners and tax collectors, they asked his disciples: "Why does he eat with tax collectors and sinners?" ¹⁷ On hearing this, Jesus said to them, "It is not the healthy who need a doctor, but the sick. I have not come to call the righteous, but sinners."
LUKE
5:27 After this, Jesus went out and saw a tax collector by the name of Levi sitting at his tax booth. "Follow me," Jesus said to him, ²⁸ and Levi got up, left everything and followed him. ²⁹ Then Levi held a great banquet for Jesus at his house, and a large crowd of tax collectors and others were eating with them. ³⁰ But the Pharisees and the teachers of the law who belonged to their sect complained to his disciples, "Why do you eat and drink with tax collectors and sinners?" ³¹ Jesus answered them, "It is not the healthy who need a doctor, but the sick. ³² I have not come to call the righteous, but sinners to repentance."
JOHN

1. Compare the accounts of Mark, Matthew, and Luke. What similarities do you find? What probably accounts for them?
2. Focus on Jesus' answer to the Pharisees at the end of the passage. In the three versions, there are small but interesting differences; what do you make of them?

5.c. Named and Unnamed Disciples

MATTHEW
10:2 These are the names of the twelve apostles: first, Simon (who is called Peter) and his brother Andrew; James son of Zebedee, and his brother John; ³ Philip and Bartholomew; Thomas and Matthew the tax collector; James son of Alphaeus, and Thaddaeus; ⁴ Simon the Zealot and Judas Iscariot, who betrayed him.
MARK
3:13 Jesus went up on a mountainside and called to him those he wanted, and they came to him. ¹⁴ He appointed twelve that they might be with him and that he might send them out to preach ¹⁵ and to have authority to drive out demons. ¹⁶ These are the twelve he appointed: Simon (to whom he gave the name Peter), ¹⁷ James son of Zebedee and his brother John (to them he gave the name Boanerges, which means "sons of thunder"), ¹⁸ Andrew, Philip, Bartholomew, Matthew, Thomas, James son of Alphaeus, Thaddaeus, Simon the Zealot ¹⁹ and Judas Iscariot, who betrayed him.
LUKE
6:12 One of those days Jesus went out to a mountainside to pray, and spent the night praying to God. ¹³ When morning came, he called his disciples to him and chose twelve of them, whom he also designated apostles: ¹⁴ Simon (whom he named Peter), his brother Andrew, James, John, Philip, Bartholomew, ¹⁵ Matthew, Thomas, James son of Alphaeus, Simon who was called the Zealot, ¹⁶ Judas son of James, and Judas Iscariot, who became a traitor. * * * Acts 1:12 Then the apostles returned to Jerusalem from the hill called the Mount of Olives, a Sabbath day's walk from the city. ¹³ When they arrived, they went upstairs to the room where they were staying. Those present were Peter, John, James and Andrew; Philip and Thomas, Bartholomew and Matthew; James son of Alphaeus and Simon the Zealot, and Judas son of James. ¹⁴ They all joined together constantly in prayer, along with the women and Mary the mother of Jesus, and with his brothers.
JOHN
1:40 Andrew, Simon Peter's brother, was one of the two who heard what John had said and who had followed Jesus. ⁴¹ The first thing Andrew did was to find his brother Simon and tell him, "We have found the Messiah" (that is, the Christ). ⁴² And he brought him to Jesus. Jesus looked at him and said, "You are Simon son of John. You will be called Cephas" (which, when translated, is Peter). ⁴³ The next day Jesus decided to leave for Galilee. Finding Philip, he said to him, "Follow me." ⁴⁴ Philip, like Andrew and Peter, was from the town of Bethsaida. ⁴⁵ Philip found Nathanael and told him, "We have found the one Moses wrote about in the Law, and about whom the prophets also wrote—Jesus of Nazareth, the son of Joseph." * * * 6:70 Then Jesus replied, "Have I not chosen you, the Twelve? Yet one of you is a devil!" ⁷¹ (He meant Judas, the son of Simon Iscariot, who, though one of the Twelve, was later to betray him.) * * * 14:22 Then Judas (not Judas Iscariot) said, "But, Lord, why do you intend to show yourself to us and not to the world?" * * * 20:24 Now Thomas (also known as Didymus), one of the Twelve, was not with the disciples when Jesus came. * * * 11:1 Now a man named Lazarus was sick. He was from Bethany, the village of Mary and her sister Martha. ³ So the sisters sent word to Jesus, "Lord, the one you love is sick." * * * 19:26 When Jesus saw his mother there, and the disciple whom he loved standing nearby, he said to her, "Woman, here is your son," ²⁷ and to the disciple, "Here is your mother." From that time on, this disciple took her into his

> home.
>
> * * *
>
> 20:1 Early on the first day of the week, while it was still dark, Mary Magdalene went to the tomb and saw that the stone had been removed from the entrance. ² So she came running to Simon Peter and the other disciple, the one Jesus loved, and said, "They have taken the Lord out of the tomb, and we don't know where they have put him!"
>
> * * *
>
> 21:20 Peter turned and saw that the disciple whom Jesus loved was following them. (This was the one who had leaned back against Jesus at the supper and had said, "Lord, who is going to betray you?") ²¹ When Peter saw him, he asked, "Lord, what about him?" ²² Jesus answered, "If I want him to remain alive until I return, what is that to you? You must follow me." ²³ Because of this, the rumor spread among the believers that this disciple would not die. But Jesus did not say that he would not die; he only said, "If I want him to remain alive until I return, what is that to you?" ²⁴ This is the disciple who testifies to these things and who wrote them down. We know that his testimony is true.

1. Note that the disciples have now become apostles. The terms are not interchangeable. A disciple is a student, a believer, a follower. An apostle is someone sent out to deliver a special, authoritative message. What wording do you see that makes this distinction?
2. Curiously, Nathanael does not appear in Matthew, Mark, or Luke. The above account could be interpreted that Nathanael did not accept Jesus' call, but John 21:2 later mentions him as a disciple. Because John names only six disciples, including Nathanael, it isn't possible to figure out which of the Twelve John omits to make room for this anomalous disciple. Matthew 10:3 (above) refers to "Philip and Bartholomew" together, while the above passage from John refers to Philip and Nathanael as being associated in some way. This has led some readers to suggest that Bartholomew and Nathanael may have been the same person, but this is far from conclusive. Is this anomaly troubling in any way? Or can it just be accepted as the kind of puzzling inconsistency one gets when there are multiple witnesses?
3. John son of Zebedee has commonly been thought to be "the disciple whom Jesus loved," but read the passages from John carefully. What do you think of the idea that in fact Lazarus was "the disciple whom Jesus loved"?

5.d. Jesus Sends Out His Disciples

MATTHEW

10:5 These twelve Jesus sent out with the following instructions: "Do not go among the Gentiles or enter any town of the Samaritans. ⁶ Go rather to the lost sheep of Israel. ⁷ As you go, proclaim this message: 'The kingdom of heaven has come near.' ⁸ Heal the sick, raise the dead, cleanse those who have leprosy, drive out demons. Freely you have received; freely give.

⁹ "Do not get any gold or silver or copper to take with you in your belts— ¹⁰ no bag for the journey or extra shirt or sandals or a staff, for the worker is worth his keep. ¹¹ Whatever town or village you enter, search there for some worthy person and stay at their house until you leave. ¹² As you enter the home, give it your greeting. ¹³ If the home is deserving, let your peace rest on it; if it is not, let your peace return to you. ¹⁴ If anyone will not welcome you or listen to your words, leave that home or town and shake the dust off your feet. ¹⁵ Truly I tell you, it will be more bearable for Sodom and Gomorrah on the day of judgment than for that town.

¹⁶ "I am sending you out like sheep among wolves. Therefore be as shrewd as snakes and as innocent as doves. ¹⁷ Be on your guard; you will be handed over to the local councils and be flogged in the synagogues. ¹⁸ On my account you will be brought before governors and kings as witnesses to them and to the Gentiles. ¹⁹ But when they arrest you, do not worry about what to say or how to say it. At that time you will be given what to say, ²⁰ for it will not be you speaking, but the Spirit of your Father speaking through you.

* * *

10:40 "Anyone who welcomes you welcomes me, and anyone who welcomes me welcomes the one who sent me. ⁴¹ Whoever welcomes a prophet as a prophet will receive a prophet's reward, and whoever welcomes a righteous person as a righteous person will receive a righteous person's reward. ⁴² And if anyone gives even a cup of cold water to one of these little ones who is my disciple, truly I tell you, that person will certainly not lose their reward."

MARK

6:6 Then Jesus went around teaching from village to village. ⁷ Calling the Twelve to him, he began to send them out two by two and gave them authority over impure spirits.

⁸ These were his instructions: "Take nothing for the journey except a staff—no bread, no bag, no money in your belts. ⁹ Wear sandals but not an extra shirt. ¹⁰ Whenever you enter a house, stay there until you leave that town. ¹¹ And if any place will not welcome you or listen to you, leave that place and shake the dust off your feet as a testimony against them."

¹² They went out and preached that people should repent. ¹³ They drove out many demons and anointed many sick people with oil and healed them.

LUKE

9:1 When Jesus had called the Twelve together, he gave them power and authority to drive out all demons and to cure diseases, ² and he sent them out to proclaim the kingdom of God and to heal the sick. ³ He told them: "Take nothing for the journey—no staff, no bag, no bread, no money, no extra shirt. ⁴ Whatever house you enter, stay there until you leave that town. ⁵ If people do not welcome you, leave their town and shake the dust off your feet as a testimony against them." ⁶ So they set out and went from village to village, proclaiming the good news and healing people everywhere.

* * *

10:1 After this the Lord appointed seventy-two others and sent them two by two ahead of him to every town and place where he was about to go. ² He told them, "The harvest is plentiful, but the workers are few. Ask the Lord of the harvest, therefore, to send out workers into his harvest field. ³ Go! I am sending you out like lambs among wolves. ⁴ Do not take a purse or bag or sandals; and do not greet anyone on the road.

⁵ "When you enter a house, first say, 'Peace to this house.' ⁶ If someone who promotes peace is there, your peace will rest on them; if not, it will return to you. ⁷ Stay there, eating and drinking whatever they give you, for the worker deserves his wages. Do not move around from house to house.

⁸ "When you enter a town and are welcomed, eat what is offered to you. ⁹ Heal the sick who are there and tell them,

'The kingdom of God has come near to you.' ¹⁰ But when you enter a town and are not welcomed, go into its streets and say, ¹¹ 'Even the dust of your town we wipe from our feet as a warning to you. Yet be sure of this: The kingdom of God has come near.' ¹² I tell you, it will be more bearable on that day for Sodom than for that town.

¹³ "Woe to you, Chorazin! Woe to you, Bethsaida! For if the miracles that were performed in you had been performed in Tyre and Sidon, they would have repented long ago, sitting in sackcloth and ashes. ¹⁴ But it will be more bearable for Tyre and Sidon at the judgment than for you. ¹⁵ And you, Capernaum, will you be lifted to the heavens? No, you will go down to Hades.

¹⁶ "Whoever listens to you listens to me; whoever rejects you rejects me; but whoever rejects me rejects him who sent me."

¹⁷ The seventy-two returned with joy and said, "Lord, even the demons submit to us in your name." ¹⁸ He replied, "I saw Satan fall like lightning from heaven. ¹⁹ I have given you authority to trample on snakes and scorpions and to overcome all the power of the enemy; nothing will harm you. ²⁰ However, do not rejoice that the spirits submit to you, but rejoice that your names are written in heaven."

²¹ At that time Jesus, full of joy through the Holy Spirit, said, "I praise you, Father, Lord of heaven and earth, because you have hidden these things from the wise and learned, and revealed them to little children. Yes, Father, for this is what you were pleased to do. ²² "All things have been committed to me by my Father. No one knows who the Son is except the Father, and no one knows who the Father is except the Son and those to whom the Son chooses to reveal him."

²³ Then he turned to his disciples and said privately, "Blessed are the eyes that see what you see. ²⁴ For I tell you that many prophets and kings wanted to see what you see but did not see it, and to hear what you hear but did not hear it."

JOHN

15:18 "If the world hates you, keep in mind that it hated me first. ¹⁹ If you belonged to the world, it would love you as its own. As it is, you do not belong to the world, but I have chosen you out of the world. That is why the world hates you. ²⁰ Remember what I told you: 'A servant is not greater than his master.' If they persecuted me, they will persecute you also. If they obeyed my teaching, they will obey yours also.

1. How many disciples did Jesus send out, according to Matthew and Mark? How many according to Luke?
2. To whom did Jesus send out his disciples, in the several accounts?
3. What similarities and what differences do you find in Jesus' instructions to the disciples in the accounts of Matthew and of Luke?
4. Shaking dust from one's feet may carry more meaning than it seems at first. Are there deeper implications apparent in the multiple accounts?
5. Are Jesus' instructions and warnings applicable to all missionaries, or do they reflect only the circumstances at that time and place?

5.e. Expect to be Persecuted

MATTHEW
10:16 "I am sending you out like sheep among wolves. Therefore be as shrewd as snakes and as innocent as doves. [17] Be on your guard; you will be handed over to the local councils and be flogged in the synagogues. [18] On my account you will be brought before governors and kings as witnesses to them and to the Gentiles. [19] But when they arrest you, do not worry about what to say or how to say it. At that time you will be given what to say, [20] for it will not be you speaking, but the Spirit of your Father speaking through you. [21] "Brother will betray brother to death, and a father his child; children will rebel against their parents and have them put to death. [22] You will be hated by everyone because of me, but the one who stands firm to the end will be saved. [23] When you are persecuted in one place, flee to another. Truly I tell you, you will not finish going through the towns of Israel before the Son of Man comes. [24] "The student is not above the teacher, nor a servant above his master. [25] It is enough for students to be like their teachers, and servants like their masters. If the head of the house has been called Beelzebul, how much more the members of his household! [26] "So do not be afraid of them, for there is nothing concealed that will not be disclosed, or hidden that will not be made known. [27] What I tell you in the dark, speak in the daylight; what is whispered in your ear, proclaim from the roofs. [28] Do not be afraid of those who kill the body but cannot kill the soul. Rather, be afraid of the One who can destroy both soul and body in hell. [29] Are not two sparrows sold for a penny? Yet not one of them will fall to the ground outside your Father's care. [30] And even the very hairs of your head are all numbered. [31] So don't be afraid; you are worth more than many sparrows. [32] "Whoever acknowledges me before others, I will also acknowledge before my Father in heaven. [33] But whoever disowns me before others, I will disown before my Father in heaven.

MARK
13:9 "You must be on your guard. You will be handed over to the local councils and flogged in the synagogues. On account of me you will stand before governors and kings as witnesses to them. [10] And the gospel must first be preached to all nations. [11] Whenever you are arrested and brought to trial, do not worry beforehand about what to say. Just say whatever is given you at the time, for it is not you speaking, but the Holy Spirit. [12] "Brother will betray brother to death, and a father his child. Children will rebel against their parents and have them put to death. [13] Everyone will hate you because of me, but the one who stands firm to the end will be saved.

LUKE
21:12 "But before all this, they will seize you and persecute you. They will hand you over to synagogues and put you in prison, and you will be brought before kings and governors, and all on account of my name. [13] And so you will bear testimony to me. [14] But make up your mind not to worry beforehand how you will defend yourselves. [15] For I will give you words and wisdom that none of your adversaries will be able to resist or contradict. [16] You will be betrayed even by parents, brothers and sisters, relatives and friends, and they will put some of you to death. [17] Everyone will hate you because of me. [18] But not a hair of your head will perish. [19] Stand firm, and you will win life.

JOHN
15:18 "If the world hates you, keep in mind that it hated me first. [19] If you belonged to the world, it would love you as its own. As it is, you do not belong to the world, but I have chosen you out of the world. That is why the world hates you. [20] Remember what I told you: 'A servant is not greater than his master.' If they persecuted me, they will persecute you also. If they obeyed my teaching, they will obey yours also. [21] They will treat you this way because of my name, for they do not know the one who sent me. [22] If I had not come and spoken to them, they would not be guilty of sin; but now they have no excuse for their sin. [23] Whoever hates me hates my Father as well. [24] If I had not done among them the works no one else did, they would not be guilty of sin. As it is, they have seen, and yet they

> have hated both me and my Father. ²⁵ But this is to fulfill what is written in their Law: 'They hated me without reason.'
>
> ²⁶ "When the Advocate comes, whom I will send to you from the Father—the Spirit of truth who goes out from the Father—he will testify about me. ²⁷ And you also must testify, for you have been with me from the beginning.
>
> * * *
>
> 16:1 "All this I have told you so that you will not fall away. ² They will put you out of the synagogue; in fact, the time is coming when anyone who kills you will think they are offering a service to God. ³ They will do such things because they have not known the Father or me. ⁴ I have told you this, so that when their time comes you will remember that I warned you about them. I did not tell you this from the beginning because I was with you, ⁵ but now I am going to him who sent me. None of you asks me, 'Where are you going?' ⁶ Rather, you are filled with grief because I have said these things. ⁷ But very truly I tell you, it is for your good that I am going away. Unless I go away, the Advocate will not come to you; but if I go, I will send him to you.

1. This set of parallel passages is an excellent example of the value of Gospel comparisons. Jesus' message to his disciples is essentially the same in each Gospel, yet each witness recalls and reports Jesus' words somewhat differently. Far from casting doubt on the historical validity of this episode, these differing accounts are considered multiple attestations. We are close to the actual words of Jesus here.
2. Do you find any significant differences among the four accounts of Jesus' warnings about persecution?

5.f. The Costs of Discipleship

MATTHEW
8:18 When Jesus saw the crowd around him, he gave orders to cross to the other side of the lake. ¹⁹ Then a teacher of the law came to him and said, "Teacher, I will follow you wherever you go." ²⁰ Jesus replied, "Foxes have dens and birds have nests, but the Son of Man has no place to lay his head." ²¹ Another disciple said to him, "Lord, first let me go and bury my father." ²² But Jesus told him, "Follow me, and let the dead bury their own dead." * * * 10:34 "Do not suppose that I have come to bring peace to the earth. I did not come to bring peace, but a sword. ³⁵ For I have come to turn "'a man against his father, a daughter against her mother, a daughter-in-law against her mother-in-law— ³⁶ a man's enemies will be the members of his own household.' ³⁷ "Anyone who loves their father or mother more than me is not worthy of me; anyone who loves their son or daughter more than me is not worthy of me. ³⁸ Whoever does not take up their cross and follow me is not worthy of me. ³⁹ Whoever finds their life will lose it, and whoever loses their life for my sake will find it. * * * 16:24 Then Jesus said to his disciples, "Whoever wants to be my disciple must deny themselves and take up their cross and follow me. ²⁵ For whoever wants to save their life will lose it, but whoever loses their life for me will find it. ²⁶ What good will it be for someone to gain the whole world, yet forfeit their soul? Or what can anyone give in exchange for their soul? ²⁷ For the Son of Man is going to come in his Father's glory with his angels, and then he will reward each person according to what they have done. * * * 19:25 When the disciples heard this, they were greatly astonished and asked, "Who then can be saved?" ²⁶ Jesus looked at them and said, "With man this is impossible, but with God all things are possible." ²⁷ Peter answered him, "We have left everything to follow you! What then will there be for us?" ²⁸ Jesus said to them, "Truly I tell you, at the renewal of all things, when the Son of Man sits on his glorious throne, you who have followed me will also sit on twelve thrones, judging the twelve tribes of Israel. ²⁹ And everyone who has left houses or brothers or sisters or father or mother or wife or children or fields for my sake will receive a hundred times as much and will inherit eternal life. ³⁰ But many who are first will be last, and many who are last will be first.

MARK
8:34 Then he called the crowd to him along with his disciples and said: "Whoever wants to be my disciple must deny themselves and take up their cross and follow me. ³⁵ For whoever wants to save their life will lose it, but whoever loses their life for me and for the gospel will save it. ³⁶ What good is it for someone to gain the whole world, yet forfeit their soul? ³⁷ Or what can anyone give in exchange for their soul? ³⁸ If anyone is ashamed of me and my words in this adulterous and sinful generation, the Son of Man will be ashamed of them when he comes in his Father's glory with the holy angels." * * * 10:26 The disciples were even more amazed, and said to each other, "Who then can be saved?" ²⁷ Jesus looked at them and said, "With man this is impossible, but not with God; all things are possible with God." ²⁸ Then Peter spoke up, "We have left everything to follow you!" ²⁹ "Truly I tell you," Jesus replied, "no one who has left home or brothers or sisters or mother or father or children or fields for me and the gospel ³⁰ will fail to receive a hundred times as much in this present age: homes, brothers, sisters, mothers, children and fields—along with persecutions—and in the age to come eternal life. ³¹ But many who are first will be last, and the last first."

LUKE
9:23 Then he said to them all: "Whoever wants to be my disciple must deny themselves and take up their cross daily and follow me. ²⁴ For whoever wants to save their life will lose it, but whoever loses their life for me will save it. ²⁵ What good is it for someone to gain the whole world, and yet lose or forfeit their very self? ²⁶ Whoever is ashamed of me and my words, the Son of Man will be ashamed of them when he comes in his glory and in the glory of the Father and of the holy angels.

***

9:57 As they were walking along the road, a man said to him, "I will follow you wherever you go." [58] Jesus replied, "Foxes have dens and birds have nests, but the Son of Man has no place to lay his head." [59] He said to another man, "Follow me." But he replied, "Lord, first let me go and bury my father." [60] Jesus said to him, "Let the dead bury their own dead, but you go and proclaim the kingdom of God." [61] Still another said, "I will follow you, Lord; but first let me go back and say goodbye to my family." [62] Jesus replied, "No one who puts a hand to the plow and looks back is fit for service in the kingdom of God."

***

12:4 "I tell you, my friends, do not be afraid of those who kill the body and after that can do no more. [5] But I will show you whom you should fear: Fear him who, after your body has been killed, has authority to throw you into hell. Yes, I tell you, fear him. [6] Are not five sparrows sold for two pennies? Yet not one of them is forgotten by God. [7] Indeed, the very hairs of your head are all numbered. Don't be afraid; you are worth more than many sparrows.

***

12:11 "When you are brought before synagogues, rulers and authorities, do not worry about how you will defend yourselves or what you will say, [12] for the Holy Spirit will teach you at that time what you should say."

***

12:49 "I have come to bring fire on the earth, and how I wish it were already kindled! [50] But I have a baptism to undergo, and what constraint I am under until it is completed! [51] Do you think I came to bring peace on earth? No, I tell you, but division. [52] From now on there will be five in one family divided against each other, three against two and two against three. [53] They will be divided, father against son and son against father, mother against daughter and daughter against mother, mother-in-law against daughter-in-law and daughter-in-law against mother-in-law."

***

14:25 Large crowds were traveling with Jesus, and turning to them he said: [26] "If anyone comes to me and does not hate father and mother, wife and children, brothers and sisters—yes, even their own life—such a person cannot be my disciple. [27] And whoever does not carry their cross and follow me cannot be my disciple.

[28] "Suppose one of you wants to build a tower. Won't you first sit down and estimate the cost to see if you have enough money to complete it? [29] For if you lay the foundation and are not able to finish it, everyone who sees it will ridicule you, [30] saying, 'This person began to build and wasn't able to finish.'

[31] "Or suppose a king is about to go to war against another king. Won't he first sit down and consider whether he is able with ten thousand men to oppose the one coming against him with twenty thousand? [32] If he is not able, he will send a delegation while the other is still a long way off and will ask for terms of peace. [33] In the same way, those of you who do not give up everything you have cannot be my disciples.

***

18:26 Those who heard this asked, "Who then can be saved?" [27] Jesus replied, "What is impossible with man is possible with God."

[28] Peter said to him, "We have left all we had to follow you!" [29] "Truly I tell you," Jesus said to them, "no one who has left home or wife or brothers or sisters or parents or children for the sake of the kingdom of God [30] will fail to receive many times as much in this age, and in the age to come eternal life."

JOHN

6:60 On hearing it, many of his disciples said, "This is a hard teaching. Who can accept it?" [61] Aware that his disciples were grumbling about this, Jesus said to them, "Does this offend you? [62] Then what if you see the Son of Man ascend to where he was before! [63] The Spirit gives life; the flesh counts for nothing. The words I have spoken to you—they are full of the Spirit and life. [64] Yet there are some of you who do not believe." For Jesus had known from the beginning which of them did not believe and who would betray him. [65] He went on to say, "This is why I told you that no one can come to me unless the Father has enabled them."

[66] From this time many of his disciples turned back and no longer followed him. [67] "You do not want to leave too, do you?" Jesus asked the Twelve. [68] Simon Peter answered him, "Lord, to whom shall we go? You have the words of eternal life. [69] We have come to believe and to know that you are the Holy One of God."

***

12:25 Anyone who loves their life will lose it, while anyone who hates their life in this world will keep it for eternal life. [26] Whoever serves me must follow me; and where I am, my servant also will be. My Father will honor the one who serves me.

> * * *
> 15:18 "If the world hates you, keep in mind that it hated me first. [19] If you belonged to the world, it would love you as its own. As it is, you do not belong to the world, but I have chosen you out of the world. That is why the world hates you. [20] Remember what I told you: 'A servant is not greater than his master.' If they persecuted me, they will persecute you also. If they obeyed my teaching, they will obey yours also. [21] They will treat you this way because of my name, for they do not know the one who sent me.

1. All four Gospels include Peter's questions concerning the commitment each of the disciples had made to Jesus. Compare the wording of Peter's question, and of Jesus' response.
2. Do you find any significant differences between the accounts of Jesus' words about his being a cause of friction among family members?
3. Compare the Synoptic versions of Jesus' telling disciples to take up their crosses. Do you find any interesting or significant differences? Is there a passage in John's Gospel that seems to correspond?

5.g. Who is the Greatest Disciple?

MATTHEW
18:1 At that time the disciples came to Jesus and asked, "Who, then, is the greatest in the kingdom of heaven?"   [2] He called a little child to him, and placed the child among them. [3] And he said: "Truly I tell you, unless you change and become like little children, you will never enter the kingdom of heaven. [4] Therefore, whoever takes the lowly position of this child is the greatest in the kingdom of heaven. [5] And whoever welcomes one such child in my name welcomes me.
MARK
9:33 They came to Capernaum. When he was in the house, he asked them, "What were you arguing about on the road?" [34] But they kept quiet because on the way they had argued about who was the greatest.   [35] Sitting down, Jesus called the Twelve and said, "Anyone who wants to be first must be the very last, and the servant of all." [36] He took a little child whom he placed among them. Taking the child in his arms, he said to them, [37] "Whoever welcomes one of these little children in my name welcomes me; and whoever welcomes me does not welcome me but the one who sent me."
LUKE
9:46 An argument started among the disciples as to which of them would be the greatest. [47] Jesus, knowing their thoughts, took a little child and had him stand beside him. [48] Then he said to them, "Whoever welcomes this little child in my name welcomes me; and whoever welcomes me welcomes the one who sent me. For it is the one who is least among you all who is the greatest."
JOHN
13:20 I tell you the truth, whoever accepts anyone I send accepts me; and whoever accepts me accepts the one who sent me.

1. What differences do you find in the versions of this short vignette?

5.h. The Death of Judas

MATTHEW
27:3 When Judas, who had betrayed him, saw that Jesus was condemned, he was seized with remorse and returned the thirty pieces of silver to the chief priests and the elders. ⁴ "I have sinned," he said, "for I have betrayed innocent blood." "What is that to us?" they replied. "That's your responsibility." ⁵ So Judas threw the money into the temple and left. Then he went away and hanged himself. ⁶ The chief priests picked up the coins and said, "It is against the law to put this into the treasury, since it is blood money." ⁷ So they decided to use the money to buy the potter's field as a burial place for foreigners. ⁸ That is why it has been called the Field of Blood to this day. ⁹ Then what was spoken by Jeremiah the prophet was fulfilled: "They took the thirty pieces of silver, the price set on him by the people of Israel, ¹⁰ and they used them to buy the potter's field, as the Lord commanded me."

MARK

LUKE
Acts 1:18 (With the payment he received for his wickedness, Judas bought a field; there he fell headlong, his body burst open and all his intestines spilled out. ¹⁹ Everyone in Jerusalem heard about this, so they called that field in their language Akeldama, that is, Field of Blood.)

JOHN

1. What do you think may account for the differences in the account of Judas' death?
2. Among the Gospel writers, Matthew is often the most ready with a connection to the Old Testament. Read Jeremiah 32; why do you suppose Matthew thought this reference germane?

Chapter 6: Healings and Resuscitations

6.a Various Healings

MATTHEW
4:23 Jesus went throughout Galilee, teaching in their synagogues, proclaiming the good news of the kingdom, and healing every disease and sickness among the people. [24] News about him spread all over Syria, and people brought to him all who were ill with various diseases, those suffering severe pain, the demon-possessed, those having seizures, and the paralyzed; and he healed them. [25] Large crowds from Galilee, the Decapolis, Jerusalem, Judea and the region across the Jordan followed him. * * * 8:14 When Jesus came into Peter's house, he saw Peter's mother-in-law lying in bed with a fever. [15] He touched her hand and the fever left her, and she got up and began to wait on him. 8:16 When evening came, many who were demon-possessed were brought to him, and he drove out the spirits with a word and healed all the sick. [17] This was to fulfill what was spoken through the prophet Isaiah: "He took up our infirmities and bore our diseases." * * * 9:35 Jesus went through all the towns and villages, teaching in their synagogues, proclaiming the good news of the kingdom and healing every disease and sickness. [36] When he saw the crowds, he had compassion on them, because they were harassed and helpless, like sheep without a shepherd. [37] Then he said to his disciples, "The harvest is plentiful but the workers are few. [38] Ask the Lord of the harvest, therefore, to send out workers into his harvest field." * * * 10:1 Jesus called his twelve disciples to him and gave them authority to drive out impure spirits and to heal every disease and sickness.
MARK
1:29 As soon as they left the synagogue, they went with James and John to the home of Simon and Andrew. [30] Simon's mother-in-law was in bed with a fever, and they immediately told Jesus about her. [31] So he went to her, took her hand and helped her up. The fever left her and she began to wait on them. [32] That evening after sunset the people brought to Jesus all the sick and demon-possessed. [33] The whole town gathered at the door, [34] and Jesus healed many who had various diseases. He also drove out many demons, but he would not let the demons speak because they knew who he was.
LUKE
4:38 Jesus left the synagogue and went to the home of Simon. Now Simon's mother-in-law was suffering from a high fever, and they asked Jesus to help her. [39] So he bent over her and rebuked the fever, and it left her. She got up at once and began to wait on them. [40] At sunset, the people brought to Jesus all who had various kinds of sickness, and laying his hands on each one, he healed them. [41] Moreover, demons came out of many people, shouting, "You are the Son of God!" But he rebuked them and would not allow them to speak, because they knew he was the Messiah.

JOHN

6:1 Some time after this, Jesus crossed to the far shore of the Sea of Galilee (that is, the Sea of Tiberias), ² and a great crowd of people followed him because they saw the signs he had performed by healing the sick.

* * *

9:1 As he went along, he saw a man blind from birth. ² His disciples asked him, "Rabbi, who sinned, this man or his parents, that he was born blind?" ³ "Neither this man nor his parents sinned," said Jesus, "but this happened so that the works of God might be displayed in him. ⁴ As long as it is day, we must do the works of him who sent me. Night is coming, when no one can work. ⁵ While I am in the world, I am the light of the world." ⁶ After saying this, he spit on the ground, made some mud with the saliva, and put it on the man's eyes. ⁷ "Go," he told him, "wash in the Pool of Siloam" (this word means "Sent"). So the man went and washed, and came home seeing.

1. Consider the accounts of Jesus curing the fever and of casting out demons. Do we have three independent accounts here?

6.b Healing a Leper

MATTHEW
8:1 When Jesus came down from the mountainside, large crowds followed him. ²A man with leprosy came and knelt before him and said, "Lord, if you are willing, you can make me clean." ³Jesus reached out his hand and touched the man. "I am willing," he said. "Be clean!" Immediately he was cleansed of his leprosy. ⁴Then Jesus said to him, "See that you don't tell anyone. But go, show yourself to the priest and offer the gift Moses commanded, as a testimony to them."

MARK
1:40 A man with leprosy came to him and begged him on his knees, "If you are willing, you can make me clean." ⁴¹Jesus was indignant. He reached out his hand and touched the man. "I am willing," he said. "Be clean!" ⁴²Immediately the leprosy left him and he was cleansed. ⁴³Jesus sent him away at once with a strong warning: ⁴⁴"See that you don't tell this to anyone. But go, show yourself to the priest and offer the sacrifices that Moses commanded for your cleansing, as a testimony to them." ⁴⁵Instead he went out and began to talk freely, spreading the news. As a result, Jesus could no longer enter a town openly but stayed outside in lonely places. Yet the people still came to him from everywhere.

LUKE
5:12 While Jesus was in one of the towns, a man came along who was covered with leprosy. When he saw Jesus, he fell with his face to the ground and begged him, "Lord, if you are willing, you can make me clean." ¹³Jesus reached out his hand and touched the man. "I am willing," he said. "Be clean!" And immediately the leprosy left him. ¹⁴Then Jesus ordered him, "Don't tell anyone, but go, show yourself to the priest and offer the sacrifices that Moses commanded for your cleansing, as a testimony to them." ¹⁵Yet the news about him spread all the more, so that crowds of people came to hear him and to be healed of their sicknesses. ¹⁶But Jesus often withdrew to lonely places and prayed.

JOHN

1. In what ways did Matthew and Luke change Mark's original account? Why do you suppose they did so?

6.c A Centurion's Faith

MATTHEW

8:5 When Jesus had entered Capernaum, a centurion came to him, asking for help. ⁶ "Lord," he said, "my servant lies at home paralyzed, suffering terribly." ⁷ Jesus said to him, "Shall I come and heal him?" ⁸ The centurion replied, "Lord, I do not deserve to have you come under my roof. But just say the word, and my servant will be healed. ⁹ For I myself am a man under authority, with soldiers under me. I tell this one, 'Go,' and he goes; and that one, 'Come,' and he comes. I say to my servant, 'Do this,' and he does it."
¹⁰ When Jesus heard this, he was amazed and said to those following him, "Truly I tell you, I have not found anyone in Israel with such great faith. ¹¹ I say to you that many will come from the east and the west, and will take their places at the feast with Abraham, Isaac and Jacob in the kingdom of heaven. ¹² But the subjects of the kingdom will be thrown outside, into the darkness, where there will be weeping and gnashing of teeth."
¹³ Then Jesus said to the centurion, "Go! Let it be done just as you believed it would." And his servant was healed at that moment.

MARK

LUKE

7:1 When Jesus had finished saying all this to the people who were listening, he entered Capernaum. ² There a centurion's servant, whom his master valued highly, was sick and about to die. ³ The centurion heard of Jesus and sent some elders of the Jews to him, asking him to come and heal his servant. ⁴ When they came to Jesus, they pleaded earnestly with him, "This man deserves to have you do this, ⁵ because he loves our nation and has built our synagogue." ⁶ So Jesus went with them.
He was not far from the house when the centurion sent friends to say to him: "Lord, don't trouble yourself, for I do not deserve to have you come under my roof. ⁷ That is why I did not even consider myself worthy to come to you. But say the word, and my servant will be healed. ⁸ For I myself am a man under authority, with soldiers under me. I tell this one, 'Go,' and he goes; and that one, 'Come,' and he comes. I say to my servant, 'Do this,' and he does it."
⁹ When Jesus heard this, he was amazed at him, and turning to the crowd following him, he said, "I tell you, I have not found such great faith even in Israel." ¹⁰ Then the men who had been sent returned to the house and found the servant well.

JOHN

4:46 Once more he visited Cana in Galilee, where he had turned the water into wine. And there was a certain royal official whose son lay sick at Capernaum. ⁴⁷ When this man heard that Jesus had arrived in Galilee from Judea, he went to him and begged him to come and heal his son, who was close to death.
⁴⁸ "Unless you people see signs and wonders," Jesus told him, "you will never believe." ⁴⁹ The royal official said, "Sir, come down before my child dies." ⁵⁰ "Go," Jesus replied, "your son will live."
The man took Jesus at his word and departed. ⁵¹ While he was still on the way, his servants met him with the news that his boy was living. ⁵² When he inquired as to the time when his son got better, they said to him, "Yesterday, at one in the afternoon, the fever left him." ⁵³ Then the father realized that this was the exact time at which Jesus had said to him, "Your son will live." So he and his whole household believed.

1. Matthew and Luke tell this story differently, but clearly it is the same event. Is John describing it, too?

6.d Pick Up Your Mat and Walk

MATTHEW
9:1 Jesus stepped into a boat, crossed over and came to his own town. ² Some men brought to him a paralyzed man, lying on a mat. When Jesus saw their faith, he said to the man, "Take heart, son; your sins are forgiven." ³ At this, some of the teachers of the law said to themselves, "This fellow is blaspheming!"   ⁴ Knowing their thoughts, Jesus said, "Why do you entertain evil thoughts in your hearts? ⁵ Which is easier: to say, 'Your sins are forgiven,' or to say, 'Get up and walk'? ⁶ But I want you to know that the Son of Man has authority on earth to forgive sins." So he said to the paralyzed man, "Get up, take your mat and go home." ⁷ Then the man got up and went home. ⁸ When the crowd saw this, they were filled with awe; and they praised God, who had given such authority to man.

MARK
2:1 A few days later, when Jesus again entered Capernaum, the people heard that he had come home. ² They gathered in such large numbers that there was no room left, not even outside the door, and he preached the word to them. ³ Some men came, bringing to him a paralyzed man, carried by four of them. ⁴ Since they could not get him to Jesus because of the crowd, they made an opening in the roof above Jesus by digging through it and then lowered the mat the man was lying on. ⁵ When Jesus saw their faith, he said to the paralyzed man, "Son, your sins are forgiven."   ⁶ Now some teachers of the law were sitting there, thinking to themselves, ⁷ "Why does this fellow talk like that? He's blaspheming! Who can forgive sins but God alone?"   ⁸ Immediately Jesus knew in his spirit that this was what they were thinking in their hearts, and he said to them, "Why are you thinking these things? ⁹ Which is easier: to say to this paralyzed man, 'Your sins are forgiven,' or to say, 'Get up, take your mat and walk'? ¹⁰ But I want you to know that the Son of Man has authority on earth to forgive sins." So he said to the man, ¹¹ "I tell you, get up, take your mat and go home." ¹² He got up, took his mat and walked out in full view of them all. This amazed everyone and they praised God, saying, "We have never seen anything like this!"

LUKE
5:17 One day Jesus was teaching, and Pharisees and teachers of the law were sitting there. They had come from every village of Galilee and from Judea and Jerusalem. And the power of the Lord was with Jesus to heal the sick.   ¹⁸ Some men came carrying a paralyzed man on a mat and tried to take him into the house to lay him before Jesus.   ¹⁹ When they could not find a way to do this because of the crowd, they went up on the roof and lowered him on his mat through the tiles into the middle of the crowd, right in front of Jesus.   ²⁰ When Jesus saw their faith, he said, "Friend, your sins are forgiven." ²¹ The Pharisees and the teachers of the law began thinking to themselves, "Who is this fellow who speaks blasphemy? Who can forgive sins but God alone?"   ²² Jesus knew what they were thinking and asked, "Why are you thinking these things in your hearts? ²³ Which is easier: to say, 'Your sins are forgiven,' or to say, 'Get up and walk'? ²⁴ But I want you to know that the Son of Man has authority on earth to forgive sins." So he said to the paralyzed man, "I tell you, get up, take your mat and go home." ²⁵ Immediately he stood up in front of them, took what he had been lying on and went home praising God.   ²⁶ Everyone was amazed and gave praise to God. They were filled with awe and said, "We have seen remarkable things today."

JOHN
5:1 Some time later, Jesus went up to Jerusalem for one of the Jewish festivals. ² Now there is in Jerusalem near the Sheep Gate a pool, which in Aramaic is called Bethesda and which is surrounded by five covered colonnades. ³ Here a great number of disabled people used to lie—the blind, the lame, the paralyzed. [4] ⁵ One who was there had been an invalid for thirty-eight years. ⁶ When Jesus saw him lying there and learned that he had been in this condition for a long time, he asked him, "Do you want to get well?"   ⁷ "Sir," the invalid replied, "I have no one to help me into the pool when the water is stirred. While I am trying to get

in, someone else goes down ahead of me." ⁸ Then Jesus said to him, "Get up! Pick up your mat and walk." ⁹ At once the man was cured; he picked up his mat and walked.

The day on which this took place was a Sabbath, ¹⁰ and so the Jewish leaders said to the man who had been healed, "It is the Sabbath; the law forbids you to carry your mat." ¹¹ But he replied, "The man who made me well said to me, 'Pick up your mat and walk.' " ¹² So they asked him, "Who is this fellow who told you to pick it up and walk?"

¹³ The man who was healed had no idea who it was, for Jesus had slipped away into the crowd that was there.

¹⁴ Later Jesus found him at the temple and said to him, "See, you are well again. Stop sinning or something worse may happen to you." ¹⁵ The man went away and told the Jewish leaders that it was Jesus who had made him well.

1. Many times when Jesus talks about the Son of Man, it is unclear whether he is speaking about himself or someone else. Do you see such ambiguity here?
2. John's account is similar to the one in the Synoptics; is he in fact reporting on the same event?

6.e Resuscitations

MATTHEW
9:18 While he was saying this, a synagogue leader came and knelt before him and said, "My daughter has just died. But come and put your hand on her, and she will live." [19] Jesus got up and went with him, and so did his disciples. [20] Just then a woman who had been subject to bleeding for twelve years came up behind him and touched the edge of his cloak. [21] She said to herself, "If I only touch his cloak, I will be healed." [22] Jesus turned and saw her. "Take heart, daughter," he said, "your faith has healed you." And the woman was healed at that moment. [23] When Jesus entered the synagogue leader's house and saw the noisy crowd and people playing pipes, [24] he said, "Go away. The girl is not dead but asleep." But they laughed at him. [25] After the crowd had been put outside, he went in and took the girl by the hand, and she got up. [26] News of this spread through all that region.

MARK
5:21 When Jesus had again crossed over by boat to the other side of the lake, a large crowd gathered around him while he was by the lake. [22] Then one of the synagogue leaders, named Jairus, came, and when he saw Jesus, he fell at his feet. [23] He pleaded earnestly with him, "My little daughter is dying. Please come and put your hands on her so that she will be healed and live." [24] So Jesus went with him. A large crowd followed and pressed around him. [25] And a woman was there who had been subject to bleeding for twelve years. [26] She had suffered a great deal under the care of many doctors and had spent all she had, yet instead of getting better she grew worse. [27] When she heard about Jesus, she came up behind him in the crowd and touched his cloak, [28] because she thought, "If I just touch his clothes, I will be healed." [29] Immediately her bleeding stopped and she felt in her body that she was freed from her suffering. [30] At once Jesus realized that power had gone out from him. He turned around in the crowd and asked, "Who touched my clothes?" [31] "You see the people crowding against you," his disciples answered, "and yet you can ask, 'Who touched me?' " [32] But Jesus kept looking around to see who had done it. [33] Then the woman, knowing what had happened to her, came and fell at his feet and, trembling with fear, told him the whole truth. [34] He said to her, "Daughter, your faith has healed you. Go in peace and be freed from your suffering." [35] While Jesus was still speaking, some people came from the house of Jairus, the synagogue leader. "Your daughter is dead," they said. "Why bother the teacher anymore?" [36] Overhearing what they said, Jesus told him, "Don't be afraid; just believe." [37] He did not let anyone follow him except Peter, James and John the brother of James. [38] When they came to the home of the synagogue leader, Jesus saw a commotion, with people crying and wailing loudly. [39] He went in and said to them, "Why all this commotion and wailing? The child is not dead but asleep." [40] But they laughed at him. After he put them all out, he took the child's father and mother and the disciples who were with him, and went in where the child was. [41] He took her by the hand and said to her, *"Talitha koum!"* (which means "Little girl, I say to you, get up!"). [42] Immediately the girl stood up and began to walk around (she was twelve years old). At this they were completely astonished. [43] He gave strict orders not to let anyone know about this, and told them to give her something to eat.

LUKE
8:40 Now when Jesus returned, a crowd welcomed him, for they were all expecting him. [41] Then a man named Jairus, a synagogue leader, came and fell at Jesus' feet, pleading with him to come to his house [42] because his only daughter, a girl of about twelve, was dying. As Jesus was on his way, the crowds almost crushed him. [43] And a woman was there who had been subject to bleeding for twelve years, but no one could heal her. [44] She came up behind him and touched the edge of his cloak, and immediately her bleeding stopped. [45] "Who touched me?" Jesus asked. When they all denied it, Peter said, "Master, the people are crowding and pressing against you." [46] But Jesus said, "Someone touched me; I know that power has gone out from me." [47] Then the woman, seeing that she could not go unnoticed, came trembling and fell at his feet. In the presence of all

the people, she told why she had touched him and how she had been instantly healed. ⁴⁸ Then he said to her, "Daughter, your faith has healed you. Go in peace."

⁴⁹ While Jesus was still speaking, someone came from the house of Jairus, the synagogue leader. "Your daughter is dead," he said. "Don't bother the teacher anymore." ⁵⁰ Hearing this, Jesus said to Jairus, "Don't be afraid; just believe, and she will be healed."

⁵¹ When he arrived at the house of Jairus, he did not let anyone go in with him except Peter, John and James, and the child's father and mother. ⁵² Meanwhile, all the people were wailing and mourning for her. "Stop wailing," Jesus said. "She is not dead but asleep."

⁵³ They laughed at him, knowing that she was dead. ⁵⁴ But he took her by the hand and said, "My child, get up!"

⁵⁵ Her spirit returned, and at once she stood up. Then Jesus told them to give her something to eat. ⁵⁶ Her parents were astonished, but he ordered them not to tell anyone what had happened.

JOHN

11:1 Now a man named Lazarus was sick. He was from Bethany, the village of Mary and her sister Martha. ² (This Mary, whose brother Lazarus now lay sick, was the same one who poured perfume on the Lord and wiped his feet with her hair.) ³ So the sisters sent word to Jesus, "Lord, the one you love is sick." ⁴ When he heard this, Jesus said, "This sickness will not end in death. No, it is for God's glory so that God's Son may be glorified through it."

* * *

11:38 Jesus, once more deeply moved, came to the tomb. It was a cave with a stone laid across the entrance. ³⁹ "Take away the stone," he said. "But, Lord," said Martha, the sister of the dead man, "by this time there is a bad odor, for he has been there four days." ⁴⁰ Then Jesus said, "Did I not tell you that if you believe, you will see the glory of God?"

⁴¹ So they took away the stone. Then Jesus looked up and said, "Father, I thank you that you have heard me. ⁴² I knew that you always hear me, but I said this for the benefit of the people standing here, that they may believe that you sent me."

⁴³ When he had said this, Jesus called in a loud voice, "Lazarus, come out!" ⁴⁴ The dead man came out, his hands and feet wrapped with strips of linen, and a cloth around his face. Jesus said to them, "Take off the grave clothes and let him go."

1. Mark and Luke give the revival of Jairus' daughter due attention, while Matthew seems to give it short shrift. Can you speculate as to why?
2. Compare the three accounts of the bleeding woman. Why do you suppose this healing appears in the middle of the revival story?
3. The Gospels contain one other revival account, that of Lazarus. Compare the two events.

6.f Jesus Heals the Blind

MATTHEW
9:27 As Jesus went on from there, two blind men followed him, calling out, "Have mercy on us, Son of David!" [28] When he had gone indoors, the blind men came to him, and he asked them, "Do you believe that I am able to do this?" "Yes, Lord," they replied. [29] Then he touched their eyes and said, "According to your faith let it be done to you"; [30] and their sight was restored. Jesus warned them sternly, "See that no one knows about this." [31] But they went out and spread the news about him all over that region. * * * 20:29 As Jesus and his disciples were leaving Jericho, a large crowd followed him. [30] Two blind men were sitting by the roadside, and when they heard that Jesus was going by, they shouted, "Lord, Son of David, have mercy on us!" [31] The crowd rebuked them and told them to be quiet, but they shouted all the louder, "Lord, Son of David, have mercy on us!" [32] Jesus stopped and called them. "What do you want me to do for you?" he asked. [33] "Lord," they answered, "we want our sight." [34] Jesus had compassion on them and touched their eyes. Immediately they received their sight and followed him.

MARK
10:46 Then they came to Jericho. As Jesus and his disciples, together with a large crowd, were leaving the city, a blind man, Bartimaeus (which means "son of Timaeus"), was sitting by the roadside begging. [47] When he heard that it was Jesus of Nazareth, he began to shout, "Jesus, Son of David, have mercy on me!" [48] Many rebuked him and told him to be quiet, but he shouted all the more, "Son of David, have mercy on me!" [49] Jesus stopped and said, "Call him." So they called to the blind man, "Cheer up! On your feet! He's calling you." [50] Throwing his cloak aside, he jumped to his feet and came to Jesus. [51] "What do you want me to do for you?" Jesus asked him. The blind man said, "Rabbi, I want to see." [52] "Go," said Jesus, "your faith has healed you." Immediately he received his sight and followed Jesus along the road.

LUKE
18:35 As Jesus approached Jericho, a blind man was sitting by the roadside begging. [36] When he heard the crowd going by, he asked what was happening. [37] They told him, "Jesus of Nazareth is passing by." [38] He called out, "Jesus, Son of David, have mercy on me!" [39] Those who led the way rebuked him and told him to be quiet, but he shouted all the more, "Son of David, have mercy on me!" [40] Jesus stopped and ordered the man to be brought to him. When he came near, Jesus asked him, [41] "What do you want me to do for you?" "Lord, I want to see," he replied. [42] Jesus said to him, "Receive your sight; your faith has healed you." [43] Immediately he received his sight and followed Jesus, praising God. When all the people saw it, they also praised God.

JOHN
9:1 As he went along, he saw a man blind from birth. [2] His disciples asked him, "Rabbi, who sinned, this man or his parents, that he was born blind?" [9:3] "Neither this man nor his parents sinned," said Jesus, "but this happened so that the works of God might be displayed in him." [6] After saying this, he spit on the ground, made some mud with the saliva, and put it on the man's eyes. [7] "Go," he told him, "wash in the Pool of Siloam" (this word means "Sent"). So the man went and washed, and came home seeing. [8] His neighbors and those who had formerly seen him begging asked, "Isn't this the same man who used to sit and beg?" [9] Some claimed that he was. Others said, "No, he only looks like him." But he himself insisted, "I am the man." [10] "How then were your eyes opened?" they asked. [11] He replied, "The man they call Jesus made some mud and put it on my eyes. He told me to go to Siloam and wash. So I went and washed, and then I could see." [12] "Where is this man?" they asked him. "I don't know," he said. [13] They brought to the Pharisees the man who had been blind. [14] Now the day on which Jesus had made the mud and opened the man's eyes was a Sabbath. [15] Therefore the Pharisees also asked him how he had received his sight. "He

put mud on my eyes," the man replied, "and I washed, and now I see." ^{16} Some of the Pharisees said, "This man is not from God, for he does not keep the Sabbath." But others asked, "How can a sinner perform such signs?" So they were divided. ^{17} Then they turned again to the blind man, "What have you to say about him? It was your eyes he opened." The man replied, "He is a prophet."

^{18} They still did not believe that he had been blind and had received his sight until they sent for the man's parents. ^{19} "Is this your son?" they asked. "Is this the one you say was born blind? How is it that now he can see?" ^{20} "We know he is our son," the parents answered, "and we know he was born blind. ^{21} But how he can see now, or who opened his eyes, we don't know. Ask him. He is of age; he will speak for himself." ^{22} His parents said this because they were afraid of the Jewish leaders, who already had decided that anyone who acknowledged that Jesus was the Messiah would be put out of the synagogue. ^{23} That was why his parents said, "He is of age; ask him."

^{24} A second time they summoned the man who had been blind. "Give glory to God by telling the truth," they said. "We know this man is a sinner." ^{25} He replied, "Whether he is a sinner or not, I don't know. One thing I do know. I was blind but now I see!" ^{26} Then they asked him, "What did he do to you? How did he open your eyes?" ^{27} He answered, "I have told you already and you did not listen. Why do you want to hear it again? Do you want to become his disciples too?"

^{28} Then they hurled insults at him and said, "You are this fellow's disciple! We are disciples of Moses! ^{29} We know that God spoke to Moses, but as for this fellow, we don't even know where he comes from." ^{30} The man answered, "Now that is remarkable! You don't know where he comes from, yet he opened my eyes. ^{31} We know that God does not listen to sinners. He listens to the godly person who does his will. ^{32} Nobody has ever heard of opening the eyes of a man born blind. ^{33} If this man were not from God, he could do nothing."

1. Taking into account the similarities and differences, how many such healings, total, do the Gospels tell about?
2. John gives an extraordinary amount of detail in his account, which could have been reported much more briefly. Why do you suppose John included so much detail?

6.g Jesus Heals a Shriveled Hand

MATTHEW
12:9 Going on from that place, he went into their synagogue, [10] and a man with a shriveled hand was there. Looking for a reason to bring charges against Jesus, they asked him, "Is it lawful to heal on the Sabbath?" [11] He said to them, "If any of you has a sheep and it falls into a pit on the Sabbath, will you not take hold of it and lift it out? [12] How much more valuable is a person than a sheep! Therefore it is lawful to do good on the Sabbath." [13] Then he said to the man, "Stretch out your hand." So he stretched it out and it was completely restored, just as sound as the other. [14] But the Pharisees went out and plotted how they might kill Jesus.
MARK
3:1 Another time Jesus went into the synagogue, and a man with a shriveled hand was there. [2] Some of them were looking for a reason to accuse Jesus, so they watched him closely to see if he would heal him on the Sabbath. [3] Jesus said to the man with the shriveled hand, "Stand up in front of everyone." [4] Then Jesus asked them, "Which is lawful on the Sabbath: to do good or to do evil, to save life or to kill?" But they remained silent. [5] He looked around at them in anger and, deeply distressed at their stubborn hearts, said to the man, "Stretch out your hand." He stretched it out, and his hand was completely restored. [6] Then the Pharisees went out and began to plot with the Herodians how they might kill Jesus.
LUKE
6:6 On another Sabbath he went into the synagogue and was teaching, and a man was there whose right hand was shriveled. [7] The Pharisees and the teachers of the law were looking for a reason to accuse Jesus, so they watched him closely to see if he would heal on the Sabbath. [8] But Jesus knew what they were thinking and said to the man with the shriveled hand, "Get up and stand in front of everyone." So he got up and stood there. [9] Then Jesus said to them, "I ask you, which is lawful on the Sabbath: to do good or to do evil, to save life or to destroy it?" [10] He looked around at them all, and then said to the man, "Stretch out your hand." He did so, and his hand was completely restored. [11] But the Pharisees and the teachers of the law were furious and began to discuss with one another what they might do to Jesus.
JOHN
5:16 So, because Jesus was doing these things on the Sabbath, the Jewish leaders began to persecute him. [17] In his defense Jesus said to them, "My Father is always at his work to this very day, and I too am working."

1. Compare the four key statements of Jesus concerning the permissibility of working on the Sabbath.

6.h Healings at Gennesaret

MATTHEW
14:34 When they had crossed over, they landed at Gennesaret. [35] And when the men of that place recognized Jesus, they sent word to all the surrounding country. People brought all their sick to him [36] and begged him to let the sick just touch the edge of his cloak, and all who touched it were healed.
MARK
6:53 When they had crossed over, they landed at Gennesaret and anchored there. [54] As soon as they got out of the boat, people recognized Jesus. [55] They ran throughout that whole region and carried the sick on mats to wherever they heard he was. [56] And wherever he went—into villages, towns or countryside—they placed the sick in the marketplaces. They begged him to let them touch even the edge of his cloak, and all who touched it were healed.
LUKE
JOHN

Chapter 7: Exorcisms

7.a Jesus Casts Out a Demon

MATTHEW
4:23 Jesus went throughout Galilee, teaching in their synagogues, proclaiming the good news of the kingdom, and healing every disease and sickness among the people. [24] News about him spread all over Syria, and people brought to him all who were ill with various diseases, those suffering severe pain, the demon-possessed, those having seizures, and the paralyzed; and he healed them. [25] Large crowds from Galilee, the Decapolis, Jerusalem, Judea and the region across the Jordan followed him.

MARK
1:23 Just then a man in their synagogue who was possessed by an impure spirit cried out, [24] "What do you want with us, Jesus of Nazareth? Have you come to destroy us? I know who you are—the Holy One of God!" [25] "Be quiet!" said Jesus sternly. "Come out of him!" [26] The impure spirit shook the man violently and came out of him with a shriek. [27] The people were all so amazed that they asked each other, "What is this? A new teaching—and with authority! He even gives orders to impure spirits and they obey him." [28] News about him spread quickly over the whole region of Galilee.

LUKE
4:33 In the synagogue there was a man possessed by a demon, an impure spirit. He cried out at the top of his voice, [34] "Go away! What do you want with us, Jesus of Nazareth? Have you come to destroy us? I know who you are—the Holy One of God!" [35] "Be quiet!" Jesus said sternly. "Come out of him!" Then the demon threw the man down before them all and came out without injuring him. [36] All the people were amazed and said to each other, "What words these are! With authority and power he gives orders to impure spirits and they come out!" [37] And the news about him spread throughout the surrounding area.

JOHN

1. Luke repeats Mark's account almost verbatim, while Matthew just includes healing those possessed by demons in a list of other healings. What might account for Matthew's de-emphasis of this remarkable healing?

7.b The Gerasene Swine

MATTHEW
8:28 When he arrived at the other side in the region of the Gadarenes, two demon-possessed men coming from the tombs met him. They were so violent that no one could pass that way. ²⁹ "What do you want with us, Son of God?" they shouted. "Have you come here to torture us before the appointed time?" ³⁰ Some distance from them a large herd of pigs was feeding. ³¹ The demons begged Jesus, "If you drive us out, send us into the herd of pigs." ³² He said to them, "Go!" So they came out and went into the pigs, and the whole herd rushed down the steep bank into the lake and died in the water. ³³ Those tending the pigs ran off, went into the town and reported all this, including what had happened to the demon-possessed men. ³⁴ Then the whole town went out to meet Jesus. And when they saw him, they pleaded with him to leave their region.

MARK
5:1 They went across the lake to the region of the Gerasenes. ² When Jesus got out of the boat, a man with an impure spirit came from the tombs to meet him. ³ This man lived in the tombs, and no one could bind him anymore, not even with a chain. ⁴ For he had often been chained hand and foot, but he tore the chains apart and broke the irons on his feet. No one was strong enough to subdue him. ⁵ Night and day among the tombs and in the hills he would cry out and cut himself with stones. ⁶ When he saw Jesus from a distance, he ran and fell on his knees in front of him. ⁷ He shouted at the top of his voice, "What do you want with me, Jesus, Son of the Most High God? In God's name don't torture me!" ⁸ For Jesus had said to him, "Come out of this man, you impure spirit!" ⁹ Then Jesus asked him, "What is your name?" "My name is Legion," he replied, "for we are many." ¹⁰ And he begged Jesus again and again not to send them out of the area. ¹¹ A large herd of pigs was feeding on the nearby hillside. ¹² The demons begged Jesus, "Send us among the pigs; allow us to go into them." ¹³ He gave them permission, and the impure spirits came out and went into the pigs. The herd, about two thousand in number, rushed down the steep bank into the lake and were drowned. ¹⁴ Those tending the pigs ran off and reported this in the town and countryside, and the people went out to see what had happened. ¹⁵ When they came to Jesus, they saw the man who had been possessed by the legion of demons, sitting there, dressed and in his right mind; and they were afraid. ¹⁶ Those who had seen it told the people what had happened to the demon-possessed man—and told about the pigs as well. ¹⁷ Then the people began to plead with Jesus to leave their region. ¹⁸ As Jesus was getting into the boat, the man who had been demon-possessed begged to go with him. ¹⁹ Jesus did not let him, but said, "Go home to your own people and tell them how much the Lord has done for you, and how he has had mercy on you." ²⁰ So the man went away and began to tell in the Decapolis how much Jesus had done for him. And all the people were amazed.

LUKE
8:26 They sailed to the region of the Gerasenes, which is across the lake from Galilee. ²⁷ When Jesus stepped ashore, he was met by a demon-possessed man from the town. For a long time this man had not worn clothes or lived in a house, but had lived in the tombs. ²⁸ When he saw Jesus, he cried out and fell at his feet, shouting at the top of his voice, "What do you want with me, Jesus, Son of the Most High God? I beg you, don't torture me!" ²⁹ For Jesus had commanded the impure spirit to come out of the man. Many times it had seized him, and though he was chained hand and foot and kept under guard, he had broken his chains and had been driven by the demon into solitary places. ³⁰ Jesus asked him, "What is your name?" "Legion," he replied, because many demons had gone into him. ³¹ And they begged Jesus repeatedly not to order them to go into the Abyss. ³² A large herd of pigs was feeding there on the hillside. The demons begged Jesus to let them go into the pigs, and he gave them permission. ³³ When the demons came out of the man, they went into the pigs, and the herd rushed down the steep bank into the lake and was drowned. ³⁴ When those tending the pigs saw what had happened, they ran off and reported this in the town and countryside,

³⁵ and the people went out to see what had happened. When they came to Jesus, they found the man from whom the demons had gone out, sitting at Jesus' feet, dressed and in his right mind; and they were afraid. ³⁶ Those who had seen it told the people how the demon-possessed man had been cured. ³⁷ Then all the people of the region of the Gerasenes asked Jesus to leave them, because they were overcome with fear. So he got into the boat and left. ³⁸ The man from whom the demons had gone out begged to go with him, but Jesus sent him away, saying, ³⁹ "Return home and tell how much God has done for you." So the man went away and told all over town how much Jesus had done for him.

JOHN

1. How many demon-possessed men were involved in this incident?
2. Again, Matthew seems to have less interest than Mark or Luke in reporting the casting out of a demon. What details do Mark or Luke include that Matthew omits? Did Matthew omit anything you consider important?

7.c Driving Out Demons

MATTHEW

9:32 While they were going out, a man who was demon-possessed and could not talk was brought to Jesus. ³³ And when the demon was driven out, the man who had been mute spoke. The crowd was amazed and said, "Nothing like this has ever been seen in Israel." ³⁴ But the Pharisees said, "It is by the prince of demons that he drives out demons."

* * *

12:22 Then they brought him a demon-possessed man who was blind and mute, and Jesus healed him, so that he could both talk and see. ²³ All the people were astonished and said, "Could this be the Son of David?" ²⁴ But when the Pharisees heard this, they said, "It is only by Beelzebul, the prince of demons, that this fellow drives out demons."
²⁵ Jesus knew their thoughts and said to them, "Every kingdom divided against itself will be ruined, and every city or household divided against itself will not stand. ²⁶ If Satan drives out Satan, he is divided against himself. How then can his kingdom stand? ²⁷ And if I drive out demons by Beelzebul, by whom do your people drive them out? So then, they will be your judges. ²⁸ But if it is by the Spirit of God that I drive out demons, then the kingdom of God has come upon you. ²⁹ "Or again, how can anyone enter a strong man's house and carry off his possessions unless he first ties up the strong man? Then he can plunder his house.

MARK

3:20 Then Jesus entered a house, and again a crowd gathered, so that he and his disciples were not even able to eat. ²¹ When his family heard about this, they went to take charge of him, for they said, "He is out of his mind." ²² And the teachers of the law who came down from Jerusalem said, "He is possessed by Beelzebul! By the prince of demons he is driving out demons."
²³ So Jesus called them over to him and began to speak to them in parables: "How can Satan drive out Satan? ²⁴ If a kingdom is divided against itself, that kingdom cannot stand. ²⁵ If a house is divided against itself, that house cannot stand. ²⁶ And if Satan opposes himself and is divided, he cannot stand; his end has come. ²⁷ In fact, no one can enter a strong man's house without first tying him up. Then he can plunder the strong man's house. ²⁸ Truly I tell you, people can be forgiven all their sins and every slander they utter, ²⁹ but whoever blasphemes against the Holy Spirit will never be forgiven; they are guilty of an eternal sin." ³⁰ He said this because they were saying, "He has an impure spirit."
³¹ Then Jesus' mother and brothers arrived. Standing outside, they sent someone in to call him. ³² A crowd was sitting around him, and they told him, "Your mother and brothers are outside looking for you." ³³ "Who are my mother and my brothers?" he asked. ³⁴ Then he looked at those seated in a circle around him and said, "Here are my mother and my brothers! ³⁵ Whoever does God's will is my brother and sister and mother."

LUKE

11:14 Jesus was driving out a demon that was mute. When the demon left, the man who had been mute spoke, and the crowd was amazed. ¹⁵ But some of them said, "By Beelzebul, the prince of demons, he is driving out demons." ¹⁶ Others tested him by asking for a sign from heaven.
¹⁷ Jesus knew their thoughts and said to them: "Any kingdom divided against itself will be ruined, and a house divided against itself will fall. ¹⁸ If Satan is divided against himself, how can his kingdom stand? I say this because you claim that I drive out demons by Beelzebul. ¹⁹ Now if I drive out demons by Beelzebul, by whom do your followers drive them out? So then, they will be your judges. ²⁰ But if I drive out demons by the finger of God, then the kingdom of God has come upon you.
²¹ "When a strong man, fully armed, guards his own house, his possessions are safe. ²² But when someone stronger attacks and overpowers him, he takes away the armor in which the man trusted and divides up his plunder.
²³ "Whoever is not with me is against me, and whoever does not gather with me scatters.
²⁴ "When an impure spirit comes out of a person, it goes through arid places seeking rest and does not find it. Then it says, 'I will return to the house I left.' ²⁵ When it arrives, it finds the house swept clean and put in order. ²⁶ Then it

goes and takes seven other spirits more wicked than itself, and they go in and live there. And the final condition of that person is worse than the first."

²⁷ As Jesus was saying these things, a woman in the crowd called out, "Blessed is the mother who gave you birth and nursed you." ²⁸ He replied, "Blessed rather are those who hear the word of God and obey it."

JOHN

1. Do you find any interesting differences in these three accounts?

7.d Jesus Heals a Demon-Possessed Girl

MATTHEW
15:21 Leaving that place, Jesus withdrew to the region of Tyre and Sidon. [22] A Canaanite woman from that vicinity came to him, crying out, "Lord, Son of David, have mercy on me! My daughter is demon-possessed and suffering terribly." [23] Jesus did not answer a word. So his disciples came to him and urged him, "Send her away, for she keeps crying out after us." [24] He answered, "I was sent only to the lost sheep of Israel." [25] The woman came and knelt before him. "Lord, help me!" she said. [26] He replied, "It is not right to take the children's bread and toss it to the dogs." [27] "Yes it is, Lord," she said. "Even the dogs eat the crumbs that fall from their master's table." [28] Then Jesus said to her, "Woman, you have great faith! Your request is granted." And her daughter was healed at that moment.

MARK
7:24 Jesus left that place and went to the vicinity of Tyre. He entered a house and did not want anyone to know it; yet he could not keep his presence secret. [25] In fact, as soon as she heard about him, a woman whose little daughter was possessed by an impure spirit came and fell at his feet. [26] The woman was a Greek, born in Syrian Phoenicia. She begged Jesus to drive the demon out of her daughter. [27] "First let the children eat all they want," he told her, "for it is not right to take the children's bread and toss it to the dogs." [28] "Lord," she replied, "even the dogs under the table eat the children's crumbs." [29] Then he told her, "For such a reply, you may go; the demon has left your daughter." [30] She went home and found her child lying on the bed, and the demon gone.

LUKE
6:17 He went down with them and stood on a level place. A large crowd of his disciples was there and a great number of people from all over Judea, from Jerusalem, and from the coastal region around Tyre and Sidon, [18] who had come to hear him and to be healed of their diseases. Those troubled by impure spirits were cured, [19] and the people all tried to touch him, because power was coming from him and healing them all.

JOHN

1. What did Jesus mean by his comment about bread and dogs, in the variations reported by Matthew and Mark? What does the episode indicate about Jesus' mission?
2. Luke seems to be talking about the same time of healing, yet he omits the episode first reported in Mark. Why do you suppose he did so?

7.e Jesus Drives Out a Boy's Demon

MATTHEW
17:14 When they came to the crowd, a man approached Jesus and knelt before him. [15] "Lord, have mercy on my son," he said. "He has seizures and is suffering greatly. He often falls into the fire or into the water. [16] I brought him to your disciples, but they could not heal him." [17] "You unbelieving and perverse generation," Jesus replied, "how long shall I stay with you? How long shall I put up with you? Bring the boy here to me." [18] Jesus rebuked the demon, and it came out of the boy, and he was healed at that moment. [19] Then the disciples came to Jesus in private and asked, "Why couldn't we drive it out?" [20] He replied, "Because you have so little faith. Truly I tell you, if you have faith as small as a mustard seed, you can say to this mountain, 'Move from here to there,' and it will move. Nothing will be impossible for you."

MARK
9:14 When they came to the other disciples, they saw a large crowd around them and the teachers of the law arguing with them. [15] As soon as all the people saw Jesus, they were overwhelmed with wonder and ran to greet him. [16] "What are you arguing with them about?" he asked. [17] A man in the crowd answered, "Teacher, I brought you my son, who is possessed by a spirit that has robbed him of speech. [18] Whenever it seizes him, it throws him to the ground. He foams at the mouth, gnashes his teeth and becomes rigid. I asked your disciples to drive out the spirit, but they could not." [19] "You unbelieving generation," Jesus replied, "how long shall I stay with you? How long shall I put up with you? Bring the boy to me." [20] So they brought him. When the spirit saw Jesus, it immediately threw the boy into a convulsion. He fell to the ground and rolled around, foaming at the mouth. [21] Jesus asked the boy's father, "How long has he been like this?" "From childhood," he answered. [22] "It has often thrown him into fire or water to kill him. But if you can do anything, take pity on us and help us." [23] "'If you can'?" said Jesus. "Everything is possible for one who believes." [24] Immediately the boy's father exclaimed, "I do believe; help me overcome my unbelief!" [25] When Jesus saw that a crowd was running to the scene, he rebuked the impure spirit. "You deaf and mute spirit," he said, "I command you, come out of him and never enter him again." [26] The spirit shrieked, convulsed him violently and came out. The boy looked so much like a corpse that many said, "He's dead." [27] But Jesus took him by the hand and lifted him to his feet, and he stood up. [28] After Jesus had gone indoors, his disciples asked him privately, "Why couldn't we drive it out?" [29] He replied, "This kind can come out only by prayer."

LUKE
9:37 The next day, when they came down from the mountain, a large crowd met him. [38] A man in the crowd called out, "Teacher, I beg you to look at my son, for he is my only child. [39] A spirit seizes him and he suddenly screams; it throws him into convulsions so that he foams at the mouth. It scarcely ever leaves him and is destroying him. [40] I begged your disciples to drive it out, but they could not." [41] "You unbelieving and perverse generation," Jesus replied, "how long shall I stay with you and put up with you? Bring your son here." [42] Even while the boy was coming, the demon threw him to the ground in a convulsion. But Jesus rebuked the impure spirit, healed the boy and gave him back to his father. [43] And they were all amazed at the greatness of God.

JOHN

1. All three Synoptic Gospels repeat Jesus' words about the unbelieving generation. About whom is he speaking and why does he use such harsh language?

2. What do you make of the fact that the disciples had been unable to cure the boy?

7.f Others Driving Out Demons

MATTHEW

MARK
9:38 "Teacher," said John, "we saw someone driving out demons in your name and we told him to stop, because he was not one of us." ³⁹ "Do not stop him," Jesus said. "For no one who does a miracle in my name can in the next moment say anything bad about me, ⁴⁰ for whoever is not against us is for us. ⁴¹ Truly I tell you, anyone who gives you a cup of water in my name because you belong to the Messiah will certainly not lose their reward.

LUKE
8:1 After this, Jesus traveled about from one town and village to another, proclaiming the good news of the kingdom of God. The Twelve were with him, ² and also some women who had been cured of evil spirits and diseases: Mary (called Magdalene) from whom seven demons had come out; ³ Joanna the wife of Chuza, the manager of Herod's household; Susanna; and many others. These women were helping to support them out of their own means. * * * 9:49 "Master," said John, "we saw someone driving out demons in your name and we tried to stop him, because he is not one of us." ⁵⁰ "Do not stop him," Jesus said, "for whoever is not against you is for you."

JOHN

1. What do you think was on the minds of John and the other disciples when they spoke to the unidentified exorcist driving out demons? How does Jesus' rejoinder relate?
2. Have you noted in this past section on the driving out of demons that John's Gospel never mentions the subject? Why do you suppose that is?

CHAPTER 8: SUPERNATURAL ACTIONS

8.a. Jesus Calms the Storm

MATTHEW
8:23 Then he got into the boat and his disciples followed him. [24] Suddenly a furious storm came up on the lake, so that the waves swept over the boat. But Jesus was sleeping. [25] The disciples went and woke him, saying, "Lord, save us! We're going to drown!" [26] He replied, "You of little faith, why are you so afraid?" Then he got up and rebuked the winds and the waves, and it was completely calm. [27] The men were amazed and asked, "What kind of man is this? Even the winds and the waves obey him!"

MARK
4:35 That day when evening came, he said to his disciples, "Let us go over to the other side." [36] Leaving the crowd behind, they took him along, just as he was, in the boat. There were also other boats with him. [37] A furious squall came up, and the waves broke over the boat, so that it was nearly swamped. [38] Jesus was in the stern, sleeping on a cushion. The disciples woke him and said to him, "Teacher, don't you care if we drown?" [39] He got up, rebuked the wind and said to the waves, "Quiet! Be still!" Then the wind died down and it was completely calm. [40] He said to his disciples, "Why are you so afraid? Do you still have no faith?" [41] They were terrified and asked each other, "Who is this? Even the wind and the waves obey him!"

LUKE
8:22 One day Jesus said to his disciples, "Let us go over to the other side of the lake." So they got into a boat and set out. [23] As they sailed, he fell asleep. A squall came down on the lake, so that the boat was being swamped, and they were in great danger. [24] The disciples went and woke him, saying, "Master, Master, we're going to drown!" He got up and rebuked the wind and the raging waters; the storm subsided, and all was calm. [25] "Where is your faith?" he asked his disciples. In fear and amazement they asked one another, "Who is this? He commands even the winds and the water, and they obey him."

JOHN

1. Can you identify any significant differences among the three passages?

8.b A Prodigious Catch of Fish

MATTHEW
13:47 "Once again, the kingdom of heaven is like a net that was let down into the lake and caught all kinds of fish. [48] When it was full, the fishermen pulled it up on the shore. Then they sat down and collected the good fish in baskets, but threw the bad away. [49] This is how it will be at the end of the age. The angels will come and separate the wicked from the righteous [50] and throw them into the blazing furnace, where there will be weeping and gnashing of teeth.

MARK

LUKE
5:1 One day as Jesus was standing by the Lake of Gennesaret, the people were crowding around him and listening to the word of God. [2] He saw at the water's edge two boats, left there by the fishermen, who were washing their nets. [3] He got into one of the boats, the one belonging to Simon, and asked him to put out a little from shore. Then he sat down and taught the people from the boat. [4] When he had finished speaking, he said to Simon, "Put out into deep water, and let down the nets for a catch." [5] Simon answered, "Master, we've worked hard all night and haven't caught anything. But because you say so, I will let down the nets." [6] When they had done so, they caught such a large number of fish that their nets began to break. [7] So they signaled their partners in the other boat to come and help them, and they came and filled both boats so full that they began to sink. [8] When Simon Peter saw this, he fell at Jesus' knees and said, "Go away from me, Lord; I am a sinful man!" [9] For he and all his companions were astonished at the catch of fish they had taken, [10] and so were James and John, the sons of Zebedee, Simon's partners. Then Jesus said to Simon, "Don't be afraid; from now on you will fish for people." [11] So they pulled their boats up on shore, left everything and followed him.

JOHN
21:1 Afterward Jesus appeared again to his disciples, by the Sea of Galilee. It happened this way: [2] Simon Peter, Thomas (also known as Didymus), Nathanael from Cana in Galilee, the sons of Zebedee, and two other disciples were together. [3] "I'm going out to fish," Simon Peter told them, and they said, "We'll go with you." So they went out and got into the boat, but that night they caught nothing. [4] Early in the morning, Jesus stood on the shore, but the disciples did not realize that it was Jesus. [5] He called out to them, "Friends, haven't you any fish?" "No," they answered. [6] He said, "Throw your net on the right side of the boat and you will find some." When they did, they were unable to haul the net in because of the large number of fish. [7] Then the disciple whom Jesus loved said to Peter, "It is the Lord!" As soon as Simon Peter heard him say, "It is the Lord," he wrapped his outer garment around him (for he had taken it off) and jumped into the water. [8] The other disciples followed in the boat, towing the net full of fish, for they were not far from shore, about a hundred yards. [9] When they landed, they saw a fire of burning coals there with fish on it, and some bread. [10] Jesus said to them, "Bring some of the fish you have just caught." [11] So Simon Peter climbed back into the boat and dragged the net ashore. It was full of large fish, 153, but even with so many the net was not torn. [12] Jesus said to them, "Come and have breakfast." None of the disciples dared ask him, "Who are you?" They knew it was the Lord. [13] Jesus came, took the bread and gave it to them, and did the same with the fish. [14] This was now the third time Jesus appeared to his disciples after he was raised from the dead.

1. The episode of the great catch of fish is remarkably similar in Luke's and John's accounts. What differences can you identify? One is especially interesting.

2. Matthew uses the simile of a net full of fish, but does not connect it with the episode reported by Luke and John. Yet does Matthew's brief version shed any light on our interpretation of the story in Luke and John?
3. Considering how so many vignettes from Jesus' ministry are found first in Mark, then embellished in Matthew and/or Luke, but omitted from John, what do we make of finding this episode only in Luke and John?

8.c Feeding the 5,000

MATTHEW

14:13 When Jesus heard what had happened, he withdrew by boat privately to a solitary place. Hearing of this, the crowds followed him on foot from the towns. [14] When Jesus landed and saw a large crowd, he had compassion on them and healed their sick.
[15] As evening approached, the disciples came to him and said, "This is a remote place, and it's already getting late. Send the crowds away, so they can go to the villages and buy themselves some food."
[16] Jesus replied, "They do not need to go away. You give them something to eat." [17] "We have here only five loaves of bread and two fish," they answered.
[18] "Bring them here to me," he said. [19] And he directed the people to sit down on the grass. Taking the five loaves and the two fish and looking up to heaven, he gave thanks and broke the loaves. Then he gave them to the disciples, and the disciples gave them to the people. [20] They all ate and were satisfied, and the disciples picked up twelve basketfuls of broken pieces that were left over. [21] The number of those who ate was about five thousand men, besides women and children.

MARK

6:30 The apostles gathered around Jesus and reported to him all they had done and taught. [31] Then, because so many people were coming and going that they did not even have a chance to eat, he said to them, "Come with me by yourselves to a quiet place and get some rest."
[32] So they went away by themselves in a boat to a solitary place. [33] But many who saw them leaving recognized them and ran on foot from all the towns and got there ahead of them. [34] When Jesus landed and saw a large crowd, he had compassion on them, because they were like sheep without a shepherd. So he began teaching them many things.
[35] By this time it was late in the day, so his disciples came to him. "This is a remote place," they said, "and it's already very late. [36] Send the people away so that they can go to the surrounding countryside and villages and buy themselves something to eat."
[37] But he answered, "You give them something to eat." They said to him, "That would take more than half a year's wages! Are we to go and spend that much on bread and give it to them to eat?"
[38] "How many loaves do you have?" he asked. "Go and see." When they found out, they said, "Five—and two fish."
[39] Then Jesus directed them to have all the people sit down in groups on the green grass. [40] So they sat down in groups of hundreds and fifties. [41] Taking the five loaves and the two fish and looking up to heaven, he gave thanks and broke the loaves. Then he gave them to his disciples to distribute to the people. He also divided the two fish among them all. [42] They all ate and were satisfied, [43] and the disciples picked up twelve basketfuls of broken pieces of bread and fish. [44] The number of the men who had eaten was five thousand.

LUKE

9:10 When the apostles returned, they reported to Jesus what they had done. Then he took them with him and they withdrew by themselves to a town called Bethsaida, [11] but the crowds learned about it and followed him. He welcomed them and spoke to them about the kingdom of God, and healed those who needed healing.
[12] Late in the afternoon the Twelve came to him and said, "Send the crowd away so they can go to the surrounding villages and countryside and find food and lodging, because we are in a remote place here."
[13] He replied, "You give them something to eat." They answered, "We have only five loaves of bread and two fish—unless we go and buy food for all this crowd." [14] (About five thousand men were there.)
But he said to his disciples, "Have them sit down in groups of about fifty each." [15] The disciples did so, and everyone sat down. [16] Taking the five loaves and the two fish and looking up to heaven, he gave thanks and broke them. Then he gave them to the disciples to distribute to the people. [17] They all ate and were satisfied, and the disciples picked up twelve basketfuls of broken pieces that were left over.

JOHN

6:1 Some time after this, Jesus crossed to the far shore of the Sea of Galilee (that is, the Sea of Tiberias), ² and a great crowd of people followed him because they saw the signs he had performed by healing the sick. ³ Then Jesus went up on a mountainside and sat down with his disciples. ⁴ The Jewish Passover Festival was near.

⁵ When Jesus looked up and saw a great crowd coming toward him, he said to Philip, "Where shall we buy bread for these people to eat?" ⁶ He asked this only to test him, for he already had in mind what he was going to do. ⁷ Philip answered him, "It would take more than half a year's wages to buy enough bread for each one to have a bite!"

⁸ Another of his disciples, Andrew, Simon Peter's brother, spoke up, ⁹ "Here is a boy with five small barley loaves and two small fish, but how far will they go among so many?"

¹⁰ Jesus said, "Have the people sit down." There was plenty of grass in that place, and they sat down (about five thousand men were there). ¹¹ Jesus then took the loaves, gave thanks, and distributed to those who were seated as much as they wanted. He did the same with the fish.

¹² When they had all had enough to eat, he said to his disciples, "Gather the pieces that are left over. Let nothing be wasted." ¹³ So they gathered them and filled twelve baskets with the pieces of the five barley loaves left over by those who had eaten.

¹⁴ After the people saw the sign Jesus performed, they began to say, "Surely this is the Prophet who is to come into the world." ¹⁵ Jesus, knowing that they intended to come and make him king by force, withdrew again to a mountain by himself.

1. Here we have one of the few episodes (aside from the Passion) about which all four Gospels give a good account. Can you find any significant differences among the four?

8.d Jesus Walks on Water

MATTHEW
14:22 Immediately Jesus made the disciples get into the boat and go on ahead of him to the other side, while he dismissed the crowd. [23] After he had dismissed them, he went up on a mountainside by himself to pray. Later that night, he was there alone, [24] and the boat was already a considerable distance from land, buffeted by the waves because the wind was against it. [25] Shortly before dawn Jesus went out to them, walking on the lake. [26] When the disciples saw him walking on the lake, they were terrified. "It's a ghost," they said, and cried out in fear. [27] But Jesus immediately said to them: "Take courage! It is I. Don't be afraid." [28] "Lord, if it's you," Peter replied, "tell me to come to you on the water." [29] "Come," he said. Then Peter got down out of the boat, walked on the water and came toward Jesus. [30] But when he saw the wind, he was afraid and, beginning to sink, cried out, "Lord, save me!" [31] Immediately Jesus reached out his hand and caught him. "You of little faith," he said, "why did you doubt?" [32] And when they climbed into the boat, the wind died down. [33] Then those who were in the boat worshiped him, saying, "Truly you are the Son of God."

MARK
6:45 Immediately Jesus made his disciples get into the boat and go on ahead of him to Bethsaida, while he dismissed the crowd. [46] After leaving them, he went up on a mountainside to pray. [47] Later that night, the boat was in the middle of the lake, and he was alone on land. [48] He saw the disciples straining at the oars, because the wind was against them. Shortly before dawn he went out to them, walking on the lake. He was about to pass by them, [49] but when they saw him walking on the lake, they thought he was a ghost. They cried out, [50] because they all saw him and were terrified. Immediately he spoke to them and said, "Take courage! It is I. Don't be afraid." [51] Then he climbed into the boat with them, and the wind died down. They were completely amazed, [52] for they had not understood about the loaves; their hearts were hardened.

LUKE
8:22 One day Jesus said to his disciples, "Let us go over to the other side of the lake." So they got into a boat and set out. [23] As they sailed, he fell asleep. A squall came down on the lake, so that the boat was being swamped, and they were in great danger. [24] The disciples went and woke him, saying, "Master, Master, we're going to drown!" He got up and rebuked the wind and the raging waters; the storm subsided, and all was calm. [25] "Where is your faith?" he asked his disciples. In fear and amazement they asked one another, "Who is this? He commands even the winds and the water, and they obey him."

JOHN
6:16 When evening came, his disciples went down to the lake, [17] where they got into a boat and set off across the lake for Capernaum. By now it was dark, and Jesus had not yet joined them. [18] A strong wind was blowing and the waters grew rough. [19] When they had rowed about three or four miles, they saw Jesus approaching the boat, walking on the water; and they were frightened. [20] But he said to them, "It is I; don't be afraid." [21] Then they were willing to take him into the boat, and immediately the boat reached the shore where they were heading.

1. Again, we are fortunate to have parallel accounts of this episode from all four Gospels. What do you see as the common factors among the four accounts? What are the differences?
2. Do you find it surprising that Mark, thought to have been Peter's assistant, omits mention of Peter's role in the story?
3. What do the disciples make of Jesus' walking on water? Do they take it as a sign of Jesus' divinity?

8.e Feeding of the 4,000

MATTHEW
15:29 Jesus left there and went along the Sea of Galilee. Then he went up on a mountainside and sat down. [30] Great crowds came to him, bringing the lame, the blind, the crippled, the mute and many others, and laid them at his feet; and he healed them. [31] The people were amazed when they saw the mute speaking, the crippled made well, the lame walking and the blind seeing. And they praised the God of Israel. [32] Jesus called his disciples to him and said, "I have compassion for these people; they have already been with me three days and have nothing to eat. I do not want to send them away hungry, or they may collapse on the way." [33] His disciples answered, "Where could we get enough bread in this remote place to feed such a crowd?" [34] "How many loaves do you have?" Jesus asked. "Seven," they replied, "and a few small fish." [35] He told the crowd to sit down on the ground. [36] Then he took the seven loaves and the fish, and when he had given thanks, he broke them and gave them to the disciples, and they in turn to the people. [37] They all ate and were satisfied. Afterward the disciples picked up seven basketfuls of broken pieces that were left over. [38] The number of those who ate was four thousand men, besides women and children. [39] After Jesus had sent the crowd away, he got into the boat and went to the vicinity of Magadan.

MARK
8:1 During those days another large crowd gathered. Since they had nothing to eat, Jesus called his disciples to him and said, [2] "I have compassion for these people; they have already been with me three days and have nothing to eat. [3] If I send them home hungry, they will collapse on the way, because some of them have come a long distance." [4] His disciples answered, "But where in this remote place can anyone get enough bread to feed them?" [5] "How many loaves do you have?" Jesus asked. "Seven," they replied. [6] He told the crowd to sit down on the ground. When he had taken the seven loaves and given thanks, he broke them and gave them to his disciples to distribute to the people, and they did so. [7] They had a few small fish as well; he gave thanks for them also and told the disciples to distribute them. [8] The people ate and were satisfied. Afterward the disciples picked up seven basketfuls of broken pieces that were left over. [9] About four thousand were present. After he had sent them away, [10] he got into the boat with his disciples and went to the region of Dalmanutha. * * * 8:19 When I broke the five loaves for the five thousand, how many basketfuls of pieces did you pick up?" "Twelve," they replied. [20] "And when I broke the seven loaves for the four thousand, how many basketfuls of pieces did you pick up?" They answered, "Seven."

LUKE

JOHN

1. This episode is obviously similar to the feeding of the 5,000 (see 8.c above). Can you find differences between this episode and the earlier one? Does the 4,000 account refer to or otherwise reflect the earlier 5,000 event?
2. How many actual mass feeding events do you suppose took place? Two, or just one? If two took place, why do you think Luke and John omitted the second one? If only one took place, why do you think Matthew and Mark repeated a near-duplicate story?

CHAPTER 9: PARABLES

9.a About Parables

MATTHEW
13:10 The disciples came to him and asked, "Why do you speak to the people in parables?" [11] He replied, "Because the knowledge of the secrets of the kingdom of heaven has been given to you, but not to them. [12] Whoever has will be given more, and they will have an abundance. Whoever does not have, even what they have will be taken from them. [13] This is why I speak to them in parables: "Though seeing, they do not see; though hearing, they do not hear or understand. [14] In them is fulfilled the prophecy of Isaiah: "'You will be ever hearing but never understanding; you will be ever seeing but never perceiving. [15] For this people's heart has become calloused; they hardly hear with their ears, and they have closed their eyes. Otherwise they might see with their eyes, hear with their ears, understand with their hearts and turn, and I would heal them.' [16] But blessed are your eyes because they see, and your ears because they hear. [17] For truly I tell you, many prophets and righteous people longed to see what you see but did not see it, and to hear what you hear but did not hear it. * * * 13:34 Jesus spoke all these things to the crowd in parables; he did not say anything to them without using a parable. [35] So was fulfilled what was spoken through the prophet: "I will open my mouth in parables, I will utter things hidden since the creation of the world."

MARK
4:10 When he was alone, the Twelve and the others around him asked him about the parables. [11] He told them, "The secret of the kingdom of God has been given to you. But to those on the outside everything is said in parables [12] so that, "'they may be ever seeing but never perceiving, and ever hearing but never understanding; otherwise they might turn and be forgiven!'" * * * 4:33 With many similar parables Jesus spoke the word to them, as much as they could understand. [34] He did not say anything to them without using a parable. But when he was alone with his own disciples, he explained everything.

LUKE
8:9 His disciples asked him what this parable meant. [10] He said, "The knowledge of the secrets of the kingdom of God has been given to you, but to others I speak in parables, so that, "'though seeing, they may not see; though hearing, they may not understand.'

JOHN
10:1 "Very truly I tell you Pharisees, anyone who does not enter the sheep pen by the gate, but climbs in by some other way, is a thief and a robber. [2] The one who enters by the gate is the shepherd of the sheep. [3] The gatekeeper opens the gate for him, and the sheep listen to his voice. He calls his own sheep by name and leads them out. [4] When he has brought out all his own, he goes on ahead of them, and his sheep follow him because they know his voice. [5] But they will never follow a stranger; in fact, they will run away from him because they do not recognize a stranger's voice." [6] Jesus used this figure of speech, but the Pharisees did not understand what he was telling them.

1. What do you see as the relationship between Mark's account, which is earlier, and Matthew's, which was written later? Did Matthew perhaps think Jesus' remarks needed amplification? Or did Mark leave parts of Jesus' remarks out?
2. John's Gospel, curiously, never reports on any parable of Jesus. Why do you suppose this is so? But some of Jesus' illuminating metaphors or word pictures – shorter than full parables – do appear in John and are included in this section for comparison.

9.b Parable of the Sower

MATTHEW

13:1 That same day Jesus went out of the house and sat by the lake. ² Such large crowds gathered around him that he got into a boat and sat in it, while all the people stood on the shore. ³ Then he told them many things in parables, saying: "A farmer went out to sow his seed. ⁴ As he was scattering the seed, some fell along the path, and the birds came and ate it up. ⁵ Some fell on rocky places, where it did not have much soil. It sprang up quickly, because the soil was shallow. ⁶ But when the sun came up, the plants were scorched, and they withered because they had no root. ⁷ Other seed fell among thorns, which grew up and choked the plants. ⁸ Still other seed fell on good soil, where it produced a crop—a hundred, sixty or thirty times what was sown. ⁹ Whoever has ears, let them hear."

¹⁸ "Listen then to what the parable of the sower means: ¹⁹ When anyone hears the message about the kingdom and does not understand it, the evil one comes and snatches away what was sown in their heart. This is the seed sown along the path. ²⁰ The seed falling on rocky ground refers to someone who hears the word and at once receives it with joy. ²¹ But since they have no root, they last only a short time. When trouble or persecution comes because of the word, they quickly fall away. ²² The seed falling among the thorns refers to someone who hears the word, but the worries of this life and the deceitfulness of wealth choke the word, making it unfruitful. ²³ But the seed falling on good soil refers to someone who hears the word and understands it. This is the one who produces a crop, yielding a hundred, sixty or thirty times what was sown."

MARK

4:1 Again Jesus began to teach by the lake. The crowd that gathered around him was so large that he got into a boat and sat in it out on the lake, while all the people were along the shore at the water's edge. ² He taught them many things by parables, and in his teaching said: ³ "Listen! A farmer went out to sow his seed. ⁴ As he was scattering the seed, some fell along the path, and the birds came and ate it up. ⁵ Some fell on rocky places, where it did not have much soil. It sprang up quickly, because the soil was shallow. ⁶ But when the sun came up, the plants were scorched, and they withered because they had no root. ⁷ Other seed fell among thorns, which grew up and choked the plants, so that they did not bear grain. ⁸ Still other seed fell on good soil. It came up, grew and produced a crop, some multiplying thirty, some sixty, some a hundred times."
⁹ Then Jesus said, "Whoever has ears to hear, let them hear."
¹³ Then Jesus said to them, "Don't you understand this parable? How then will you understand any parable? ¹⁴ The farmer sows the word. ¹⁵ Some people are like seed along the path, where the word is sown. As soon as they hear it, Satan comes and takes away the word that was sown in them. ¹⁶ Others, like seed sown on rocky places, hear the word and at once receive it with joy. ¹⁷ But since they have no root, they last only a short time. When trouble or persecution comes because of the word, they quickly fall away. ¹⁸ Still others, like seed sown among thorns, hear the word; ¹⁹ but the worries of this life, the deceitfulness of wealth and the desires for other things come in and choke the word, making it unfruitful. ²⁰ Others, like seed sown on good soil, hear the word, accept it, and produce a crop—some thirty, some sixty, some a hundred times what was sown."

LUKE

8:4 While a large crowd was gathering and people were coming to Jesus from town after town, he told this parable: ⁵ "A farmer went out to sow his seed. As he was scattering the seed, some fell along the path; it was trampled on, and the birds ate it up. ⁶ Some fell on rocky ground, and when it came up, the plants withered because they had no moisture. ⁷ Other seed fell among thorns, which grew up with it and choked the plants. ⁸ Still other seed fell on good soil. It came up and yielded a crop, a hundred times more than was sown."
When he said this, he called out, "Whoever has ears to hear, let them hear."
¹¹ "This is the meaning of the parable: The seed is the word of God. ¹² Those along the path are the ones who hear, and then the devil comes and takes away the word from their hearts, so that they may not believe and be saved. ¹³ Those on the rocky ground are the ones who receive the word with joy when they hear it, but they have no root. They believe for a while, but in the time of testing they fall away. ¹⁴ The seed that fell among thorns stands for those

who hear, but as they go on their way they are choked by life's worries, riches and pleasures, and they do not mature. ¹⁵ But the seed on good soil stands for those with a noble and good heart, who hear the word, retain it, and by persevering produce a crop.

JOHN

4:34 "My food," said Jesus, "is to do the will of him who sent me and to finish his work. ³⁵ Don't you have a saying, 'It's still four months until harvest'? I tell you, open your eyes and look at the fields! They are ripe for harvest. ³⁶ Even now the one who reaps draws a wage and harvests a crop for eternal life, so that the sower and the reaper may be glad together. ³⁷ Thus the saying 'One sows and another reaps' is true. ³⁸ I sent you to reap what you have not worked for. Others have done the hard work, and you have reaped the benefits of their labor."

1. Do you find any significant differences among the three versions of this parable?
2. The passage from John is not another version of the parable, but is there anything about the quotation that leads you to conclude it does in fact reflect the thinking and words of Jesus?

9.c Parable of the Mustard Seed

MATTHEW
13:31 He told them another parable: "The kingdom of heaven is like a mustard seed, which a man took and planted in his field. [32] Though it is the smallest of all seeds, yet when it grows, it is the largest of garden plants and becomes a tree, so that the birds come and perch in its branches."
MARK
4:30 Again he said, "What shall we say the kingdom of God is like, or what parable shall we use to describe it? [31] It is like a mustard seed, which is the smallest of all seeds on earth. [32] Yet when planted, it grows and becomes the largest of all garden plants, with such big branches that the birds can perch in its shade."
LUKE
13:18 Then Jesus asked, "What is the kingdom of God like? What shall I compare it to? [19] It is like a mustard seed, which a man took and planted in his garden. It grew and became a tree, and the birds perched in its branches." * * * 17:5 The apostles said to the Lord, "Increase our faith!" [6] He replied, "If you have faith as small as a mustard seed, you can say to this mulberry tree, 'Be uprooted and planted in the sea,' and it will obey you.
JOHN

1. Do you see any significant differences among the versions of this parable?

9.d Parable of the Yeast

MATTHEW
13:33 He told them still another parable: "The kingdom of heaven is like yeast that a woman took and mixed into about sixty pounds of flour until it worked all through the dough."
MARK
8:14 The disciples had forgotten to bring bread, except for one loaf they had with them in the boat. [15] "Be careful," Jesus warned them. "Watch out for the yeast of the Pharisees and that of Herod." [16] They discussed this with one another and said, "It is because we have no bread." [17] Aware of their discussion, Jesus asked them: "Why are you talking about having no bread? Do you still not see or understand? Are your hearts hardened? [18] Do you have eyes but fail to see, and ears but fail to hear? And don't you remember? [19] When I broke the five loaves for the five thousand, how many basketfuls of pieces did you pick up?" "Twelve," they replied. [20] "And when I broke the seven loaves for the four thousand, how many basketfuls of pieces did you pick up?" They answered, "Seven." [21] He said to them, "Do you still not understand?"
LUKE
13:20 Again he asked, "What shall I compare the kingdom of God to? [21] It is like yeast that a woman took and mixed into about sixty pounds of flour until it worked all through the dough."
JOHN
6:31 "Our ancestors ate the manna in the wilderness; as it is written: 'He gave them bread from heaven to eat.'" [32] Jesus said to them, "Very truly I tell you, it is not Moses who has given you the bread from heaven, but it is my Father who gives you the true bread from heaven. [33] For the bread of God is the bread that comes down from heaven and gives life to the world." [34] "Sir," they said, "always give us this bread." [35] Then Jesus declared, "I am the bread of life. Whoever comes to me will never go hungry, and whoever believes in me will never be thirsty.

1. Which two of these passages are directly comparable to one another?
2. Does the passage from Mark relate in any way to the others?
3. Does the passage from John relate in any way to the others?

9.e Parable of the Lost Sheep

MATTHEW
18:10 "See that you do not despise one of these little ones. For I tell you that their angels in heaven always see the face of my Father in heaven. [11]   12 "What do you think? If a man owns a hundred sheep, and one of them wanders away, will he not leave the ninety-nine on the hills and go to look for the one that wandered off? 13 And if he finds it, truly I tell you, he is happier about that one sheep than about the ninety-nine that did not wander off. 14 In the same way your Father in heaven is not willing that any of these little ones should perish.

MARK
6:34 When Jesus landed and saw a large crowd, he had compassion on them, because they were like sheep without a shepherd. So he began teaching them many things.   * * *   14:27 "You will all fall away," Jesus told them, "for it is written: "'I will strike the shepherd, and the sheep will be scattered.'

LUKE
15:1 Now the tax collectors and sinners were all gathering around to hear Jesus. 2 But the Pharisees and the teachers of the law muttered, "This man welcomes sinners and eats with them."   3 Then Jesus told them this parable: 4 "Suppose one of you has a hundred sheep and loses one of them. Doesn't he leave the ninety-nine in the open country and go after the lost sheep until he finds it? 5 And when he finds it, he joyfully puts it on his shoulders 6 and goes home. Then he calls his friends and neighbors together and says, 'Rejoice with me; I have found my lost sheep.' 7 I tell you that in the same way there will be more rejoicing in heaven over one sinner who repents than over ninety-nine righteous persons who do not need to repent.

JOHN
10:21 Then came the Festival of Dedication at Jerusalem. It was winter, 23 and Jesus was in the temple courts walking in Solomon's Colonnade. 24 The Jews who were there gathered around him, saying, "How long will you keep us in suspense? If you are the Messiah, tell us plainly."   25 Jesus answered, "I did tell you, but you do not believe. The works I do in my Father's name testify about me, 26 but you do not believe because you are not my sheep. 27 My sheep listen to my voice; I know them, and they follow me. 28 I give them eternal life, and they shall never perish; no one will snatch them out of my hand. 29 My Father, who has given them to me, is greater than all; no one can snatch them out of my Father's hand. 30 I and the Father are one."

1. Matthew and Luke tell the same parable, and in nearly identical terms. What do you find that is comparable in the passages from Mark and John?
2. What does the similarity in metaphors suggest about the origin of all four passages?

9.f Parable of the Two Sons

MATTHEW
21:33 "Listen to another parable: There was a landowner who planted a vineyard. He put a wall around it, dug a winepress in it and built a watchtower. Then he rented the vineyard to some farmers and moved to another place. [34] When the harvest time approached, he sent his servants to the tenants to collect his fruit. [35] "The tenants seized his servants; they beat one, killed another, and stoned a third. [36] Then he sent other servants to them, more than the first time, and the tenants treated them the same way. [37] Last of all, he sent his son to them. 'They will respect my son,' he said. [38] "But when the tenants saw the son, they said to each other, 'This is the heir. Come, let's kill him and take his inheritance.' [39] So they took him and threw him out of the vineyard and killed him. [40] "Therefore, when the owner of the vineyard comes, what will he do to those tenants?" [41] "He will bring those wretches to a wretched end," they replied, "and he will rent the vineyard to other tenants, who will give him his share of the crop at harvest time." [42] Jesus said to them, "Have you never read in the Scriptures: "'The stone the builders rejected has become the cornerstone; the Lord has done this, and it is marvelous in our eyes'? [43] "Therefore I tell you that the kingdom of God will be taken away from you and given to a people who will produce its fruit. [44] Anyone who falls on this stone will be broken to pieces; anyone on whom it falls will be crushed." [45] When the chief priests and the Pharisees heard Jesus' parables, they knew he was talking about them. [46] They looked for a way to arrest him, but they were afraid of the crowd because the people held that he was a prophet.
MARK
12:1 Jesus then began to speak to them in parables: "A man planted a vineyard. He put a wall around it, dug a pit for the winepress and built a watchtower. Then he rented the vineyard to some farmers and moved to another place. [2] At harvest time he sent a servant to the tenants to collect from them some of the fruit of the vineyard. [3] But they seized him, beat him and sent him away empty-handed. [4] Then he sent another servant to them; they struck this man on the head and treated him shamefully. [5] He sent still another, and that one they killed. He sent many others; some of them they beat, others they killed. [6] "He had one left to send, a son, whom he loved. He sent him last of all, saying, 'They will respect my son.' [7] "But the tenants said to one another, 'This is the heir. Come, let's kill him, and the inheritance will be ours.' [8] So they took him and killed him, and threw him out of the vineyard. [9] "What then will the owner of the vineyard do? He will come and kill those tenants and give the vineyard to others. [10] Haven't you read this passage of Scripture: "'The stone the builders rejected has become the cornerstone; [11] the Lord has done this, and it is marvelous in our eyes'?" [12] Then the chief priests, the teachers of the law and the elders looked for a way to arrest him because they knew he had spoken the parable against them. But they were afraid of the crowd; so they left him and went away.
LUKE
20:9 He went on to tell the people this parable: "A man planted a vineyard, rented it to some farmers and went away for a long time. [10] At harvest time he sent a servant to the tenants so they would give him some of the fruit of the vineyard. But the tenants beat him and sent him away empty-handed. [11] He sent another servant, but that one also they beat and treated shamefully and sent away empty-handed. [12] He sent still a third, and they wounded him and threw him out. [13] "Then the owner of the vineyard said, 'What shall I do? I will send my son, whom I love; perhaps they will respect him.' [14] "But when the tenants saw him, they talked the matter over. 'This is the heir,' they said. 'Let's kill him, and the inheritance will be ours.' [15] So they threw him out of the vineyard and killed him. "What then will the owner of the vineyard do to them? [16] He will come and kill those tenants and give the vineyard to others." When the people heard this, they said, "God forbid!" [17] Jesus looked directly at them and asked, "Then what is the meaning of that which is written: "'The stone the builders rejected has become the cornerstone'? [18] Everyone who falls on that stone will be broken to pieces; anyone

on whom it falls will be crushed."

¹⁹ The teachers of the law and the chief priests looked for a way to arrest him immediately, because they knew he had spoken this parable against them. But they were afraid of the people.

JOHN

1. Do you see any significant differences among the three versions of the parable?

9.g Parable of the Banquet

MATTHEW

22:1 Jesus spoke to them again in parables, saying: [2] "The kingdom of heaven is like a king who prepared a wedding banquet for his son. [3] He sent his servants to those who had been invited to the banquet to tell them to come, but they refused to come.

[4] "Then he sent some more servants and said, 'Tell those who have been invited that I have prepared my dinner: My oxen and fattened cattle have been butchered, and everything is ready. Come to the wedding banquet.'

[5] "But they paid no attention and went off—one to his field, another to his business. [6] The rest seized his servants, mistreated them and killed them. [7] The king was enraged. He sent his army and destroyed those murderers and burned their city.

[8] "Then he said to his servants, 'The wedding banquet is ready, but those I invited did not deserve to come. [9] So go to the street corners and invite to the banquet anyone you find.' [10] So the servants went out into the streets and gathered all the people they could find, the bad as well as the good, and the wedding hall was filled with guests.

[11] "But when the king came in to see the guests, he noticed a man there who was not wearing wedding clothes. [12] He asked, 'How did you get in here without wedding clothes, friend?' The man was speechless. [13] "Then the king told the attendants, 'Tie him hand and foot, and throw him outside, into the darkness, where there will be weeping and gnashing of teeth.'

[14] "For many are invited, but few are chosen."

MARK

LUKE

14:15 When one of those at the table with him heard this, he said to Jesus, "Blessed is the one who will eat at the feast in the kingdom of God." [16] Jesus replied: "A certain man was preparing a great banquet and invited many guests. [17] At the time of the banquet he sent his servant to tell those who had been invited, 'Come, for everything is now ready.'

[18] "But they all alike began to make excuses. The first said, 'I have just bought a field, and I must go and see it. Please excuse me.' [19] "Another said, 'I have just bought five yoke of oxen, and I'm on my way to try them out. Please excuse me.' [20] "Still another said, 'I just got married, so I can't come.'

[21] "The servant came back and reported this to his master. Then the owner of the house became angry and ordered his servant, 'Go out quickly into the streets and alleys of the town and bring in the poor, the crippled, the blind and the lame.' [22] "'Sir,' the servant said, 'what you ordered has been done, but there is still room.'

[23] "Then the master told his servant, 'Go out to the roads and country lanes and compel them to come in, so that my house will be full. [24] I tell you, not one of those who were invited will get a taste of my banquet.'"

JOHN

1. How do Matthew and Luke approach the matter of invitation vs. compulsion? Is there a significant difference between them?
2. The excuses offered are different in the two versions: in Matthew the vineyard owner is a king, in Luke he is just a landowner. Do these differences affect the meaning of the parable in any way?
3. Do you suppose that Jesus told this parable on just one occasion, or did he probably use it on a number of occasions? On what factors do you base your answer?

9.h Parable of the Talents

MATTHEW
25:14 "Again, it will be like a man going on a journey, who called his servants and entrusted his wealth to them. [15] To one he gave five bags of gold, to another two bags, and to another one bag, each according to his ability. Then he went on his journey. [16] The man who had received five bags of gold went at once and put his money to work and gained five bags more. [17] So also, the one with two bags of gold gained two more. [18] But the man who had received one bag went off, dug a hole in the ground and hid his master's money. [19] "After a long time the master of those servants returned and settled accounts with them. [20] The man who had received five bags of gold brought the other five. 'Master,' he said, 'you entrusted me with five bags of gold. See, I have gained five more.' [21] "His master replied, 'Well done, good and faithful servant! You have been faithful with a few things; I will put you in charge of many things. Come and share your master's happiness!' [22] "The man with two bags of gold also came. 'Master,' he said, 'you entrusted me with two bags of gold; see, I have gained two more.' [23] "His master replied, 'Well done, good and faithful servant! You have been faithful with a few things; I will put you in charge of many things. Come and share your master's happiness!' [24] "Then the man who had received one bag of gold came. 'Master,' he said, 'I knew that you are a hard man, harvesting where you have not sown and gathering where you have not scattered seed. [25] So I was afraid and went out and hid your gold in the ground. See, here is what belongs to you.' [26] "His master replied, 'You wicked, lazy servant! So you knew that I harvest where I have not sown and gather where I have not scattered seed? [27] Well then, you should have put my money on deposit with the bankers, so that when I returned I would have received it back with interest. [28] "'So take the bag of gold from him and give it to the one who has ten bags. [29] For whoever has will be given more, and they will have an abundance. Whoever does not have, even what they have will be taken from them. [30] And throw that worthless servant outside, into the darkness, where there will be weeping and gnashing of teeth.'
MARK
LUKE
19:11 While they were listening to this, he went on to tell them a parable, because he was near Jerusalem and the people thought that the kingdom of God was going to appear at once. [12] He said: "A man of noble birth went to a distant country to have himself appointed king and then to return. [13] So he called ten of his servants and gave them ten minas. 'Put this money to work,' he said, 'until I come back.' [14] "But his subjects hated him and sent a delegation after him to say, 'We don't want this man to be our king.' [15] "He was made king, however, and returned home. Then he sent for the servants to whom he had given the money, in order to find out what they had gained with it. [16] "The first one came and said, 'Sir, your mina has earned ten more.' [17] "'Well done, my good servant!' his master replied. 'Because you have been trustworthy in a very small matter, take charge of ten cities.' [18] "The second came and said, 'Sir, your mina has earned five more.' [19] "His master answered, 'You take charge of five cities.' [20] "Then another servant came and said, 'Sir, here is your mina; I have kept it laid away in a piece of cloth. [21] I was afraid of you, because you are a hard man. You take out what you did not put in and reap what you did not sow.' [22] "His master replied, 'I will judge you by your own words, you wicked servant! You knew, did you, that I am a hard man, taking out what I did not put in, and reaping what I did not sow? [23] Why then didn't you put my money on deposit, so that when I came back, I could have collected it with interest?' [24] "Then he said to those standing by, 'Take his mina away from him and give it to the one who has ten minas.' [25] "'Sir,' they said, 'he already has ten!' [26] "He replied, 'I tell you that to everyone who has, more will be given, but as for the one who has nothing, even what they have will be taken away. [27] But those enemies of mine who did not want me to be king over them—bring them here and kill them in front of me.'"

JOHN

1. There are differences between the two versions of the parable. Are they significant?

Chapter 10: Proper Actions and Attitudes

10.a The Beatitudes

MATTHEW
5:1 Now when Jesus saw the crowds, he went up on a mountainside and sat down. His disciples came to him, [2] and he began to teach them. He said: [3] "Blessed are the poor in spirit, for theirs is the kingdom of heaven. [4] Blessed are those who mourn, for they will be comforted. [5] Blessed are the meek, for they will inherit the earth. [6] Blessed are those who hunger and thirst for righteousness, for they will be filled. [7] Blessed are the merciful, for they will be shown mercy. [8] Blessed are the pure in heart, for they will see God. [9] Blessed are the peacemakers, for they will be called children of God. [10] Blessed are those who are persecuted because of righteousness, for theirs is the kingdom of heaven. [11] "Blessed are you when people insult you, persecute you and falsely say all kinds of evil against you because of me. [12] Rejoice and be glad, because great is your reward in heaven, for in the same way they persecuted the prophets who were before you.

MARK

LUKE
6:17 He went down with them and stood on a level place. A large crowd of his disciples was there and a great number of people from all over Judea, from Jerusalem, and from the coastal region around Tyre and Sidon, [18] who had come to hear him and to be healed of their diseases. Those troubled by impure spirits were cured, [19] and the people all tried to touch him, because power was coming from him and healing them all. [20] Looking at his disciples, he said: "Blessed are you who are poor, for yours is the kingdom of God. [21] Blessed are you who hunger now, for you will be satisfied. Blessed are you who weep now, for you will laugh. [22] Blessed are you when people hate you, when they exclude you and insult you and reject your name as evil, because of the Son of Man. [23] "Rejoice in that day and leap for joy, because great is your reward in heaven. For that is how their ancestors treated the prophets.

JOHN

1. There are differences between the two accounts of Jesus' words, but do you find any actual contradictions? Are the two sets of categories different in some way? Do the two versions say the same things about who is blessed?
2. What is the full meaning of "blessed" in both accounts? Is it something more or different than happy or fortunate?
3. Matthew's account is completely upbeat, assuring a good outcome for all the categories of people he mentions, while Luke's is balanced between good outcomes for some and adverse outcomes for others. What do you make of Jesus' "woe to you" warnings in Luke?
4. Is there a difference in meaning between the "poor" and the "poor in spirit?" What about those who "hunger now" vs. those who "hunger and thirst for righteousness?"
5. Focus on the two two-verse passages concerning those who suffer on account of Christ (Matthew 5:11-12 and Luke 6:22-23). Is there something that seems unique about this pair of passages?
6. Matthew relates that this event took place on a mountainside, while Luke says Jesus came down from a mountainside to a level place to speak (it's sometimes called the Sermon on the Plain). Is there any significance to this difference, or is it probably another example of minor discrepancies that often arise when multiple witnesses describe an event? Do you think these are two accounts of the same event, or accounts of two different but similar events?
7. The episode does not appear in Mark. What does that indicate about its origin, i.e. about how Matthew and Luke learned of it?

10.b The Salt of the Earth

MATTHEW
5:13 "You are the salt of the earth. But if the salt loses its saltiness, how can it be made salty again? It is no longer good for anything, except to be thrown out and trampled underfoot.
MARK
9:49 Everyone will be salted with fire. [50] "Salt is good, but if it loses its saltiness, how can you make it salty again? Have salt among yourselves, and be at peace with each other."
LUKE
14:34 "Salt is good, but if it loses its saltiness, how can it be made salty again? [35] It is fit neither for the soil nor for the manure pile; it is thrown out. "Whoever has ears to hear, let them hear."
JOHN

1. What attributes of salt does Jesus use in talking about his disciples and other believers, as conveyed in these closely parallel passages in Mark, Matthew, and Luke?
2. What do you make of the differences in the three versions of this brief episode?

10.c Resolving Grievances

MATTHEW
5:21 "You have heard that it was said to the people long ago, 'You shall not murder, and anyone who murders will be subject to judgment.' ²² But I tell you that anyone who is angry with a brother or sister will be subject to judgment. Again, anyone who says to a brother or sister, 'Raca,' is answerable to the court. And anyone who says, 'You fool!' will be in danger of the fire of hell. ²³ "Therefore, if you are offering your gift at the altar and there remember that your brother or sister has something against you, ²⁴ leave your gift there in front of the altar. First go and be reconciled to them; then come and offer your gift. ²⁵ "Settle matters quickly with your adversary who is taking you to court. Do it while you are still together on the way, or your adversary may hand you over to the judge, and the judge may hand you over to the officer, and you may be thrown into prison. ²⁶ Truly I tell you, you will not get out until you have paid the last penny.
MARK
11:25 And when you stand praying, if you hold anything against anyone, forgive them, so that your Father in heaven may forgive you your sins."
LUKE
12:57 "Why don't you judge for yourselves what is right? ⁵⁸ As you are going with your adversary to the magistrate, try hard to be reconciled on the way, or your adversary may drag you off to the judge, and the judge turn you over to the officer, and the officer throw you into prison. ⁵⁹ I tell you, you will not get out until you have paid the last penny."
JOHN

1. The versions of Matthew and Luke have differences, but they obviously came from the same source. How does Jesus' teaching in Mark relate to those in Matthew and Luke?

10.d Avoiding Temptation

MATTHEW
5:27 "You have heard that it was said, 'You shall not commit adultery.' [28] But I tell you that anyone who looks at a woman lustfully has already committed adultery with her in his heart. [29] If your right eye causes you to stumble, gouge it out and throw it away. It is better for you to lose one part of your body than for your whole body to be thrown into hell. [30] And if your right hand causes you to stumble, cut it off and throw it away. It is better for you to lose one part of your body than for your whole body to go into hell. * * * 18:6 "If anyone causes one of these little ones—those who believe in me—to stumble, it would be better for them to have a large millstone hung around their neck and to be drowned in the depths of the sea. [7] Woe to the world because of the things that cause people to stumble! Such things must come, but woe to the person through whom they come! [8] If your hand or your foot causes you to stumble, cut it off and throw it away. It is better for you to enter life maimed or crippled than to have two hands or two feet and be thrown into eternal fire. [9] And if your eye causes you to stumble, gouge it out and throw it away. It is better for you to enter life with one eye than to have two eyes and be thrown into the fire of hell.
MARK
9:42 "If anyone causes one of these little ones—those who believe in me—to stumble, it would be better for them if a large millstone were hung around their neck and they were thrown into the sea. [43] If your hand causes you to stumble, cut it off. It is better for you to enter life maimed than with two hands to go into hell, where the fire never goes out. [[44]] [45] And if your foot causes you to stumble, cut it off. It is better for you to enter life crippled than to have two feet and be thrown into hell. [[46]] [47] And if your eye causes you to stumble, pluck it out. It is better for you to enter the kingdom of God with one eye than to have two eyes and be thrown into hell, [48] where "'the worms that eat them do not die, and the fire is not quenched.'
LUKE
17:1 Jesus said to his disciples: "Things that cause people to stumble are bound to come, but woe to anyone through whom they come. [2] It would be better for them to be thrown into the sea with a millstone tied around their neck than to cause one of these little ones to stumble. [3] So watch yourselves.
JOHN

1. (An alternative translation for "stumble" is "sin.") What differences do you see in the three versions of this teaching?

10.e Divorce

MATTHEW

5:31 "It has been said, 'Anyone who divorces his wife must give her a certificate of divorce.' ³² But I tell you that anyone who divorces his wife, except for sexual immorality, makes her the victim of adultery, and anyone who marries a divorced woman commits adultery.

* * *

19:3 Some Pharisees came to him to test him. They asked, "Is it lawful for a man to divorce his wife for any and every reason?"
⁴ "Haven't you read," he replied, "that at the beginning the Creator 'made them male and female,' ⁵ and said, 'For this reason a man will leave his father and mother and be united to his wife, and the two will become one flesh'? ⁶ So they are no longer two, but one flesh. Therefore what God has joined together, let no one separate."
⁷ "Why then," they asked, "did Moses command that a man give his wife a certificate of divorce and send her away?"
⁸ Jesus replied, "Moses permitted you to divorce your wives because your hearts were hard. But it was not this way from the beginning. ⁹ I tell you that anyone who divorces his wife, except for sexual immorality, and marries another woman commits adultery."

MARK

10:2 Some Pharisees came and tested him by asking, "Is it lawful for a man to divorce his wife?" ³ "What did Moses command you?" he replied. ⁴ They said, "Moses permitted a man to write a certificate of divorce and send her away."
⁵ "It was because your hearts were hard that Moses wrote you this law," Jesus replied. ⁶ "But at the beginning of creation God 'made them male and female.' ⁷ 'For this reason a man will leave his father and mother and be united to his wife, ⁸ and the two will become one flesh.' So they are no longer two, but one flesh. ⁹ Therefore what God has joined together, let no one separate."
¹⁰ When they were in the house again, the disciples asked Jesus about this. ¹¹ He answered, "Anyone who divorces his wife and marries another woman commits adultery against her. ¹² And if she divorces her husband and marries another man, she commits adultery."

LUKE

16:18 "Anyone who divorces his wife and marries another woman commits adultery, and the man who marries a divorced woman commits adultery.

JOHN

1. Note the differences and similarities in the four passages.
2. What does it mean when Jesus says in Mark and Matthew that divorce was permitted under the Law of Moses because "your hearts were hard?" (Rather than take the Pharisees' word for what the Law said, read the original passage for yourself in Deuteronomy 24:1-4.) Did God later change his mind, were circumstances changing, or did the Pharisees mischaracterize the Law on this?
3. As reported by Mark and Luke, God's prohibition of divorce apparently applies to all situations and conditions. But Matthew includes additional words of Jesus that allow for divorce under certain circumstances. What are the possible justifications for divorce, according to Matthew's report of Jesus' words?

10.f. Love Your Enemies

MATTHEW
5:38 "You have heard that it was said, 'Eye for eye, and tooth for tooth.' [39] But I tell you, do not resist an evil person. If anyone slaps you on the right cheek, turn to them the other cheek also. [40] And if anyone wants to sue you and take your shirt, hand over your coat as well. [41] If anyone forces you to go one mile, go with them two miles. [42] Give to the one who asks you, and do not turn away from the one who wants to borrow from you. [43] "You have heard that it was said, 'Love your neighbor and hate your enemy.' [44] But I tell you, love your enemies and pray for those who persecute you, [45] that you may be children of your Father in heaven. He causes his sun to rise on the evil and the good, and sends rain on the righteous and the unrighteous. [46] If you love those who love you, what reward will you get? Are not even the tax collectors doing that? [47] And if you greet only your own people, what are you doing more than others? Do not even pagans do that? [48] Be perfect, therefore, as your heavenly Father is perfect.

MARK

LUKE
6:27 "But to you who are listening I say: Love your enemies, do good to those who hate you, [28] bless those who curse you, pray for those who mistreat you. [29] If someone slaps you on one cheek, turn to them the other also. If someone takes your coat, do not withhold your shirt from them. [30] Give to everyone who asks you, and if anyone takes what belongs to you, do not demand it back. [31] Do to others as you would have them do to you. [32] "If you love those who love you, what credit is that to you? Even sinners love those who love them. [33] And if you do good to those who are good to you, what credit is that to you? Even sinners do that. [34] And if you lend to those from whom you expect repayment, what credit is that to you? Even sinners lend to sinners, expecting to be repaid in full. [35] But love your enemies, do good to them, and lend to them without expecting to get anything back. Then your reward will be great, and you will be children of the Most High, because he is kind to the ungrateful and wicked. [36] Be merciful, just as your Father is merciful.

JOHN

1. Identify the statements in Matthew's and Luke's accounts that are essentially identical to one another. Which statements are similar to each other but contain differences in nuance or perspective? Which statements are unique to one or another of the accounts?
2. The two passages end with teachings that are similar in structure but that contain a different key word (Matthew 5:48 and Luke 6:36). Jesus' call to be merciful (in Luke) appears easy to understand, but what does Jesus mean in Matthew when he calls us to be perfect? In the context of Jesus' teaching, are the two words actually as different in meaning as they first appear?

10.g. The Lord's Prayer

MATTHEW
6:9 "This, then, is how you should pray: "'Our Father in heaven, hallowed be your name,   ¹⁰ your kingdom come, your will be done,   on earth as it is in heaven.   ¹¹ Give us today our daily bread.   ¹² And forgive us our debts, as we also have forgiven our debtors.   ¹³ And lead us not into temptation, but deliver us from the evil one.'
MARK
LUKE
11:1 One day Jesus was praying in a certain place. When he finished, one of his disciples said to him, "Lord, teach us to pray, just as John taught his disciples."   ² He said to them, "When you pray, say: "'Father, hallowed be your name, your kingdom come.   ³ Give us each day our daily bread.   ⁴ Forgive us our sins, for we also forgive everyone who sins against us.   And lead us not into temptation.'"
JOHN

1. Identify and consider the similarities and differences in the two versions of the Lord's prayer.

10.h Forgiveness

MATTHEW
6:14 For if you forgive other people when they sin against you, your heavenly Father will also forgive you. [15] But if you do not forgive others their sins, your Father will not forgive your sins. * * * 18:21 Then Peter came to Jesus and asked, "Lord, how many times shall I forgive my brother or sister who sins against me? Up to seven times?" [22] Jesus answered, "I tell you, not seven times, but seventy-seven times. [23] "Therefore, the kingdom of heaven is like a king who wanted to settle accounts with his servants. [24] As he began the settlement, a man who owed him ten thousand bags of gold was brought to him. [25] Since he was not able to pay, the master ordered that he and his wife and his children and all that he had be sold to repay the debt. [26] "At this the servant fell on his knees before him. 'Be patient with me,' he begged, 'and I will pay back everything.' [27] The servant's master took pity on him, canceled the debt and let him go. [28] "But when that servant went out, he found one of his fellow servants who owed him a hundred silver coins. He grabbed him and began to choke him. 'Pay back what you owe me!' he demanded. [29] "His fellow servant fell to his knees and begged him, 'Be patient with me, and I will pay it back.' [30] "But he refused. Instead, he went off and had the man thrown into prison until he could pay the debt. [31] When the other servants saw what had happened, they were outraged and went and told their master everything that had happened. [32] "Then the master called the servant in. 'You wicked servant,' he said, 'I canceled all that debt of yours because you begged me to. [33] Shouldn't you have had mercy on your fellow servant just as I had on you?' [34] In anger his master handed him over to the jailers to be tortured, until he should pay back all he owed. [35] "This is how my heavenly Father will treat each of you unless you forgive your brother or sister from your heart."

MARK
11:25 And when you stand praying, if you hold anything against anyone, forgive them, so that your Father in heaven may forgive you your sins."

LUKE
6:37 "Do not judge, and you will not be judged. Do not condemn, and you will not be condemned. Forgive, and you will be forgiven. * * * 17:3 "If your brother or sister sins against you, rebuke them; and if they repent, forgive them. [4] Even if they sin against you seven times in a day and seven times come back to you saying 'I repent,' you must forgive them."

JOHN

1. Note that Matthew does not only repeat Jesus' basic teaching on forgiveness, but also quotes a parable as illustration.

10.i Treasure in Heaven

MATTHEW
6:19 "Do not store up for yourselves treasures on earth, where moths and vermin destroy, and where thieves break in and steal. [20] But store up for yourselves treasures in heaven, where moths and vermin do not destroy, and where thieves do not break in and steal. [21] For where your treasure is, there your heart will be also.

MARK
10:21 Jesus looked at him and loved him. "One thing you lack," he said. "Go, sell everything you have and give to the poor, and you will have treasure in heaven. Then come, follow me."

LUKE
12:13 Someone in the crowd said to him, "Teacher, tell my brother to divide the inheritance with me." [14] Jesus replied, "Man, who appointed me a judge or an arbiter between you?" [15] Then he said to them, "Watch out! Be on your guard against all kinds of greed; life does not consist in an abundance of possessions."   [16] And he told them this parable: "The ground of a certain rich man yielded an abundant harvest. [17] He thought to himself, 'What shall I do? I have no place to store my crops.' [18] "Then he said, 'This is what I'll do. I will tear down my barns and build bigger ones, and there I will store my surplus grain. [19] And I'll say to myself, "You have plenty of grain laid up for many years. Take life easy; eat, drink and be merry."'   [20] "But God said to him, 'You fool! This very night your life will be demanded from you. Then who will get what you have prepared for yourself?' [21] "This is how it will be with whoever stores up things for themselves but is not rich toward God."   * * *   12:32 "Do not be afraid, little flock, for your Father has been pleased to give you the kingdom. [33] Sell your possessions and give to the poor. Provide purses for yourselves that will not wear out, a treasure in heaven that will never fail, where no thief comes near and no moth destroys. [34] For where your treasure is, there your heart will be also.

JOHN

1. These are not three versions of the same saying, but rather are different instances in which Jesus discussed generosity. What similarities or differences can you identify?
2. Do you see any variations in the account of the encounter with the rich man, as found in Mark, Matthew, and Luke? It may be helpful to check your Bible for the full texts of the three passages.
3. The passages in Matthew 6 and Luke 12 offer further insight into what Jesus means by "treasure in heaven." Their quotations of Jesus in different contexts suggest that this was a metaphor that Jesus used on several occasions. How do you define or describe "treasure in heaven?"

10.j Serving Two Masters

MATTHEW
6:24 "No one can serve two masters. Either you will hate the one and love the other, or you will be devoted to the one and despise the other. You cannot serve both God and money.
MARK
LUKE
16:13 "No one can serve two masters. Either you will hate the one and love the other, or you will be devoted to the one and despise the other. You cannot serve both God and money."   [14] The Pharisees, who loved money, heard all this and were sneering at Jesus. [15] He said to them, "You are the ones who justify yourselves in the eyes of others, but God knows your hearts. What people value highly is detestable in God's sight.
JOHN

1. Note how Luke adds a vignette to the basic teaching.

10.k. Do Not Worry

MATTHEW

6:25 "Therefore I tell you, do not worry about your life, what you will eat or drink; or about your body, what you will wear. Is not life more than food, and the body more than clothes? [26] Look at the birds of the air; they do not sow or reap or store away in barns, and yet your heavenly Father feeds them. Are you not much more valuable than they? [27] Can any one of you by worrying add a single hour to your life?

[28] "And why do you worry about clothes? See how the flowers of the field grow. They do not labor or spin. [29] Yet I tell you that not even Solomon in all his splendor was dressed like one of these. [30] If that is how God clothes the grass of the field, which is here today and tomorrow is thrown into the fire, will he not much more clothe you—you of little faith? [31] So do not worry, saying, 'What shall we eat?' or 'What shall we drink?' or 'What shall we wear?' [32] For the pagans run after all these things, and your heavenly Father knows that you need them. [33] But seek first his kingdom and his righteousness, and all these things will be given to you as well. [34] Therefore do not worry about tomorrow, for tomorrow will worry about itself. Each day has enough trouble of its own.

MARK

LUKE

12:22 Then Jesus said to his disciples: "Therefore I tell you, do not worry about your life, what you will eat; or about your body, what you will wear. [23] For life is more than food, and the body more than clothes. [24] Consider the ravens: They do not sow or reap, they have no storeroom or barn; yet God feeds them. And how much more valuable you are than birds! [25] Who of you by worrying can add a single hour to your life? [26] Since you cannot do this very little thing, why do you worry about the rest?

[27] "Consider how the wild flowers grow. They do not labor or spin. Yet I tell you, not even Solomon in all his splendor was dressed like one of these. [28] If that is how God clothes the grass of the field, which is here today, and tomorrow is thrown into the fire, how much more will he clothe you—you of little faith! [29] And do not set your heart on what you will eat or drink; do not worry about it. [30] For the pagan world runs after all such things, and your Father knows that you need them. [31] But seek his kingdom, and these things will be given to you as well.

[32] "Do not be afraid, little flock, for your Father has been pleased to give you the kingdom. [33] Sell your possessions and give to the poor. Provide purses for yourselves that will not wear out, a treasure in heaven that will never fail, where no thief comes near and no moth destroys. [34] For where your treasure is, there your heart will be also.

JOHN

1. Consider the similarities and differences in the two versions.

10.1 Do Not Judge

MATTHEW
7:1 "Do not judge, or you too will be judged. ²For in the same way you judge others, you will be judged, and with the measure you use, it will be measured to you.   ³ "Why do you look at the speck of sawdust in your brother's eye and pay no attention to the plank in your own eye? ⁴ How can you say to your brother, 'Let me take the speck out of your eye,' when all the time there is a plank in your own eye? ⁵ You hypocrite, first take the plank out of your own eye, and then you will see clearly to remove the speck from your brother's eye.
MARK
4:24 "Consider carefully what you hear," he continued. "With the measure you use, it will be measured to you—and even more. ²⁵ Whoever has will be given more; whoever does not have, even what they have will be taken from them."
LUKE
6:37 "Do not judge, and you will not be judged. Do not condemn, and you will not be condemned. Forgive, and you will be forgiven. ³⁸ Give, and it will be given to you. A good measure, pressed down, shaken together and running over, will be poured into your lap. For with the measure you use, it will be measured to you."   ⁴¹ "Why do you look at the speck of sawdust in your brother's eye and pay no attention to the plank in your own eye? ⁴² How can you say to your brother, 'Brother, let me take the speck out of your eye,' when you yourself fail to see the plank in your own eye? You hypocrite, first take the plank out of your eye, and then you will see clearly to remove the speck from your brother's eye.
JOHN
8:2 (passage is absent from the oldest manuscripts) At dawn he appeared again in the temple courts, where all the people gathered around him, and he sat down to teach them. ³ The teachers of the law and the Pharisees brought in a woman caught in adultery. They made her stand before the group ⁴ and said to Jesus, "Teacher, this woman was caught in the act of adultery. ⁵ In the Law Moses commanded us to stone such women. Now what do you say?" ⁶ They were using this question as a trap, in order to have a basis for accusing him.   But Jesus bent down and started to write on the ground with his finger. ⁷ When they kept on questioning him, he straightened up and said to them, "Let any one of you who is without sin be the first to throw a stone at her." ⁸ Again he stooped down and wrote on the ground.   ⁹ At this, those who heard began to go away one at a time, the older ones first, until only Jesus was left, with the woman still standing there. ¹⁰ Jesus straightened up and asked her, "Woman, where are they? Has no one condemned you?" ¹¹ "No one, sir," she said. "Then neither do I condemn you," Jesus declared. "Go now and leave your life of sin."

1. Consider the short passage in Mark as the core of the ideas developed in Matthew and Luke. What additional insights have they provided?
2. What is the relationship between the Synoptic passages and the passage from John?

10.m Prayer

MATTHEW
7:7 "Ask and it will be given to you; seek and you will find; knock and the door will be opened to you. [8] For everyone who asks receives; the one who seeks finds; and to the one who knocks, the door will be opened. [9] "Which of you, if your son asks for bread, will give him a stone? [10] Or if he asks for a fish, will give him a snake? [11] If you, then, though you are evil, know how to give good gifts to your children, how much more will your Father in heaven give good gifts to those who ask him!   * * *   18:19 "Again, truly I tell you that if two of you on earth agree about anything they ask for, it will be done for them by my Father in heaven. [20] For where two or three gather in my name, there am I with them."

MARK
11:22 "Have faith in God," Jesus answered. [23] "Truly I tell you, if anyone says to this mountain, 'Go, throw yourself into the sea,' and does not doubt in their heart but believes that what they say will happen, it will be done for them. [24] Therefore I tell you, whatever you ask for in prayer, believe that you have received it, and it will be yours. [25] And when you stand praying, if you hold anything against anyone, forgive them, so that your Father in heaven may forgive you your sins."

LUKE
11:5 Then Jesus said to them, "Suppose you have a friend, and you go to him at midnight and say, 'Friend, lend me three loaves of bread; [6] a friend of mine on a journey has come to me, and I have no food to offer him.' [7] And suppose the one inside answers, 'Don't bother me. The door is already locked, and my children and I are in bed. I can't get up and give you anything.' [8] I tell you, even though he will not get up and give you the bread because of friendship, yet because of your shameless audacity he will surely get up and give you as much as you need.   [9] "So I say to you: Ask and it will be given to you; seek and you will find; knock and the door will be opened to you. [10] For everyone who asks receives; the one who seeks finds; and to the one who knocks, the door will be opened. [11] "Which of you fathers, if your son asks for a fish, will give him a snake instead? [12] Or if he asks for an egg, will give him a scorpion? [13] If you then, though you are evil, know how to give good gifts to your children, how much more will your Father in heaven give the Holy Spirit to those who ask him!"   * * *   18:1 Then Jesus told his disciples a parable to show them that they should always pray and not give up. [2] He said: "In a certain town there was a judge who neither feared God nor cared what people thought. [3] And there was a widow in that town who kept coming to him with the plea, 'Grant me justice against my adversary.'   [4] "For some time he refused. But finally he said to himself, 'Even though I don't fear God or care what people think, [5] yet because this widow keeps bothering me, I will see that she gets justice, so that she won't eventually come and attack me!'"   [6] And the Lord said, "Listen to what the unjust judge says. [7] And will not God bring about justice for his chosen ones, who cry out to him day and night? Will he keep putting them off? [8] I tell you, he will see that they get justice, and quickly. However, when the Son of Man comes, will he find faith on the earth?"

JOHN
16:23 In that day you will no longer ask me anything. Very truly I tell you, my Father will give you whatever you ask in my name. [24] Until now you have not asked for anything in my name. Ask and you will receive, and your joy will be complete.   [25] "Though I have been speaking figuratively, a time is coming when I will no longer use this kind of language but will tell you plainly about my Father. [26] In that day you will ask in my name. I am not saying that I will ask the Father on your behalf. [27] No, the Father himself loves you because you have loved me and have believed that I came from God.

1. This is a classic instance in which the four Gospels offer witnesses that are each unique in some ways and overlapping or duplicative in others. What is Jesus' teaching on prayer that you can gather from all the witnesses together?

10.n Do unto Others

MATTHEW
7:12 So in everything, do to others what you would have them do to you, for this sums up the Law and the Prophets.

MARK

LUKE
6:27 "But to you who are listening I say: Love your enemies, do good to those who hate you, [28] bless those who curse you, pray for those who mistreat you. [29] If someone slaps you on one cheek, turn to them the other also. If someone takes your coat, do not withhold your shirt from them. [30] Give to everyone who asks you, and if anyone takes what belongs to you, do not demand it back. [31] Do to others as you would have them do to you. [32] "If you love those who love you, what credit is that to you? Even sinners love those who love them. [33] And if you do good to those who are good to you, what credit is that to you? Even sinners do that. [34] And if you lend to those from whom you expect repayment, what credit is that to you? Even sinners lend to sinners, expecting to be repaid in full. [35] But love your enemies, do good to them, and lend to them without expecting to get anything back. Then your reward will be great, and you will be children of the Most High, because he is kind to the ungrateful and wicked. [36] Be merciful, just as your Father is merciful.

JOHN

1. Do these two teachings express the same idea, or are there differences?

10.0 The Narrow Gate

MATTHEW
7:13 "Enter through the narrow gate. For wide is the gate and broad is the road that leads to destruction, and many enter through it. [14] But small is the gate and narrow the road that leads to life, and only a few find it.

MARK

LUKE
13:22 Then Jesus went through the towns and villages, teaching as he made his way to Jerusalem. [23] Someone asked him, "Lord, are only a few people going to be saved?"   He said to them, [24] "Make every effort to enter through the narrow door, because many, I tell you, will try to enter and will not be able to. [25] Once the owner of the house gets up and closes the door, you will stand outside knocking and pleading, 'Sir, open the door for us.' "But he will answer, 'I don't know you or where you come from.' [26] "Then you will say, 'We ate and drank with you, and you taught in our streets.' [27] "But he will reply, 'I don't know you or where you come from. Away from me, all you evildoers!'   [28] "There will be weeping there, and gnashing of teeth, when you see Abraham, Isaac and Jacob and all the prophets in the kingdom of God, but you yourselves thrown out. [29] People will come from east and west and north and south, and will take their places at the feast in the kingdom of God. [30] Indeed there are those who are last who will be first, and first who will be last."

JOHN
10:1 "Very truly I tell you Pharisees, anyone who does not enter the sheep pen by the gate, but climbs in by some other way, is a thief and a robber. [2] The one who enters by the gate is the shepherd of the sheep. [3] The gatekeeper opens the gate for him, and the sheep listen to his voice. He calls his own sheep by name and leads them out. [4] When he has brought out all his own, he goes on ahead of them, and his sheep follow him because they know his voice. [5] But they will never follow a stranger; in fact, they will run away from him because they do not recognize a stranger's voice." [6] Jesus used this figure of speech, but the Pharisees did not understand what he was telling them. [7] Therefore Jesus said again, "Very truly I tell you, I am the gate for the sheep. [8] All who have come before me are thieves and robbers, but the sheep have not listened to them. [9] I am the gate; whoever enters through me will be saved. They will come in and go out, and find pasture. [10] The thief comes only to steal and kill and destroy; I have come that they may have life, and have it to the full.

1. Does Jesus mean the same thing by "gate" or "door" in each passage?

10.p Building on Rock

MATTHEW
7:24 "Therefore everyone who hears these words of mine and puts them into practice is like a wise man who built his house on the rock. ²⁵ The rain came down, the streams rose, and the winds blew and beat against that house; yet it did not fall, because it had its foundation on the rock. ²⁶ But everyone who hears these words of mine and does not put them into practice is like a foolish man who built his house on sand. ²⁷ The rain came down, the streams rose, and the winds blew and beat against that house, and it fell with a great crash."

MARK

LUKE
6:46 "Why do you call me, 'Lord, Lord,' and do not do what I say? ⁴⁷ As for everyone who comes to me and hears my words and puts them into practice, I will show you what they are like. ⁴⁸ They are like a man building a house, who dug down deep and laid the foundation on rock. When a flood came, the torrent struck that house but could not shake it, because it was well built. ⁴⁹ But the one who hears my words and does not put them into practice is like a man who built a house on the ground without a foundation. The moment the torrent struck that house, it collapsed and its destruction was complete."

JOHN

1. Note the differences of detail between the two versions. What explanations can you think of that might account for such differences?

10.q Fasting

MATTHEW
9:14 Then John's disciples came and asked him, "How is it that we and the Pharisees fast often, but your disciples do not fast?" [15] Jesus answered, "How can the guests of the bridegroom mourn while he is with them? The time will come when the bridegroom will be taken from them; then they will fast. [16] "No one sews a patch of unshrunk cloth on an old garment, for the patch will pull away from the garment, making the tear worse. [17] Neither do people pour new wine into old wineskins. If they do, the skins will burst; the wine will run out and the wineskins will be ruined. No, they pour new wine into new wineskins, and both are preserved.
MARK
2:18 Now John's disciples and the Pharisees were fasting. Some people came and asked Jesus, "How is it that John's disciples and the disciples of the Pharisees are fasting, but yours are not?" [19] Jesus answered, "How can the guests of the bridegroom fast while he is with them? They cannot, so long as they have him with them. [20] But the time will come when the bridegroom will be taken from them, and on that day they will fast. [21] "No one sews a patch of unshrunk cloth on an old garment. Otherwise, the new piece will pull away from the old, making the tear worse. [22] And no one pours new wine into old wineskins. Otherwise, the wine will burst the skins, and both the wine and the wineskins will be ruined. No, they pour new wine into new wineskins."
LUKE
5:33 They said to him, "John's disciples often fast and pray, and so do the disciples of the Pharisees, but yours go on eating and drinking." [34] Jesus answered, "Can you make the friends of the bridegroom fast while he is with them? [35] But the time will come when the bridegroom will be taken from them; in those days they will fast." [36] He told them this parable: "No one tears a piece out of a new garment to patch an old one. Otherwise, they will have torn the new garment, and the patch from the new will not match the old. [37] And no one pours new wine into old wineskins. Otherwise, the new wine will burst the skins; the wine will run out and the wineskins will be ruined. [38] No, new wine must be poured into new wineskins. [39] And no one after drinking old wine wants the new, for they say, 'The old is better.'"
JOHN

1. Do you find any significant differences between these three two-part passages?
2. What is the connection between the first part of each passage and the second part? Do the variations among the three versions provide you any help?

10.r That Which Defiles

MATTHEW
15:1 Then some Pharisees and teachers of the law came to Jesus from Jerusalem and asked, ² "Why do your disciples break the tradition of the elders? They don't wash their hands before they eat!" ³ Jesus replied, "And why do you break the command of God for the sake of your tradition? ⁴ For God said, 'Honor your father and mother' and 'Anyone who curses their father or mother is to be put to death.' ⁵ But you say that if anyone declares that what might have been used to help their father or mother is 'devoted to God,' ⁶ they are not to 'honor their father or mother' with it. Thus you nullify the word of God for the sake of your tradition. ⁷ You hypocrites! Isaiah was right when he prophesied about you: ⁸ "'These people honor me with their lips, but their hearts are far from me. ⁹ They worship me in vain; their teachings are merely human rules.'" ¹⁰ Jesus called the crowd to him and said, "Listen and understand. ¹¹ What goes into someone's mouth does not defile them, but what comes out of their mouth, that is what defiles them." ¹² Then the disciples came to him and asked, "Do you know that the Pharisees were offended when they heard this?" ¹³ He replied, "Every plant that my heavenly Father has not planted will be pulled up by the roots. ¹⁴ Leave them; they are blind guides. If the blind lead the blind, both will fall into a pit." ¹⁵ Peter said, "Explain the parable to us." ¹⁶ "Are you still so dull?" Jesus asked them. ¹⁷ "Don't you see that whatever enters the mouth goes into the stomach and then out of the body? ¹⁸ But the things that come out of a person's mouth come from the heart, and these defile them. ¹⁹ For out of the heart come evil thoughts—murder, adultery, sexual immorality, theft, false testimony, slander. ²⁰ These are what defile a person; but eating with unwashed hands does not defile them."
MARK
7:1 The Pharisees and some of the teachers of the law who had come from Jerusalem gathered around Jesus ² and saw some of his disciples eating food with hands that were defiled, that is, unwashed. ³ (The Pharisees and all the Jews do not eat unless they give their hands a ceremonial washing, holding to the tradition of the elders. ⁴ When they come from the marketplace they do not eat unless they wash. And they observe many other traditions, such as the washing of cups, pitchers and kettles.) ⁵ So the Pharisees and teachers of the law asked Jesus, "Why don't your disciples live according to the tradition of the elders instead of eating their food with defiled hands?" ⁶ He replied, "Isaiah was right when he prophesied about you hypocrites; as it is written: "'These people honor me with their lips, but their hearts are far from me. ⁷ They worship me in vain; their teachings are merely human rules.' ⁸ You have let go of the commands of God and are holding on to human traditions." ⁹ And he continued, "You have a fine way of setting aside the commands of God in order to observe your own traditions! ¹⁰ For Moses said, 'Honor your father and mother,' and, 'Anyone who curses their father or mother is to be put to death.' ¹¹ But you say that if anyone declares that what might have been used to help their father or mother is Corban (that is, devoted to God)— ¹² then you no longer let them do anything for their father or mother. ¹³ Thus you nullify the word of God by your tradition that you have handed down. And you do many things like that." ¹⁴ Again Jesus called the crowd to him and said, "Listen to me, everyone, and understand this. ¹⁵ Nothing outside a person can defile them by going into them. Rather, it is what comes out of a person that defiles them." [¹⁶] ¹⁷ After he had left the crowd and entered the house, his disciples asked him about this parable. ¹⁸ "Are you so dull?" he asked. "Don't you see that nothing that enters a person from the outside can defile them? ¹⁹ For it doesn't go into their heart but into their stomach, and then out of the body." (In saying this, Jesus declared all foods clean.) ²⁰ He went on: "What comes out of a person is what defiles them. ²¹ For it is from within, out of a person's heart, that evil thoughts come—sexual immorality, theft, murder, ²² adultery, greed, malice, deceit, lewdness, envy, slander, arrogance and folly. ²³ All these evils come from inside and defile a person."

LUKE
11:37 When Jesus had finished speaking, a Pharisee invited him to eat with him; so he went in and reclined at the table. ³⁸ But the Pharisee was surprised when he noticed that Jesus did not first wash before the meal. ³⁹ Then the Lord said to him, "Now then, you Pharisees clean the outside of the cup and dish, but inside you are full of greed and wickedness. ⁴⁰ You foolish people! Did not the one who made the outside make the inside also? ⁴¹ But now as for what is inside you—be generous to the poor, and everything will be clean for you.
JOHN

1. Mark and Matthew make it clear than Jesus is abrogating – or at least de-emphasizing – a Jewish dietary law. Why do you suppose Luke leaves this issue unremarked?
2. What other differences or similarities do you find among the three passages?

10.s Dealing with Sin

MATTHEW
18:15 "If your brother or sister sins, go and point out their fault, just between the two of you. If they listen to you, you have won them over. [16] But if they will not listen, take one or two others along, so that 'every matter may be established by the testimony of two or three witnesses.' [17] If they still refuse to listen, tell it to the church; and if they refuse to listen even to the church, treat them as you would a pagan or a tax collector.
MARK
11:25 And when you stand praying, if you hold anything against anyone, forgive them, so that your Father in heaven may forgive you your sins."
LUKE
17:3 "If your brother or sister sins against you, rebuke them; and if they repent, forgive them. [4] Even if they sin against you seven times in a day and seven times come back to you saying 'I repent,' you must forgive them."
JOHN
20:23 If you forgive anyone's sins, their sins are forgiven; if you do not forgive them, they are not forgiven."

1. Perhaps not surprisingly, all four of the passages on dealing with the sin of others are unique. Do you see similarities? What do you make of the differences?

10.t Let the Children Come

MATTHEW
19:13 Then people brought little children to Jesus for him to place his hands on them and pray for them. But the disciples rebuked them. [14] Jesus said, "Let the little children come to me, and do not hinder them, for the kingdom of heaven belongs to such as these." [15] When he had placed his hands on them, he went on from there.
MARK
10:13 People were bringing little children to Jesus for him to place his hands on them, but the disciples rebuked them. [14] When Jesus saw this, he was indignant. He said to them, "Let the little children come to me, and do not hinder them, for the kingdom of God belongs to such as these. [15] Truly I tell you, anyone who will not receive the kingdom of God like a little child will never enter it." [16] And he took the children in his arms, placed his hands on them and blessed them.
LUKE
18:15 People were also bringing babies to Jesus for him to place his hands on them. When the disciples saw this, they rebuked them. [16] But Jesus called the children to him and said, "Let the little children come to me, and do not hinder them, for the kingdom of God belongs to such as these. [17] Truly I tell you, anyone who will not receive the kingdom of God like a little child will never enter it."
JOHN

1. Do you find any differences among the three passages?

10.u The Eye of the Needle

MATTHEW
19:16 Just then a man came up to Jesus and asked, "Teacher, what good thing must I do to get eternal life?" [17] "Why do you ask me about what is good?" Jesus replied. "There is only One who is good. If you want to enter life, keep the commandments." [18] "Which ones?" he inquired. Jesus replied, "'You shall not murder, you shall not commit adultery, you shall not steal, you shall not give false testimony, [19] honor your father and mother,' and 'love your neighbor as yourself.'" [20] "All these I have kept," the young man said. "What do I still lack?" [21] Jesus answered, "If you want to be perfect, go, sell your possessions and give to the poor, and you will have treasure in heaven. Then come, follow me." [22] When the young man heard this, he went away sad, because he had great wealth. [23] Then Jesus said to his disciples, "Truly I tell you, it is hard for someone who is rich to enter the kingdom of heaven. [24] Again I tell you, it is easier for a camel to go through the eye of a needle than for someone who is rich to enter the kingdom of God." [25] When the disciples heard this, they were greatly astonished and asked, "Who then can be saved?" [26] Jesus looked at them and said, "With man this is impossible, but with God all things are possible."

MARK
10:17 As Jesus started on his way, a man ran up to him and fell on his knees before him. "Good teacher," he asked, "what must I do to inherit eternal life?" [18] "Why do you call me good?" Jesus answered. "No one is good—except God alone. [19] You know the commandments: 'You shall not murder, you shall not commit adultery, you shall not steal, you shall not give false testimony, you shall not defraud, honor your father and mother.'" [20] "Teacher," he declared, "all these I have kept since I was a boy." [21] Jesus looked at him and loved him. "One thing you lack," he said. "Go, sell everything you have and give to the poor, and you will have treasure in heaven. Then come, follow me." [22] At this the man's face fell. He went away sad, because he had great wealth. [23] Jesus looked around and said to his disciples, "How hard it is for the rich to enter the kingdom of God!" [24] The disciples were amazed at his words. But Jesus said again, "Children, how hard it is to enter the kingdom of God! [25] It is easier for a camel to go through the eye of a needle than for someone who is rich to enter the kingdom of God." [26] The disciples were even more amazed, and said to each other, "Who then can be saved?" [27] Jesus looked at them and said, "With man this is impossible, but not with God; all things are possible with God."

LUKE
18:18 A certain ruler asked him, "Good teacher, what must I do to inherit eternal life?" [19] "Why do you call me good?" Jesus answered. "No one is good—except God alone. [20] You know the commandments: 'You shall not commit adultery, you shall not murder, you shall not steal, you shall not give false testimony, honor your father and mother.'" [21] "All these I have kept since I was a boy," he said. [22] When Jesus heard this, he said to him, "You still lack one thing. Sell everything you have and give to the poor, and you will have treasure in heaven. Then come, follow me." [23] When he heard this, he became very sad, because he was very wealthy. [24] Jesus looked at him and said, "How hard it is for the rich to enter the kingdom of God! [25] Indeed, it is easier for a camel to go through the eye of a needle than for someone who is rich to enter the kingdom of God." [26] Those who heard this asked, "Who then can be saved?" [27] Jesus replied, "What is impossible with man is possible with God."

JOHN

1. What differences do you find among the three versions of this episode?

10.v Render unto Caesar

MATTHEW
22:15 Then the Pharisees went out and laid plans to trap him in his words. [16] They sent their disciples to him along with the Herodians. "Teacher," they said, "we know that you are a man of integrity and that you teach the way of God in accordance with the truth. You aren't swayed by others, because you pay no attention to who they are. [17] Tell us then, what is your opinion? Is it right to pay the imperial tax to Caesar or not?" [18] But Jesus, knowing their evil intent, said, "You hypocrites, why are you trying to trap me? [19] Show me the coin used for paying the tax." They brought him a denarius, [20] and he asked them, "Whose image is this? And whose inscription?" [21] "Caesar's," they replied. Then he said to them, "So give back to Caesar what is Caesar's, and to God what is God's." [22] When they heard this, they were amazed. So they left him and went away.
MARK
12:13 Later they sent some of the Pharisees and Herodians to Jesus to catch him in his words. [14] They came to him and said, "Teacher, we know that you are a man of integrity. You aren't swayed by others, because you pay no attention to who they are; but you teach the way of God in accordance with the truth. Is it right to pay the imperial tax to Caesar or not? [15] Should we pay or shouldn't we?" But Jesus knew their hypocrisy. "Why are you trying to trap me?" he asked. "Bring me a denarius and let me look at it." [16] They brought the coin, and he asked them, "Whose image is this? And whose inscription?" "Caesar's," they replied. [17] Then Jesus said to them, "Give back to Caesar what is Caesar's and to God what is God's." And they were amazed at him.
LUKE
20:20 Keeping a close watch on him, they sent spies, who pretended to be sincere. They hoped to catch Jesus in something he said, so that they might hand him over to the power and authority of the governor. [21] So the spies questioned him: "Teacher, we know that you speak and teach what is right, and that you do not show partiality but teach the way of God in accordance with the truth. [22] Is it right for us to pay taxes to Caesar or not?" [23] He saw through their duplicity and said to them, [24] "Show me a denarius. Whose image and inscription are on it?" "Caesar's," they replied. [25] He said to them, "Then give back to Caesar what is Caesar's, and to God what is God's." [26] They were unable to trap him in what he had said there in public. And astonished by his answer, they became silent.
JOHN

1. Identify the differences among the three versions.

10.w Marriage at the Resurrection

MATTHEW
22:23 That same day the Sadducees, who say there is no resurrection, came to him with a question. [24] "Teacher," they said, "Moses told us that if a man dies without having children, his brother must marry the widow and raise up offspring for him. [25] Now there were seven brothers among us. The first one married and died, and since he had no children, he left his wife to his brother. [26] The same thing happened to the second and third brother, right on down to the seventh. [27] Finally, the woman died. [28] Now then, at the resurrection, whose wife will she be of the seven, since all of them were married to her?" [29] Jesus replied, "You are in error because you do not know the Scriptures or the power of God. [30] At the resurrection people will neither marry nor be given in marriage; they will be like the angels in heaven. [31] But about the resurrection of the dead—have you not read what God said to you, [32] 'I am the God of Abraham, the God of Isaac, and the God of Jacob'? He is not the God of the dead but of the living." [33] When the crowds heard this, they were astonished at his teaching.

MARK
12:18 Then the Sadducees, who say there is no resurrection, came to him with a question. [19] "Teacher," they said, "Moses wrote for us that if a man's brother dies and leaves a wife but no children, the man must marry the widow and raise up offspring for his brother. [20] Now there were seven brothers. The first one married and died without leaving any children. [21] The second one married the widow, but he also died, leaving no child. It was the same with the third. [22] In fact, none of the seven left any children. Last of all, the woman died too. [23] At the resurrection whose wife will she be, since the seven were married to her?" [24] Jesus replied, "Are you not in error because you do not know the Scriptures or the power of God? [25] When the dead rise, they will neither marry nor be given in marriage; they will be like the angels in heaven. [26] Now about the dead rising—have you not read in the Book of Moses, in the account of the burning bush, how God said to him, 'I am the God of Abraham, the God of Isaac, and the God of Jacob'? [27] He is not the God of the dead, but of the living. You are badly mistaken!"

LUKE
20:27 Some of the Sadducees, who say there is no resurrection, came to Jesus with a question. [28] "Teacher," they said, "Moses wrote for us that if a man's brother dies and leaves a wife but no children, the man must marry the widow and raise up offspring for his brother. [29] Now there were seven brothers. The first one married a woman and died childless. [30] The second [31] and then the third married her, and in the same way the seven died, leaving no children. [32] Finally, the woman died too. [33] Now then, at the resurrection whose wife will she be, since the seven were married to her?" [34] Jesus replied, "The people of this age marry and are given in marriage. [35] But those who are considered worthy of taking part in the age to come and in the resurrection from the dead will neither marry nor be given in marriage, [36] and they can no longer die; for they are like the angels. They are God's children, since they are children of the resurrection. [37] But in the account of the burning bush, even Moses showed that the dead rise, for he calls the Lord 'the God of Abraham, and the God of Isaac, and the God of Jacob.' [38] He is not the God of the dead, but of the living, for to him all are alive." [39] Some of the teachers of the law responded, "Well said, teacher!" [40] And no one dared to ask him any more questions.

JOHN

1. Compare Jesus' teaching in the three versions.

10.x The Greatest Commandments

MATTHEW
22:34 Hearing that Jesus had silenced the Sadducees, the Pharisees got together. [35] One of them, an expert in the law, tested him with this question: [36] "Teacher, which is the greatest commandment in the Law?" [37] Jesus replied: "'Love the Lord your God with all your heart and with all your soul and with all your mind.' [38] This is the first and greatest commandment. [39] And the second is like it: 'Love your neighbor as yourself.' [40] All the Law and the Prophets hang on these two commandments."

MARK
12:28 One of the teachers of the law came and heard them debating. Noticing that Jesus had given them a good answer, he asked him, "Of all the commandments, which is the most important?" [29] "The most important one," answered Jesus, "is this: 'Hear, O Israel: The Lord our God, the Lord is one. [30] Love the Lord your God with all your heart and with all your soul and with all your mind and with all your strength.' [31] The second is this: 'Love your neighbor as yourself.' There is no commandment greater than these." [32] "Well said, teacher," the man replied. "You are right in saying that God is one and there is no other but him. [33] To love him with all your heart, with all your understanding and with all your strength, and to love your neighbor as yourself is more important than all burnt offerings and sacrifices." [34] When Jesus saw that he had answered wisely, he said to him, "You are not far from the kingdom of God." And from then on no one dared ask him any more questions.

LUKE
10:25 On one occasion an expert in the law stood up to test Jesus. "Teacher," he asked, "what must I do to inherit eternal life?" [26] "What is written in the Law?" he replied. "How do you read it?" [27] He answered, "'Love the Lord your God with all your heart and with all your soul and with all your strength and with all your mind'; and, 'Love your neighbor as yourself.'" [28] "You have answered correctly," Jesus replied. "Do this and you will live."

JOHN

1. Are there significant differences among the three versions of Jesus' teaching?

10.y The Widow's Mite

MATTHEW

MARK
12:41 Jesus sat down opposite the place where the offerings were put and watched the crowd putting their money into the temple treasury. Many rich people threw in large amounts. ⁴² But a poor widow came and put in two very small copper coins, worth only a few cents. ⁴³ Calling his disciples to him, Jesus said, "Truly I tell you, this poor widow has put more into the treasury than all the others. ⁴⁴ They all gave out of their wealth; but she, out of her poverty, put in everything—all she had to live on."

LUKE
21:1 As Jesus looked up, he saw the rich putting their gifts into the temple treasury. ² He also saw a poor widow put in two very small copper coins. ³ "Truly I tell you," he said, "this poor widow has put in more than all the others. ⁴ All these people gave their gifts out of their wealth; but she out of her poverty put in all she had to live on."

JOHN

1. Do you find any variation between the two accounts?
2. Have you noticed how few comparable passages in Section 10 have been drawn from John's Gospel? How would you generalize a description of the passages in this section? Why do you suppose John all but omitted any comparable passages?

Chapter 11: Curses and Imprecations

11.a Known by their Fruit

MATTHEW
7:15 "Watch out for false prophets. They come to you in sheep's clothing, but inwardly they are ferocious wolves. 16 By their fruit you will recognize them. Do people pick grapes from thornbushes, or figs from thistles? 17 Likewise, every good tree bears good fruit, but a bad tree bears bad fruit. 18 A good tree cannot bear bad fruit, and a bad tree cannot bear good fruit. 19 Every tree that does not bear good fruit is cut down and thrown into the fire. 20 Thus, by their fruit you will recognize them. 21 "Not everyone who says to me, 'Lord, Lord,' will enter the kingdom of heaven, but only the one who does the will of my Father who is in heaven. 22 Many will say to me on that day, 'Lord, Lord, did we not prophesy in your name and in your name drive out demons and in your name perform many miracles?' 23 Then I will tell them plainly, 'I never knew you. Away from me, you evildoers!' * * * 12:33 "Make a tree good and its fruit will be good, or make a tree bad and its fruit will be bad, for a tree is recognized by its fruit. 34 You brood of vipers, how can you who are evil say anything good? For the mouth speaks what the heart is full of. 35 A good man brings good things out of the good stored up in him, and an evil man brings evil things out of the evil stored up in him. 36 But I tell you that everyone will have to give account on the day of judgment for every empty word they have spoken. 37 For by your words you will be acquitted, and by your words you will be condemned."
MARK
LUKE
6:43 "No good tree bears bad fruit, nor does a bad tree bear good fruit. 44 Each tree is recognized by its own fruit. People do not pick figs from thornbushes, or grapes from briers. 45 A good man brings good things out of the good stored up in his heart, and an evil man brings evil things out of the evil stored up in his heart. For the mouth speaks what the heart is full of.
JOHN
15:1 "I am the true vine, and my Father is the gardener. 2 He cuts off every branch in me that bears no fruit, while every branch that does bear fruit he prunes so that it will be even more fruitful. 3 You are already clean because of the word I have spoken to you. 4 Remain in me, as I also remain in you. No branch can bear fruit by itself; it must remain in the vine. Neither can you bear fruit unless you remain in me. 5 "I am the vine; you are the branches. If you remain in me and I in you, you will bear much fruit; apart from me you can do nothing. 6 If you do not remain in me, you are like a branch that is thrown away and withers; such branches are picked up, thrown into the fire and burned. 7 If you remain in me and my words remain in you, ask whatever you wish, and it will be done for you. 8 This is to my Father's glory, that you bear much fruit, showing yourselves to be my disciples.

1. What thoughts does Matthew develop in his longer accounts than does Luke in his single, short account?

2. Are there further ideas developed in the similar passage in John? Are there important ideas omitted from John's passage that Matthew or Luke include?

11.b The Sign of Jonah

MATTHEW
12:38 Then some of the Pharisees and teachers of the law said to him, "Teacher, we want to see a sign from you." [39] He answered, "A wicked and adulterous generation asks for a sign! But none will be given it except the sign of the prophet Jonah. [40] For as Jonah was three days and three nights in the belly of a huge fish, so the Son of Man will be three days and three nights in the heart of the earth. [41] The men of Nineveh will stand up at the judgment with this generation and condemn it; for they repented at the preaching of Jonah, and now something greater than Jonah is here. [42] The Queen of the South will rise at the judgment with this generation and condemn it; for she came from the ends of the earth to listen to Solomon's wisdom, and now something greater than Solomon is here. * * * 16:1 The Pharisees and Sadducees came to Jesus and tested him by asking him to show them a sign from heaven. [2] He replied, "When evening comes, you say, 'It will be fair weather, for the sky is red,' [3] and in the morning, 'Today it will be stormy, for the sky is red and overcast.' You know how to interpret the appearance of the sky, but you cannot interpret the signs of the times. [4] A wicked and adulterous generation looks for a sign, but none will be given it except the sign of Jonah." Jesus then left them and went away.

MARK

LUKE
11:29 As the crowds increased, Jesus said, "This is a wicked generation. It asks for a sign, but none will be given it except the sign of Jonah. [30] For as Jonah was a sign to the Ninevites, so also will the Son of Man be to this generation. [31] The Queen of the South will rise at the judgment with the people of this generation and condemn them, for she came from the ends of the earth to listen to Solomon's wisdom; and now something greater than Solomon is here. [32] The men of Nineveh will stand up at the judgment with this generation and condemn it, for they repented at the preaching of Jonah; and now something greater than Jonah is here.

JOHN

1. Does the second passage in Matthew – not reflected in the other Gospels – cast additional light on Jesus' meaning?
2. Do you find significant differences between the passage from Matthew 12 and the one from Luke?

11.c The Yeast of the Pharisees

MATTHEW
16:5 When they went across the lake, the disciples forgot to take bread. ⁶"Be careful," Jesus said to them. "Be on your guard against the yeast of the Pharisees and Sadducees." ⁷ They discussed this among themselves and said, "It is because we didn't bring any bread." ⁸ Aware of their discussion, Jesus asked, "You of little faith, why are you talking among yourselves about having no bread? ⁹ Do you still not understand? Don't you remember the five loaves for the five thousand, and how many basketfuls you gathered? ¹⁰ Or the seven loaves for the four thousand, and how many basketfuls you gathered? ¹¹ How is it you don't understand that I was not talking to you about bread? But be on your guard against the yeast of the Pharisees and Sadducees." ¹² Then they understood that he was not telling them to guard against the yeast used in bread, but against the teaching of the Pharisees and Sadducees.

MARK
8:14 The disciples had forgotten to bring bread, except for one loaf they had with them in the boat. ¹⁵"Be careful," Jesus warned them. "Watch out for the yeast of the Pharisees and that of Herod." ¹⁶ They discussed this with one another and said, "It is because we have no bread." ¹⁷ Aware of their discussion, Jesus asked them: "Why are you talking about having no bread? Do you still not see or understand? Are your hearts hardened? ¹⁸ Do you have eyes but fail to see, and ears but fail to hear? And don't you remember? ¹⁹ When I broke the five loaves for the five thousand, how many basketfuls of pieces did you pick up?" "Twelve," they replied. ²⁰ "And when I broke the seven loaves for the four thousand, how many basketfuls of pieces did you pick up?" They answered, "Seven." ²¹ He said to them, "Do you still not understand?"

LUKE
12:1 Meanwhile, when a crowd of many thousands had gathered, so that they were trampling on one another, Jesus began to speak first to his disciples, saying: "Be on your guard against the yeast of the Pharisees, which is hypocrisy. ² There is nothing concealed that will not be disclosed, or hidden that will not be made known. ³ What you have said in the dark will be heard in the daylight, and what you have whispered in the ear in the inner rooms will be proclaimed from the roofs.

JOHN

1. Jesus' term "the yeast of the Pharisees" is obscure in meaning. Does Luke's report of another occasion on which Jesus used the term cast further light on its meaning?

11.d Cleansing the Temple

MATTHEW
21:12 Jesus entered the temple courts and drove out all who were buying and selling there. He overturned the tables of the money changers and the benches of those selling doves. [13] "It is written," he said to them, "'My house will be called a house of prayer,' but you are making it 'a den of robbers.'" [14] The blind and the lame came to him at the temple, and he healed them. [15] But when the chief priests and the teachers of the law saw the wonderful things he did and the children shouting in the temple courts, "Hosanna to the Son of David," they were indignant. [16] "Do you hear what these children are saying?" they asked him. "Yes," replied Jesus, "have you never read, "'From the lips of children and infants you, Lord, have called forth your praise'?" [17] And he left them and went out of the city to Bethany, where he spent the night.

MARK
11:15 On reaching Jerusalem, Jesus entered the temple courts and began driving out those who were buying and selling there. He overturned the tables of the money changers and the benches of those selling doves, [16] and would not allow anyone to carry merchandise through the temple courts. [17] And as he taught them, he said, "Is it not written: 'My house will be called a house of prayer for all nations'? But you have made it 'a den of robbers.'" [18] The chief priests and the teachers of the law heard this and began looking for a way to kill him, for they feared him, because the whole crowd was amazed at his teaching. [19] When evening came, Jesus and his disciples went out of the city.

LUKE
19:45 When Jesus entered the temple courts, he began to drive out those who were selling. [46] "It is written," he said to them, "'My house will be a house of prayer'; but you have made it 'a den of robbers.'"

JOHN
2:13 When it was almost time for the Jewish Passover, Jesus went up to Jerusalem. [14] In the temple courts he found people selling cattle, sheep and doves, and others sitting at tables exchanging money. [15] So he made a whip out of cords, and drove all from the temple courts, both sheep and cattle; he scattered the coins of the money changers and overturned their tables. [16] To those who sold doves he said, "Get these out of here! Stop turning my Father's house into a market!" [17] His disciples remembered that it is written: "Zeal for your house will consume me." [18] The Jews then responded to him, "What sign can you show us to prove your authority to do all this?" [19] Jesus answered them, "Destroy this temple, and I will raise it again in three days." [20] They replied, "It has taken forty-six years to build this temple, and you are going to raise it in three days?" [21] But the temple he had spoken of was his body. [22] After he was raised from the dead, his disciples recalled what he had said. Then they believed the scripture and the words that Jesus had spoken.

1. Compare the four accounts of Jesus' cleansing of the temple. What common factors do you find? What differences?
2. Note that the Synoptics report that the cleansing took place near the end of Jesus' ministry, just before the crucifixion, while John places the event near the start of Jesus' ministry. What do you make of this inconsistency? Some readers note this difference and to resolve the inconsistency conclude there were two such incidents; is that a plausible interpretation?

11.e Jesus Curses the Fig Tree

MATTHEW
21:18 Early in the morning, as Jesus was on his way back to the city, he was hungry. [19] Seeing a fig tree by the road, he went up to it but found nothing on it except leaves. Then he said to it, "May you never bear fruit again!" Immediately the tree withered. [20] When the disciples saw this, they were amazed. "How did the fig tree wither so quickly?" they asked. [21] Jesus replied, "Truly I tell you, if you have faith and do not doubt, not only can you do what was done to the fig tree, but also you can say to this mountain, 'Go, throw yourself into the sea,' and it will be done. [22] If you believe, you will receive whatever you ask for in prayer."

MARK
11:12 The next day as they were leaving Bethany, Jesus was hungry. [13] Seeing in the distance a fig tree in leaf, he went to find out if it had any fruit. When he reached it, he found nothing but leaves, because it was not the season for figs. [14] Then he said to the tree, "May no one ever eat fruit from you again." And his disciples heard him say it. In the morning, as they went along, they saw the fig tree withered from the roots. [21] Peter remembered and said to Jesus, "Rabbi, look! The fig tree you cursed has withered!" [22] "Have faith in God," Jesus answered. [23] "Truly I tell you, if anyone says to this mountain, 'Go, throw yourself into the sea,' and does not doubt in their heart but believes that what they say will happen, it will be done for them. [24] Therefore I tell you, whatever you ask for in prayer, believe that you have received it, and it will be yours.

LUKE
13:6 Then he told this parable: "A man had a fig tree growing in his vineyard, and he went to look for fruit on it but did not find any. [7] So he said to the man who took care of the vineyard, 'For three years now I've been coming to look for fruit on this fig tree and haven't found any. Cut it down! Why should it use up the soil?' [8] "'Sir,' the man replied, 'leave it alone for one more year, and I'll dig around it and fertilize it. [9] If it bears fruit next year, fine! If not, then cut it down.'"

JOHN

1. Matthew and Mark give parallel accounts of this episode, while Luke's account differs. Do the differing versions help in interpreting the passage?

11.f Woe to Pharisees and Teachers of the Law

MATTHEW

23:1 Then Jesus said to the crowds and to his disciples: ² "The teachers of the law and the Pharisees sit in Moses' seat. ³ So you must be careful to do everything they tell you. But do not do what they do, for they do not practice what they preach. ⁴ They tie up heavy, cumbersome loads and put them on other people's shoulders, but they themselves are not willing to lift a finger to move them.

⁵ "Everything they do is done for people to see: They make their phylacteries wide and the tassels on their garments long; ⁶ they love the place of honor at banquets and the most important seats in the synagogues; ⁷ they love to be greeted with respect in the marketplaces and to be called 'Rabbi' by others.

⁸ "But you are not to be called 'Rabbi,' for you have one Teacher, and you are all brothers. ⁹ And do not call anyone on earth 'father,' for you have one Father, and he is in heaven. ¹⁰ Nor are you to be called instructors, for you have one Instructor, the Messiah. ¹¹ The greatest among you will be your servant. ¹² For those who exalt themselves will be humbled, and those who humble themselves will be exalted.

¹³ "Woe to you, teachers of the law and Pharisees, you hypocrites! You shut the door of the kingdom of heaven in people's faces. You yourselves do not enter, nor will you let those enter who are trying to. [14]

¹⁵ "Woe to you, teachers of the law and Pharisees, you hypocrites! You travel over land and sea to win a single convert, and when you have succeeded, you make them twice as much a child of hell as you are.

¹⁶ "Woe to you, blind guides! You say, 'If anyone swears by the temple, it means nothing; but anyone who swears by the gold of the temple is bound by that oath.' ¹⁷ You blind fools! Which is greater: the gold, or the temple that makes the gold sacred? ¹⁸ You also say, 'If anyone swears by the altar, it means nothing; but anyone who swears by the gift on the altar is bound by that oath.' ¹⁹ You blind men! Which is greater: the gift, or the altar that makes the gift sacred? ²⁰ Therefore, anyone who swears by the altar swears by it and by everything on it. ²¹ And anyone who swears by the temple swears by it and by the one who dwells in it. ²² And anyone who swears by heaven swears by God's throne and by the one who sits on it.

²³ "Woe to you, teachers of the law and Pharisees, you hypocrites! You give a tenth of your spices—mint, dill and cumin. But you have neglected the more important matters of the law—justice, mercy and faithfulness. You should have practiced the latter, without neglecting the former. ²⁴ You blind guides! You strain out a gnat but swallow a camel.

²⁵ "Woe to you, teachers of the law and Pharisees, you hypocrites! You clean the outside of the cup and dish, but inside they are full of greed and self-indulgence. ²⁶ Blind Pharisee! First clean the inside of the cup and dish, and then the outside also will be clean.

²⁷ "Woe to you, teachers of the law and Pharisees, you hypocrites! You are like whitewashed tombs, which look beautiful on the outside but on the inside are full of the bones of the dead and everything unclean. ²⁸ In the same way, on the outside you appear to people as righteous but on the inside you are full of hypocrisy and wickedness.

²⁹ "Woe to you, teachers of the law and Pharisees, you hypocrites! You build tombs for the prophets and decorate the graves of the righteous. ³⁰ And you say, 'If we had lived in the days of our ancestors, we would not have taken part with them in shedding the blood of the prophets.' ³¹ So you testify against yourselves that you are the descendants of those who murdered the prophets. ³² Go ahead, then, and complete what your ancestors started! ³³ "You snakes! You brood of vipers! How will you escape being condemned to hell? ³⁴ Therefore I am sending you prophets and sages and teachers. Some of them you will kill and crucify; others you will flog in your synagogues and pursue from town to town. ³⁵ And so upon you will come all the righteous blood that has been shed on earth, from the blood of righteous Abel to the blood of Zechariah son of Berekiah, whom you murdered between the temple and the altar. ³⁶ Truly I tell you, all this will come on this generation.

MARK

12:38 As he taught, Jesus said, "Watch out for the teachers of the law. They like to walk around in flowing robes and be greeted with respect in the marketplaces, ³⁹ and have the most important seats in the synagogues and the places of honor at banquets. ⁴⁰ They devour widows' houses and for a show make lengthy prayers. These men will be punished most severely."

LUKE

11:42 "Woe to you Pharisees, because you give God a tenth of your mint, rue and all other kinds of garden herbs, but you neglect justice and the love of God. You should have practiced the latter without leaving the former undone. [43] "Woe to you Pharisees, because you love the most important seats in the synagogues and respectful greetings in the marketplaces. [44] "Woe to you, because you are like unmarked graves, which people walk over without knowing it."

[45] One of the experts in the law answered him, "Teacher, when you say these things, you insult us also." [46] Jesus replied, "And you experts in the law, woe to you, because you load people down with burdens they can hardly carry, and you yourselves will not lift one finger to help them.

[47] "Woe to you, because you build tombs for the prophets, and it was your ancestors who killed them. [48] So you testify that you approve of what your ancestors did; they killed the prophets, and you build their tombs. [49] Because of this, God in his wisdom said, 'I will send them prophets and apostles, some of whom they will kill and others they will persecute.' [50] Therefore this generation will be held responsible for the blood of all the prophets that has been shed since the beginning of the world, [51] from the blood of Abel to the blood of Zechariah, who was killed between the altar and the sanctuary. Yes, I tell you, this generation will be held responsible for it all.

[52] "Woe to you experts in the law, because you have taken away the key to knowledge. You yourselves have not entered, and you have hindered those who were entering."

[53] When Jesus went outside, the Pharisees and the teachers of the law began to oppose him fiercely and to besiege him with questions, [54] waiting to catch him in something he might say.

* * *

18:9 To some who were confident of their own righteousness and looked down on everyone else, Jesus told this parable: [10] "Two men went up to the temple to pray, one a Pharisee and the other a tax collector. [11] The Pharisee stood by himself and prayed: 'God, I thank you that I am not like other people—robbers, evildoers, adulterers—or even like this tax collector. [12] I fast twice a week and give a tenth of all I get.'

[13] "But the tax collector stood at a distance. He would not even look up to heaven, but beat his breast and said, 'God, have mercy on me, a sinner.' [14] "I tell you that this man, rather than the other, went home justified before God. For all those who exalt themselves will be humbled, and those who humble themselves will be exalted."

* * *

20:45 While all the people were listening, Jesus said to his disciples, [46] "Beware of the teachers of the law. They like to walk around in flowing robes and love to be greeted with respect in the marketplaces and have the most important seats in the synagogues and the places of honor at banquets. [47] They devour widows' houses and for a show make lengthy prayers. These men will be punished most severely."

JOHN

9:40 Some Pharisees who were with him heard him say this and asked, "What? Are we blind too?" [41] Jesus said, "If you were blind, you would not be guilty of sin; but now that you claim you can see, your guilt remains.

* * *

10:1 "Very truly I tell you Pharisees, anyone who does not enter the sheep pen by the gate, but climbs in by some other way, is a thief and a robber. [2] The one who enters by the gate is the shepherd of the sheep. [3] The gatekeeper opens the gate for him, and the sheep listen to his voice. He calls his own sheep by name and leads them out. [4] When he has brought out all his own, he goes on ahead of them, and his sheep follow him because they know his voice. [5] But they will never follow a stranger; in fact, they will run away from him because they do not recognize a stranger's voice." [6] Jesus used this figure of speech, but the Pharisees did not understand what he was telling them.

1. Does Mark's brief report of Jesus' words capture all of what is contained in the longer accounts of Matthew and Luke? If not, what are important ideas that they included, which Mark did not?
2. Matthew and Luke report two series of imprecations ("Woe to you..."). Are their two accounts the same, or do they differ in some ways?
3. Note that Luke not only reports Jesus' curses in parallel to those in Matthew and Mark, but also includes two other passages on the same subject. Do these additional accounts add to our understanding of Jesus' judgment?

4. Jesus' words as reported by John differ from those in the Synoptics. Is his meaning the same or different?

CHAPTER 12: THE END TIMES

12.a End Times: Only the Father Knows When

MATTHEW
16:28 "Truly I tell you, some who are standing here will not taste death before they see the Son of Man coming in his kingdom."   * * *   24:34 Truly I tell you, this generation will certainly not pass away until all these things have happened. [35] Heaven and earth will pass away, but my words will never pass away. [36] "But about that day or hour no one knows, not even the angels in heaven, nor the Son, but only the Father.
MARK
9:1 And he said to them, "Truly I tell you, some who are standing here will not taste death before they see that the kingdom of God has come with power."   * * *   13:30 Truly I tell you, this generation will certainly not pass away until all these things have happened. [31] Heaven and earth will pass away, but my words will never pass away. [32] "But about that day or hour no one knows, not even the angels in heaven, nor the Son, but only the Father. [33] Be on guard! Be alert! You do not know when that time will come. [34] It's like a man going away: He leaves his house and puts his servants in charge, each with their assigned task, and tells the one at the door to keep watch.
LUKE
9:27 "Truly I tell you, some who are standing here will not taste death before they see the kingdom of God."   * * *   21:32 "Truly I tell you, this generation will certainly not pass away until all these things have happened. [33] Heaven and earth will pass away, but my words will never pass away.
JOHN

1. Do you find any significant or interesting differences among these highly parallel sayings?
2. What do the several passages indicate about Jesus' role in the end times?
3. The Synoptics clearly report that Jesus preached that the end times were near, yet John – ostensibly also the author of *Revelation* – is silent on the topic. What do you make of this?

12.b End Times: the Temple

MATTHEW
24:1 Jesus left the temple and was walking away when his disciples came up to him to call his attention to its buildings. ² "Do you see all these things?" he asked. "Truly I tell you, not one stone here will be left on another; every one will be thrown down." ³ As Jesus was sitting on the Mount of Olives, the disciples came to him privately. "Tell us," they said, "when will this happen, and what will be the sign of your coming and of the end of the age?"
MARK
13:1 As Jesus was leaving the temple, one of his disciples said to him, "Look, Teacher! What massive stones! What magnificent buildings!" ² "Do you see all these great buildings?" replied Jesus. "Not one stone here will be left on another; every one will be thrown down."
LUKE
21:5 Some of his disciples were remarking about how the temple was adorned with beautiful stones and with gifts dedicated to God. But Jesus said, ⁶ "As for what you see here, the time will come when not one stone will be left on another; every one of them will be thrown down."
JOHN
2:18 The Jews then responded to him, "What sign can you show us to prove your authority to do all this?" ¹⁹ Jesus answered them, "Destroy this temple, and I will raise it again in three days." ²⁰ They replied, "It has taken forty-six years to build this temple, and you are going to raise it in three days?" ²¹ But the temple he had spoken of was his body. ²² After he was raised from the dead, his disciples recalled what he had said. Then they believed the scripture and the words that Jesus had spoken.

1. Do you identify any differences among the accounts in Matthew, Mark, and Luke?
2. How does the meaning of the passage in John compare with those in the Synoptics?

12.c End Times: Deception

MATTHEW
24:4 Jesus answered: "Watch out that no one deceives you. [5] For many will come in my name, claiming, 'I am the Messiah,' and will deceive many. [6] You will hear of wars and rumors of wars, but see to it that you are not alarmed. Such things must happen, but the end is still to come. [7] Nation will rise against nation, and kingdom against kingdom. There will be famines and earthquakes in various places. [8] All these are the beginning of birth pains.

MARK
13:5 Jesus said to them: "Watch out that no one deceives you. [6] Many will come in my name, claiming, 'I am he,' and will deceive many. [7] When you hear of wars and rumors of wars, do not be alarmed. Such things must happen, but the end is still to come. [8] Nation will rise against nation, and kingdom against kingdom. There will be earthquakes in various places, and famines. These are the beginning of birth pains.

LUKE
21:7 "Teacher," they asked, "when will these things happen? And what will be the sign that they are about to take place?" [8] He replied: "Watch out that you are not deceived. For many will come in my name, claiming, 'I am he,' and, 'The time is near.' Do not follow them. [9] When you hear of wars and uprisings, do not be frightened. These things must happen first, but the end will not come right away." [10] Then he said to them: "Nation will rise against nation, and kingdom against kingdom. [11] There will be great earthquakes, famines and pestilences in various places, and fearful events and great signs from heaven. * * * 21:20 "When you see Jerusalem being surrounded by armies, you will know that its desolation is near. [21] Then let those who are in Judea flee to the mountains, let those in the city get out, and let those in the country not enter the city. [22] For this is the time of punishment in fulfillment of all that has been written. [23] How dreadful it will be in those days for pregnant women and nursing mothers! There will be great distress in the land and wrath against this people. [24] They will fall by the sword and will be taken as prisoners to all the nations. Jerusalem will be trampled on by the Gentiles until the times of the Gentiles are fulfilled.

JOHN

1. Do you see any significant differences among these three similar accounts?
2. These passages are reminiscent of *Revelation*, yet John – to whom *Revelation* is commonly attributed – has nothing to say on the subject. What do you make of this?

12.d End Times: Persecution

MATTHEW
24:9 "Then you will be handed over to be persecuted and put to death, and you will be hated by all nations because of me. [10] At that time many will turn away from the faith and will betray and hate each other, [11] and many false prophets will appear and deceive many people. [12] Because of the increase of wickedness, the love of most will grow cold, [13] but the one who stands firm to the end will be saved. [14] And this gospel of the kingdom will be preached in the whole world as a testimony to all nations, and then the end will come.
MARK
13:9 "You must be on your guard. You will be handed over to the local councils and flogged in the synagogues. On account of me you will stand before governors and kings as witnesses to them. [10] And the gospel must first be preached to all nations. [11] Whenever you are arrested and brought to trial, do not worry beforehand about what to say. Just say whatever is given you at the time, for it is not you speaking, but the Holy Spirit. [12] "Brother will betray brother to death, and a father his child. Children will rebel against their parents and have them put to death. [13] Everyone will hate you because of me, but the one who stands firm to the end will be saved.
LUKE
21:12 "But before all this, they will seize you and persecute you. They will hand you over to synagogues and put you in prison, and you will be brought before kings and governors, and all on account of my name. [13] And so you will bear testimony to me. [14] But make up your mind not to worry beforehand how you will defend yourselves. [15] For I will give you words and wisdom that none of your adversaries will be able to resist or contradict. [16] You will be betrayed even by parents, brothers and sisters, relatives and friends, and they will put some of you to death. [17] Everyone will hate you because of me. [18] But not a hair of your head will perish. [19] Stand firm, and you will win life.
JOHN

1. Can you identify any significant differences among these three passages?

12.e End Times: Hurry!

MATTHEW
24:15 "So when you see standing in the holy place 'the abomination that causes desolation,' spoken of through the prophet Daniel—let the reader understand— [16] then let those who are in Judea flee to the mountains. [17] Let no one on the housetop go down to take anything out of the house. [18] Let no one in the field go back to get their cloak. [19] How dreadful it will be in those days for pregnant women and nursing mothers! [20] Pray that your flight will not take place in winter or on the Sabbath. [21] For then there will be great distress, unequaled from the beginning of the world until now—and never to be equaled again.

MARK
13:14 "When you see 'the abomination that causes desolation' standing where it does not belong—let the reader understand—then let those who are in Judea flee to the mountains. [15] Let no one on the housetop go down or enter the house to take anything out. [16] Let no one in the field go back to get their cloak. [17] How dreadful it will be in those days for pregnant women and nursing mothers! [18] Pray that this will not take place in winter, [19] because those will be days of distress unequaled from the beginning, when God created the world, until now—and never to be equaled again.

LUKE
17:30 "It will be just like this on the day the Son of Man is revealed. [31] On that day no one who is on the housetop, with possessions inside, should go down to get them. Likewise, no one in the field should go back for anything. [32] Remember Lot's wife! [33] Whoever tries to keep their life will lose it, and whoever loses their life will preserve it. [34] I tell you, on that night two people will be in one bed; one will be taken and the other left. [35] Two women will be grinding grain together; one will be taken and the other left."

JOHN

1. Matthew evidently chose to use the passage reported by Mark without any significant change. Luke chose to use a different source. What differences do you see between the quotation in Luke and those in Matthew and Mark?

12.f End Times: False Messiahs

MATTHEW
24:22 "If those days had not been cut short, no one would survive, but for the sake of the elect those days will be shortened. [23] At that time if anyone says to you, 'Look, here is the Messiah!' or, 'There he is!' do not believe it. [24] For false messiahs and false prophets will appear and perform great signs and wonders to deceive, if possible, even the elect. [25] See, I have told you ahead of time.
MARK
13:20 "If the Lord had not cut short those days, no one would survive. But for the sake of the elect, whom he has chosen, he has shortened them. [21] At that time if anyone says to you, 'Look, here is the Messiah!' or, 'Look, there he is!' do not believe it. [22] For false messiahs and false prophets will appear and perform signs and wonders to deceive, if possible, even the elect. [23] So be on your guard; I have told you everything ahead of time.
LUKE
17:20 Once, on being asked by the Pharisees when the kingdom of God would come, Jesus replied, "The coming of the kingdom of God is not something that can be observed, [21] nor will people say, 'Here it is,' or 'There it is,' because the kingdom of God is in your midst."   [22] Then he said to his disciples, "The time is coming when you will long to see one of the days of the Son of Man, but you will not see it. [23] People will tell you, 'There he is!' or 'Here he is!' Do not go running off after them. [24] For the Son of Man in his day will be like the lightning, which flashes and lights up the sky from one end to the other. [25] But first he must suffer many things and be rejected by this generation.
JOHN

1. Again, Matthew repeated Mark nearly verbatim, while Luke quoted from a different source. Do you see any differences in Jesus' meaning?

12.g End Times: Keep Watch

MATTHEW
24:26 "So if anyone tells you, 'There he is, out in the wilderness,' do not go out; or, 'Here he is, in the inner rooms,' do not believe it. ²⁷ For as lightning that comes from the east is visible even in the west, so will be the coming of the Son of Man. ²⁸ Wherever there is a carcass, there the vultures will gather. 24:42 "Therefore keep watch, because you do not know on what day your Lord will come. ⁴³ But understand this: If the owner of the house had known at what time of night the thief was coming, he would have kept watch and would not have let his house be broken into. ⁴⁴ So you also must be ready, because the Son of Man will come at an hour when you do not expect him. * * * 25:1 "At that time the kingdom of heaven will be like ten virgins who took their lamps and went out to meet the bridegroom. ² Five of them were foolish and five were wise. ³ The foolish ones took their lamps but did not take any oil with them. ⁴ The wise ones, however, took oil in jars along with their lamps. ⁵ The bridegroom was a long time in coming, and they all became drowsy and fell asleep. ⁶ "At midnight the cry rang out: 'Here's the bridegroom! Come out to meet him!' ⁷ "Then all the virgins woke up and trimmed their lamps. ⁸ The foolish ones said to the wise, 'Give us some of your oil; our lamps are going out.' ⁹ "'No,' they replied, 'there may not be enough for both us and you. Instead, go to those who sell oil and buy some for yourselves.' ¹⁰ "But while they were on their way to buy the oil, the bridegroom arrived. The virgins who were ready went in with him to the wedding banquet. And the door was shut. ¹¹ "Later the others also came. 'Lord, Lord,' they said, 'open the door for us!' ¹² "But he replied, 'Truly I tell you, I don't know you.' ¹³ "Therefore keep watch, because you do not know the day or the hour.
MARK
13:35 "Therefore keep watch because you do not know when the owner of the house will come back—whether in the evening, or at midnight, or when the rooster crows, or at dawn. ³⁶ If he comes suddenly, do not let him find you sleeping. ³⁷ What I say to you, I say to everyone: 'Watch!'"
LUKE
21:34 "Be careful, or your hearts will be weighed down with carousing, drunkenness and the anxieties of life, and that day will close on you suddenly like a trap. ³⁵ For it will come on all those who live on the face of the whole earth. ³⁶ Be always on the watch, and pray that you may be able to escape all that is about to happen, and that you may be able to stand before the Son of Man."
JOHN

1. At first glance, the three passages are quite different. But are there differences in Jesus' meaning?
2. How do you account for the parable-like illustration in Matthew, when Mark and Luke report no such words?

12.h End Times: The Son of Man Comes

MATTHEW
24:29 "Immediately after the distress of those days 'the sun will be darkened, and the moon will not give its light; the stars will fall from the sky, and the heavenly bodies will be shaken.' [30] "Then will appear the sign of the Son of Man in heaven. And then all the peoples of the earth will mourn when they see the Son of Man coming on the clouds of heaven, with power and great glory. [31] And he will send his angels with a loud trumpet call, and they will gather his elect from the four winds, from one end of the heavens to the other.
MARK
13:24 "But in those days, following that distress, "'the sun will be darkened, and the moon will not give its light; [25] the stars will fall from the sky, and the heavenly bodies will be shaken.' [26] "At that time people will see the Son of Man coming in clouds with great power and glory. [27] And he will send his angels and gather his elect from the four winds, from the ends of the earth to the ends of the heavens.
LUKE
21:25 "There will be signs in the sun, moon and stars. On the earth, nations will be in anguish and perplexity at the roaring and tossing of the sea. [26] People will faint from terror, apprehensive of what is coming on the world, for the heavenly bodies will be shaken. [27] At that time they will see the Son of Man coming in a cloud with power and great glory. [28] When these things begin to take place, stand up and lift up your heads, because your redemption is drawing near."
JOHN
5:24 "Very truly I tell you, whoever hears my word and believes him who sent me has eternal life and will not be judged but has crossed over from death to life. [25] Very truly I tell you, a time is coming and has now come when the dead will hear the voice of the Son of God and those who hear will live. [26] For as the Father has life in himself, so he has granted the Son also to have life in himself. [27] And he has given him authority to judge because he is the Son of Man. [28] "Do not be amazed at this, for a time is coming when all who are in their graves will hear his voice [29] and come out—those who have done what is good will rise to live, and those who have done what is evil will rise to be condemned. [30] By myself I can do nothing; I judge only as I hear, and my judgment is just, for I seek not to please myself but him who sent me.

1. What common messages do you find in the four passages?
2. Do you find any differences in meaning among the four?

12.i End Times: The Fig Tree

MATTHEW
24:32 "Now learn this lesson from the fig tree: As soon as its twigs get tender and its leaves come out, you know that summer is near. [33] Even so, when you see all these things, you know that it is near, right at the door.
MARK
13:28 "Now learn this lesson from the fig tree: As soon as its twigs get tender and its leaves come out, you know that summer is near. [29] Even so, when you see these things happening, you know that it is near, right at the door.
LUKE
21:29 He told them this parable: "Look at the fig tree and all the trees. [30] When they sprout leaves, you can see for yourselves and know that summer is near. [31] Even so, when you see these things happening, you know that the kingdom of God is near.
JOHN

1. Matthew repeats Mark verbatim. Luke's report is somewhat different, however. What do you make of it?

12.j End Times: As in the Days of Noah

MATTHEW
24:37 As it was in the days of Noah, so it will be at the coming of the Son of Man. [38] For in the days before the flood, people were eating and drinking, marrying and giving in marriage, up to the day Noah entered the ark; [39] and they knew nothing about what would happen until the flood came and took them all away. That is how it will be at the coming of the Son of Man. [40] Two men will be in the field; one will be taken and the other left. [41] Two women will be grinding with a hand mill; one will be taken and the other left.
MARK
LUKE
17:26 "Just as it was in the days of Noah, so also will it be in the days of the Son of Man. [27] People were eating, drinking, marrying and being given in marriage up to the day Noah entered the ark. Then the flood came and destroyed them all. [28] "It was the same in the days of Lot. People were eating and drinking, buying and selling, planting and building. [29] But the day Lot left Sodom, fire and sulfur rained down from heaven and destroyed them all.
JOHN

1. What differences do you find in the two passages?
2. Why do you suppose Mark omitted this passage? Based on the topic, it is unlikely that it originated with the Q source.

CHAPTER 13: THE NATURE OF CHRIST

13.a The Fulfillment of the Law and Prophets

MATTHEW
4:16 He went to Nazareth, where he had been brought up, and on the Sabbath day he went into the synagogue, as was his custom. He stood up to read, [17] and the scroll of the prophet Isaiah was handed to him. Unrolling it, he found the place where it is written: [18] "The Spirit of the Lord is on me, because he has anointed me to proclaim good news to the poor. He has sent me to proclaim freedom for the prisoners and recovery of sight for the blind, to set the oppressed free, [19] to proclaim the year of the Lord's favor." [20] Then he rolled up the scroll, gave it back to the attendant and sat down. The eyes of everyone in the synagogue were fastened on him. [21] He began by saying to them, "Today this scripture is fulfilled in your hearing."   * * *   5:17 "Do not think that I have come to abolish the Law or the Prophets; I have not come to abolish them but to fulfill them. [18] For truly I tell you, until heaven and earth disappear, not the smallest letter, not the least stroke of a pen, will by any means disappear from the Law until everything is accomplished. [19] Therefore anyone who sets aside one of the least of these commands and teaches others accordingly will be called least in the kingdom of heaven, but whoever practices and teaches these commands will be called great in the kingdom of heaven. [20] For I tell you that unless your righteousness surpasses that of the Pharisees and the teachers of the law, you will certainly not enter the kingdom of heaven.

MARK

LUKE
16:16 "The Law and the Prophets were proclaimed until John. Since that time, the good news of the kingdom of God is being preached, and everyone is forcing their way into it. [17] It is easier for heaven and earth to disappear than for the least stroke of a pen to drop out of the Law.   * * *   24:44 He said to them, "This is what I told you while I was still with you: Everything must be fulfilled that is written about me in the Law of Moses, the Prophets and the Psalms."

JOHN

1. These are quite different quotations, but all have to do with Christ as the fulfillment of the Law. Do you see any differences in meaning among the four quotations?

13.b The Light

MATTHEW

5:14 "You are the light of the world. A town built on a hill cannot be hidden. [15] Neither do people light a lamp and put it under a bowl. Instead they put it on its stand, and it gives light to everyone in the house. [16] In the same way, let your light shine before others, that they may see your good deeds and glorify your Father in heaven.

* * *

6:22 "The eye is the lamp of the body. If your eyes are healthy, your whole body will be full of light. [23] But if your eyes are unhealthy, your whole body will be full of darkness. If then the light within you is darkness, how great is that darkness!"

MARK

4:21 He said to them, "Do you bring in a lamp to put it under a bowl or a bed? Instead, don't you put it on its stand? [22] For whatever is hidden is meant to be disclosed, and whatever is concealed is meant to be brought out into the open. [23] If anyone has ears to hear, let them hear."

LUKE

8:16 "No one lights a lamp and hides it in a clay jar or puts it under a bed. Instead, they put it on a stand, so that those who come in can see the light. [17] For there is nothing hidden that will not be disclosed, and nothing concealed that will not be known or brought out into the open. [18] Therefore consider carefully how you listen. Whoever has will be given more; whoever does not have, even what they think they have will be taken from them."

* * *

11:33 "No one lights a lamp and puts it in a place where it will be hidden, or under a bowl. Instead they put it on its stand, so that those who come in may see the light. [34] Your eye is the lamp of your body. When your eyes are healthy, your whole body also is full of light. But when they are unhealthy, your body also is full of darkness. [35] See to it, then, that the light within you is not darkness. [36] Therefore, if your whole body is full of light, and no part of it dark, it will be just as full of light as when a lamp shines its light on you."

JOHN

1:4 In him was life, and that life was the light of all mankind. [5] The light shines in the darkness, and the darkness has not overcome it. [6] There was a man sent from God whose name was John. [7] He came as a witness to testify concerning that light, so that through him all might believe. [8] He himself was not the light; he came only as a witness to the light. [9] The true light that gives light to everyone was coming into the world.

* * *

3:19 This is the verdict: Light has come into the world, but people loved darkness instead of light because their deeds were evil. [20] Everyone who does evil hates the light, and will not come into the light for fear that their deeds will be exposed. [21] But whoever lives by the truth comes into the light, so that it may be seen plainly that what they have done has been done in the sight of God.

* * *

5:35 John was a lamp that burned and gave light, and you chose for a time to enjoy his light.

* * *

8:12 When Jesus spoke again to the people, he said, "I am the light of the world. Whoever follows me will never walk in darkness, but will have the light of life."

* * *

9:4 As long as it is day, we must do the works of him who sent me. Night is coming, when no one can work. [5] While I am in the world, I am the light of the world."

* * *

12:35 Then Jesus told them, "You are going to have the light just a little while longer. Walk while you have the light, before darkness overtakes you. Whoever walks in the dark does not know where they are going. [36] Believe in the light while you have the light, so that you may become children of light." When he had finished speaking, Jesus left and hid himself from them.

* * *

12:46 I have come into the world as a light, so that no one who believes in me should stay in darkness.

1. Jesus often used the metaphor of light. Can you identify any differences in the meaning of this metaphor in the passages quoted?
2. What are the similarities among the passages in the four Gospels? What aspects are unique to each?
3. As quoted in Matthew and Luke, what does Jesus mean by light and darkness? Who is Jesus speaking to? Who is to preserve, show, or spread this light?
4. As quoted in John, Jesus uses the metaphor of light to describe himself rather than others. Is his meaning of "light" different in any way from those uses of the term in Matthew and Luke?

13.c Teaching with Authority

MATTHEW
7:28 When Jesus had finished saying these things, the crowds were amazed at his teaching, [29] because he taught as one who had authority, and not as their teachers of the law.
MARK
1:21 They went to Capernaum, and when the Sabbath came, Jesus went into the synagogue and began to teach. [22] The people were amazed at his teaching, because he taught them as one who had authority, not as the teachers of the law.
LUKE
4:31 Then he went down to Capernaum, a town in Galilee, and on the Sabbath he taught the people. [32] They were amazed at his teaching, because his words had authority.
JOHN
5:16 So, because Jesus was doing these things on the Sabbath, the Jewish leaders began to persecute him. [17] In his defense Jesus said to them, "My Father is always at his work to this very day, and I too am working." [18] For this reason they tried all the more to kill him; not only was he breaking the Sabbath, but he was even calling God his own Father, making himself equal with God. [19] Jesus gave them this answer: "Very truly I tell you, the Son can do nothing by himself; he can do only what he sees his Father doing, because whatever the Father does the Son also does. [20] For the Father loves the Son and shows him all he does. Yes, and he will show him even greater works than these, so that you will be amazed. [21] For just as the Father raises the dead and gives them life, even so the Son gives life to whom he is pleased to give it. [22] Moreover, the Father judges no one, but has entrusted all judgment to the Son, [23] that all may honor the Son just as they honor the Father. Whoever does not honor the Son does not honor the Father, who sent him. * * * 7:28 Then Jesus, still teaching in the temple courts, cried out, "Yes, you know me, and you know where I am from. I am not here on my own authority, but he who sent me is true. You do not know him, [29] but I know him because I am from him and he sent me." * * * 14:10 Don't you believe that I am in the Father, and that the Father is in me? The words I say to you I do not speak on my own authority. Rather, it is the Father, living in me, who is doing his work.

1. The hearers of Jesus as reported in the Synoptics remarked upon his evident authority. As quoted in John, Jesus explains this authority. What are its sources and attributes?
2. Do you think the hearers of Jesus in the Synoptics had a fairly complete understanding of his authority?

13.d Did Jesus Consider Himself the Messiah?

MATTHEW
11:2 When John, who was in prison, heard about the deeds of the Messiah, he sent his disciples [3] to ask him, "Are you the one who is to come, or should we expect someone else?" [4] Jesus replied, "Go back and report to John what you hear and see: [5] The blind receive sight, the lame walk, those who have leprosy are cleansed, the deaf hear, the dead are raised, and the good news is proclaimed to the poor. [6] Blessed is anyone who does not stumble on account of me."   [7] As John's disciples were leaving, Jesus began to speak to the crowd about John: "What did you go out into the wilderness to see? A reed swayed by the wind? [8] If not, what did you go out to see? A man dressed in fine clothes? No, those who wear fine clothes are in kings' palaces. [9] Then what did you go out to see? A prophet? Yes, I tell you, and more than a prophet. [10] This is the one about whom it is written: "'I will send my messenger ahead of you, who will prepare your way before you.'   * * *   16:15 "But what about you?" he asked. "Who do you say I am?" [16] Simon Peter answered, "You are the Messiah, the Son of the living God." [17] Jesus replied, "Blessed are you, Simon son of Jonah, for this was not revealed to you by flesh and blood, but by my Father in heaven…. [20] Then he ordered his disciples not to tell anyone that he was the Messiah.   * * *   24:4 Jesus answered: "Watch out that no one deceives you. [5] For many will come in my name, claiming, 'I am the Messiah,' and will deceive many.   * * *   26:63 The high priest said to him, "I charge you under oath by the living God: Tell us if you are the Messiah, the Son of God." [64] "You have said so," Jesus replied. "But I say to all of you: From now on you will see the Son of Man sitting at the right hand of the Mighty One and coming on the clouds of heaven."
MARK
8:29 "But what about you?" he asked. "Who do you say I am?" Peter answered, "You are the Messiah." [30] Jesus warned them not to tell anyone about him.   * * *   9:41 Truly I tell you, anyone who gives you a cup of water in my name because you belong to the Messiah will certainly not lose their reward.   * * *   13:21 At that time if anyone says to you, 'Look, here is the Messiah!' or, 'Look, there he is!' do not believe it. [22] For false messiahs and false prophets will appear and perform signs and wonders to deceive, if possible, even the elect. [23] So be on your guard; I have told you everything ahead of time…. [26] "At that time people will see the Son of Man coming in clouds with great power and glory. [27] And he will send his angels and gather his elect from the four winds, from the ends of the earth to the ends of the heavens.   * * *   14:61 Again the high priest asked him, "Are you the Messiah, the Son of the Blessed One?" [62] "I am," said Jesus. "And you will see the Son of Man sitting at the right hand of the Mighty One and coming on the clouds of heaven."
LUKE
4:41 Moreover, demons came out of many people, shouting, "You are the Son of God!" But he rebuked them and would not allow them to speak, because they knew he was the Messiah.   * * *   9:20 "But what about you?" he asked. "Who do you say I am?" Peter answered, "God's Messiah." [21] Jesus strictly warned them not to tell this to anyone. [22] And he said, "The Son of Man must suffer many things and be rejected by the elders, the chief priests and the teachers of the law, and he must be killed and on the third day be raised to life."   * * *

22:67 "If you are the Messiah," they said, "tell us." Jesus answered, "If I tell you, you will not believe me, [68] and if I asked you, you would not answer. [69] But from now on, the Son of Man will be seated at the right hand of the mighty God." [70] They all asked, "Are you then the Son of God?" He replied, "You say that I am."

* * *

24:26 "Did not the Messiah have to suffer these things and then enter his glory?" [27] And beginning with Moses and all the Prophets, he explained to them what was said in all the Scriptures concerning himself.... [45] Then he opened their minds so they could understand the Scriptures. [46] He told them, "This is what is written: The Messiah will suffer and rise from the dead on the third day, [47] and repentance for the forgiveness of sins will be preached in his name to all nations, beginning at Jerusalem. [48] You are witnesses of these things.

JOHN

10:24 The Jews who were there gathered around him, saying, "How long will you keep us in suspense? If you are the Messiah, tell us plainly." [25] Jesus answered, "I did tell you, but you do not believe. The works I do in my Father's name testify about me, [26] but you do not believe because you are not my sheep. [27] My sheep listen to my voice; I know them, and they follow me. [28] I give them eternal life, and they shall never perish; no one will snatch them out of my hand. [29] My Father, who has given them to me, is greater than all; no one can snatch them out of my Father's hand. [30] I and the Father are one."

1. Many modern biblical scholars maintain that Jesus never thought of himself as the Messiah. What response would you give them?
2. Can you identify any differences – or at least nuances – in what "Messiah" means, in the passages from the Gospels?
3. Compare the words of Jesus in response to the high priest, as reported in the Synoptic accounts.

13.e The Father and the Son

MATTHEW
11:27 "All things have been committed to me by my Father. No one knows the Son except the Father, and no one knows the Father except the Son and those to whom the Son chooses to reveal him.

MARK
13:32 "But about that day or hour no one knows, not even the angels in heaven, nor the Son, but only the Father. * * * 14:36 *"Abba*, Father," he said, "everything is possible for you. Take this cup from me. Yet not what I will, but what you will."

LUKE
10:22 "All things have been committed to me by my Father. No one knows who the Son is except the Father, and no one knows who the Father is except the Son and those to whom the Son chooses to reveal him."

JOHN
3:34 For the one whom God has sent speaks the words of God, for God gives the Spirit without limit. [35] The Father loves the Son and has placed everything in his hands. [36] Whoever believes in the Son has eternal life, but whoever rejects the Son will not see life, for God's wrath remains on them. * * * 7:28 Then Jesus, still teaching in the temple courts, cried out, "Yes, you know me, and you know where I am from. I am not here on my own authority, but he who sent me is true. You do not know him, [29] but I know him because I am from him and he sent me." * * * 10:14 "I am the good shepherd; I know my sheep and my sheep know me— [15] just as the Father knows me and I know the Father—and I lay down my life for the sheep. [16] I have other sheep that are not of this sheep pen. I must bring them also. They too will listen to my voice, and there shall be one flock and one shepherd. [17] The reason my Father loves me is that I lay down my life—only to take it up again. [18] No one takes it from me, but I lay it down of my own accord. I have authority to lay it down and authority to take it up again. This command I received from my Father." * * * 13:3 Jesus knew that the Father had put all things under his power, and that he had come from God and was returning to God. * * * 17:1 After Jesus said this, he looked toward heaven and prayed: "Father, the hour has come. Glorify your Son, that your Son may glorify you. [2] For you granted him authority over all people that he might give eternal life to all those you have given him. [3] Now this is eternal life: that they know you, the only true God, and Jesus Christ, whom you have sent. [4] I have brought you glory on earth by finishing the work you gave me to do. [5] And now, Father, glorify me in your presence with the glory I had with you before the world began. * * * 17:24 "Father, I want those you have given me to be with me where I am, and to see my glory, the glory you have given me because you loved me before the creation of the world. [25] "Righteous Father, though the world does not know you, I know you, and they know that you have sent me. [26] I have made you known to them, and will continue to make you known in order that the love you have for me may be in them and that I myself may be in them."

1. As reflected in the Synoptics, what is the relationship between the Father and the Son?
2. How does this view compare with the relationship reflected in John?

13.f The Lord of the Sabbath

MATTHEW
12:1 At that time Jesus went through the grainfields on the Sabbath. His disciples were hungry and began to pick some heads of grain and eat them. [2] When the Pharisees saw this, they said to him, "Look! Your disciples are doing what is unlawful on the Sabbath." [3] He answered, "Haven't you read what David did when he and his companions were hungry? [4] He entered the house of God, and he and his companions ate the consecrated bread—which was not lawful for them to do, but only for the priests. [5] Or haven't you read in the Law that the priests on Sabbath duty in the temple desecrate the Sabbath and yet are innocent? [6] I tell you that something greater than the temple is here. [7] If you had known what these words mean, 'I desire mercy, not sacrifice,' you would not have condemned the innocent. [8] For the Son of Man is Lord of the Sabbath."

MARK
2:23 One Sabbath Jesus was going through the grainfields, and as his disciples walked along, they began to pick some heads of grain. [24] The Pharisees said to him, "Look, why are they doing what is unlawful on the Sabbath?" [25] He answered, "Have you never read what David did when he and his companions were hungry and in need? [26] In the days of Abiathar the high priest, he entered the house of God and ate the consecrated bread, which is lawful only for priests to eat. And he also gave some to his companions." [27] Then he said to them, "The Sabbath was made for man, not man for the Sabbath. [28] So the Son of Man is Lord even of the Sabbath."

LUKE
6:1 One Sabbath Jesus was going through the grainfields, and his disciples began to pick some heads of grain, rub them in their hands and eat the kernels. [2] Some of the Pharisees asked, "Why are you doing what is unlawful on the Sabbath?" [3] Jesus answered them, "Have you never read what David did when he and his companions were hungry? [4] He entered the house of God, and taking the consecrated bread, he ate what is lawful only for priests to eat. And he also gave some to his companions." [5] Then Jesus said to them, "The Son of Man is Lord of the Sabbath."

JOHN
5:8 Then Jesus said to him, "Get up! Pick up your mat and walk." [9] At once the man was cured; he picked up his mat and walked. The day on which this took place was a Sabbath, [10] and so the Jewish leaders said to the man who had been healed, "It is the Sabbath; the law forbids you to carry your mat." [11] But he replied, "The man who made me well said to me, 'Pick up your mat and walk.' "   ***   5:16 So, because Jesus was doing these things on the Sabbath, the Jewish leaders began to persecute him. [17] In his defense Jesus said to them, "My Father is always at his work to this very day, and I too am working." [18] For this reason they tried all the more to kill him; not only was he breaking the Sabbath, but he was even calling God his own Father, making himself equal with God.   ***   7:23 "Now if a boy can be circumcised on the Sabbath so that the law of Moses may not be broken, why are you angry with me for healing a man's whole body on the Sabbath? [24] Stop judging by mere appearances, but instead judge correctly."

1. Do you find any differences in the meaning of "Lord of the Sabbath" among the three Synoptic accounts?
2. John does not record the term "Lord of the Sabbath." Is there any difference in Jesus' idea of the Sabbath as reported in John vs. that in the Synoptics?

13.g Jesus Fulfills Isaiah's Prophecy

MATTHEW
12:15 Aware of this, Jesus withdrew from that place. A large crowd followed him, and he healed all who were ill. [16] He warned them not to tell others about him. [17] This was to fulfill what was spoken through the prophet Isaiah: [18] "Here is my servant whom I have chosen, the one I love, in whom I delight; I will put my Spirit on him, and he will proclaim justice to the nations. [19] He will not quarrel or cry out; no one will hear his voice in the streets. [20] A bruised reed he will not break, and a smoldering wick he will not snuff out, till he has brought justice through to victory. [21] In his name the nations will put their hope." (Isaiah 42:1-4)
MARK
1:1 The beginning of the good news about Jesus the Messiah, the Son of God, [2] as it is written in Isaiah the prophet: "I will send my messenger ahead of you, who will prepare your way"— [3] "a voice of one calling in the wilderness, 'Prepare the way for the Lord, make straight paths for him.'" (Isaiah 40:3, Malachi 3:1)
LUKE
4:14 Jesus returned to Galilee in the power of the Spirit, and news about him spread through the whole countryside. [15] He was teaching in their synagogues, and everyone praised him. [16] He went to Nazareth, where he had been brought up, and on the Sabbath day he went into the synagogue, as was his custom. He stood up to read, [17] and the scroll of the prophet Isaiah was handed to him. Unrolling it, he found the place where it is written: [18] "The Spirit of the Lord is on me, because he has anointed me to proclaim good news to the poor. He has sent me to proclaim freedom for the prisoners and recovery of sight for the blind, to set the oppressed free, [19] to proclaim the year of the Lord's favor." [20] Then he rolled up the scroll, gave it back to the attendant and sat down. The eyes of everyone in the synagogue were fastened on him. [21] He began by saying to them, "Today this scripture is fulfilled in your hearing." (Isaiah 61:1-2)
JOHN
Even after Jesus had performed so many signs in their presence, they still would not believe in him. [38] This was to fulfill the word of Isaiah the prophet: "Lord, who has believed our message and to whom has the arm of the Lord been revealed?" [39] For this reason they could not believe, because, as Isaiah says elsewhere: [40] "He has blinded their eyes and hardened their hearts, so they can neither see with their eyes, nor understand with their hearts, nor turn—and I would heal them." [41] Isaiah said this because he saw Jesus' glory and spoke about him. (Isaiah 53:1)

1. Each of the Gospels cites a different passage of Isaiah. What do you see as the commonalities among them? Are there significant differences?

13.h The Unforgiveable Sin

MATTHEW
12:30 "Whoever is not with me is against me, and whoever does not gather with me scatters. [31] And so I tell you, every kind of sin and slander can be forgiven, but blasphemy against the Spirit will not be forgiven. [32] Anyone who speaks a word against the Son of Man will be forgiven, but anyone who speaks against the Holy Spirit will not be forgiven, either in this age or in the age to come.
MARK
3:28 Truly I tell you, people can be forgiven all their sins and every slander they utter, [29] but whoever blasphemes against the Holy Spirit will never be forgiven; they are guilty of an eternal sin."
LUKE
12:8 "I tell you, whoever publicly acknowledges me before others, the Son of Man will also acknowledge before the angels of God. [9] But whoever disowns me before others will be disowned before the angels of God. [10] And everyone who speaks a word against the Son of Man will be forgiven, but anyone who blasphemes against the Holy Spirit will not be forgiven.
JOHN

1. Do you find any shades of difference among the three passages?

13.i Giving Signs

MATTHEW

12:38 Then some of the Pharisees and teachers of the law said to him, "Teacher, we want to see a sign from you." [39] He answered, "A wicked and adulterous generation asks for a sign! But none will be given it except the sign of the prophet Jonah.

* * *

16:1 The Pharisees and Sadducees came to Jesus and tested him by asking him to show them a sign from heaven. [2] He replied, "When evening comes, you say, 'It will be fair weather, for the sky is red,' [3] and in the morning, 'Today it will be stormy, for the sky is red and overcast.' You know how to interpret the appearance of the sky, but you cannot interpret the signs of the times. [4] A wicked and adulterous generation looks for a sign, but none will be given it except the sign of Jonah." Jesus then left them and went away.

MARK

8:11 The Pharisees came and began to question Jesus. To test him, they asked him for a sign from heaven. [12] He sighed deeply and said, "Why does this generation ask for a sign? Truly I tell you, no sign will be given to it." [13] Then he left them, got back into the boat and crossed to the other side.

* * *

16:15 He said to them, "Go into all the world and preach the gospel to all creation. [16] Whoever believes and is baptized will be saved, but whoever does not believe will be condemned. [17] And these signs will accompany those who believe: In my name they will drive out demons; they will speak in new tongues; [18] they will pick up snakes with their hands; and when they drink deadly poison, it will not hurt them at all; they will place their hands on sick people, and they will get well." (Passage absent from earliest manuscripts of Mark.)

LUKE

11:16 Others tested him by asking for a sign from heaven.

* * *

11:29 As the crowds increased, Jesus said, "This is a wicked generation. It asks for a sign, but none will be given it except the sign of Jonah.

* * *

23:8 When Herod saw Jesus, he was greatly pleased, because for a long time he had been wanting to see him. From what he had heard about him, he hoped to see him perform a sign of some sort. [9] He plied him with many questions, but Jesus gave him no answer.

JOHN

2:11 What Jesus did here in Cana of Galilee was the first of the signs through which he revealed his glory; and his disciples believed in him.

* * *

2:18 The Jews then responded to him, "What sign can you show us to prove your authority to do all this?" [19] Jesus answered them, "Destroy this temple, and I will raise it again in three days."

* * *

2:23 Now while he was in Jerusalem at the Passover Festival, many people saw the signs he was performing and believed in his name.

* * *

3:1 Now there was a Pharisee, a man named Nicodemus who was a member of the Jewish ruling council. [2] He came to Jesus at night and said, "Rabbi, we know that you are a teacher who has come from God. For no one could perform the signs you are doing if God were not with him."

* * *

4:48 "Unless you people see signs and wonders," Jesus told him, "you will never believe." [49] The royal official said, "Sir, come down before my child dies." [50] "Go," Jesus replied, "your son will live." [54] This was the second sign Jesus performed after coming from Judea to Galilee.

* * *

6:1 Some time after this, Jesus crossed to the far shore of the Sea of Galilee (that is, the Sea of Tiberias), ² and a great crowd of people followed him because they saw the signs he had performed by healing the sick.

* * *

6:14 After the people saw the sign Jesus performed, they began to say, "Surely this is the Prophet who is to come into the world."

* * *

6:26 Jesus answered, "Very truly I tell you, you are looking for me, not because you saw the signs I performed but because you ate the loaves and had your fill. ³⁰ So they asked him, "What sign then will you give that we may see it and believe you? What will you do? ³¹ Our ancestors ate the manna in the wilderness; as it is written: 'He gave them bread from heaven to eat.'" ³² Jesus said to them, "Very truly I tell you, it is not Moses who has given you the bread from heaven, but it is my Father who gives you the true bread from heaven.

* * *

7:30 At this they tried to seize him, but no one laid a hand on him, because his hour had not yet come. ³¹ Still, many in the crowd believed in him. They said, "When the Messiah comes, will he perform more signs than this man?"

* * *

9:16 Some of the Pharisees said, "This man is not from God, for he does not keep the Sabbath." But others asked, "How can a sinner perform such signs?" So they were divided.

* * *

11:47 Then the chief priests and the Pharisees called a meeting of the Sanhedrin. "What are we accomplishing?" they asked. "Here is this man performing many signs. ⁴⁸ If we let him go on like this, everyone will believe in him, and then the Romans will come and take away both our temple and our nation."

* * *

12:17 Now the crowd that was with him when he called Lazarus from the tomb and raised him from the dead continued to spread the word. ¹⁸ Many people, because they had heard that he had performed this sign, went out to meet him.

* * *

12:37 Even after Jesus had performed so many signs in their presence, they still would not believe in him.

* * *

20:30 Jesus performed many other signs in the presence of his disciples, which are not recorded in this book.

1. Jesus is quoted several times in each of the Synoptics to the effect that people should not require signs from him and that he will perform none. Yet in John, Jesus says nothing against signs and performs many. What do you make of this difference?

13.j Who Are My Mother and Brothers?

MATTHEW
12:46 While Jesus was still talking to the crowd, his mother and brothers stood outside, wanting to speak to him. [47] Someone told him, "Your mother and brothers are standing outside, wanting to speak to you." [48] He replied to him, "Who is my mother, and who are my brothers?" [49] Pointing to his disciples, he said, "Here are my mother and my brothers. [50] For whoever does the will of my Father in heaven is my brother and sister and mother."
MARK
3:31 Then Jesus' mother and brothers arrived. Standing outside, they sent someone in to call him. [32] A crowd was sitting around him, and they told him, "Your mother and brothers are outside looking for you." [33] "Who are my mother and my brothers?" he asked. [34] Then he looked at those seated in a circle around him and said, "Here are my mother and my brothers! [35] Whoever does God's will is my brother and sister and mother."
LUKE
8:19 Now Jesus' mother and brothers came to see him, but they were not able to get near him because of the crowd. [20] Someone told him, "Your mother and brothers are standing outside, wanting to see you." [21] He replied, "My mother and brothers are those who hear God's word and put it into practice."
JOHN

1. Compare Jesus' words as quoted in these three passages.

13.k Prophet Not Honored in His Home Town

MATTHEW
13:53 When Jesus had finished these parables, he moved on from there. ⁵⁴ Coming to his hometown, he began teaching the people in their synagogue, and they were amazed. "Where did this man get this wisdom and these miraculous powers?" they asked. ⁵⁵ "Isn't this the carpenter's son? Isn't his mother's name Mary, and aren't his brothers James, Joseph, Simon and Judas? ⁵⁶ Aren't all his sisters with us? Where then did this man get all these things?" ⁵⁷ And they took offense at him. But Jesus said to them, "A prophet is not without honor except in his own town and in his own home." ⁵⁸ And he did not do many miracles there because of their lack of faith.

MARK
6:1 Jesus left there and went to his hometown, accompanied by his disciples. ² When the Sabbath came, he began to teach in the synagogue, and many who heard him were amazed. "Where did this man get these things?" they asked. "What's this wisdom that has been given him? What are these remarkable miracles he is performing? ³ Isn't this the carpenter? Isn't this Mary's son and the brother of James, Joseph, Judas and Simon? Aren't his sisters here with us?" And they took offense at him. ⁴ Jesus said to them, "A prophet is not without honor except in his own town, among his relatives and in his own home." ⁵ He could not do any miracles there, except lay his hands on a few sick people and heal them. ⁶ He was amazed at their lack of faith.

LUKE
4:14 Jesus returned to Galilee in the power of the Spirit, and news about him spread through the whole countryside. ¹⁵ He was teaching in their synagogues, and everyone praised him. ¹⁶ He went to Nazareth, where he had been brought up, and on the Sabbath day he went into the synagogue, as was his custom. He stood up to read, ¹⁷ and the scroll of the prophet Isaiah was handed to him. Unrolling it, he found the place where it is written: ¹⁸ "The Spirit of the Lord is on me, because he has anointed me to proclaim good news to the poor. He has sent me to proclaim freedom for the prisoners and recovery of sight for the blind, to set the oppressed free, ¹⁹ to proclaim the year of the Lord's favor." ²⁰ Then he rolled up the scroll, gave it back to the attendant and sat down. The eyes of everyone in the synagogue were fastened on him. ²¹ He began by saying to them, "Today this scripture is fulfilled in your hearing." ²² All spoke well of him and were amazed at the gracious words that came from his lips. "Isn't this Joseph's son?" they asked. ²³ Jesus said to them, "Surely you will quote this proverb to me: 'Physician, heal yourself!' And you will tell me, 'Do here in your hometown what we have heard that you did in Capernaum.'" ²⁴ "Truly I tell you," he continued, "no prophet is accepted in his hometown. ²⁵ I assure you that there were many widows in Israel in Elijah's time, when the sky was shut for three and a half years and there was a severe famine throughout the land. ²⁶ Yet Elijah was not sent to any of them, but to a widow in Zarephath in the region of Sidon. ²⁷ And there were many in Israel with leprosy in the time of Elisha the prophet, yet not one of them was cleansed—only Naaman the Syrian." ²⁸ All the people in the synagogue were furious when they heard this. ²⁹ They got up, drove him out of the town, and took him to the brow of the hill on which the town was built, in order to throw him off the cliff. ³⁰ But he walked right through the crowd and went on his way.

JOHN
4:43 After the two days he left for Galilee. ⁴⁴ (Now Jesus himself had pointed out that a prophet has no honor in his own country.) ⁴⁵ When he arrived in Galilee, the Galileans welcomed him. They had seen all that he had done in Jerusalem at the Passover Festival, for they also had been there.

1. Matthew repeats Mark's account of this encounter nearly word for word, yet Luke provides context and followup that are both unique and significant. What may explain the difference in the account in Mark-Matthew vs. the account in Luke?
2. John's brief reference to this period is not entirely consistent with the Synoptic writers, and can even be interpreted as self-contradictory. What are we to make of John's report?

13.1 Who Do You Say I Am?

MATTHEW

16:13 When Jesus came to the region of Caesarea Philippi, he asked his disciples, "Who do people say the Son of Man is?" [14] They replied, "Some say John the Baptist; others say Elijah; and still others, Jeremiah or one of the prophets."
[15] "But what about you?" he asked. "Who do you say I am?" [16] Simon Peter answered, "You are the Messiah, the Son of the living God."
[17] Jesus replied, "Blessed are you, Simon son of Jonah, for this was not revealed to you by flesh and blood, but by my Father in heaven. [18] And I tell you that you are Peter, and on this rock I will build my church, and the gates of Hades will not overcome it. [19] I will give you the keys of the kingdom of heaven; whatever you bind on earth will be bound in heaven, and whatever you loose on earth will be loosed in heaven." [20] Then he ordered his disciples not to tell anyone that he was the Messiah.

MARK

8:27 Jesus and his disciples went on to the villages around Caesarea Philippi. On the way he asked them, "Who do people say I am?" [28] They replied, "Some say John the Baptist; others say Elijah; and still others, one of the prophets."
[29] "But what about you?" he asked. "Who do you say I am?" Peter answered, "You are the Messiah."
[30] Jesus warned them not to tell anyone about him.

LUKE

9:18 Once when Jesus was praying in private and his disciples were with him, he asked them, "Who do the crowds say I am?" [19] They replied, "Some say John the Baptist; others say Elijah; and still others, that one of the prophets of long ago has come back to life."
[20] "But what about you?" he asked. "Who do you say I am?" Peter answered, "God's Messiah." [21] Jesus strictly warned them not to tell this to anyone.

JOHN

4:9 The Samaritan woman said to him, "You are a Jew and I am a Samaritan woman. How can you ask me for a drink?" (For Jews do not associate with Samaritans.) [10] Jesus answered her, "If you knew the gift of God and who it is that asks you for a drink, you would have asked him and he would have given you living water."
[11] "Sir," the woman said, "you have nothing to draw with and the well is deep. Where can you get this living water? [12] Are you greater than our father Jacob, who gave us the well and drank from it himself, as did also his sons and his livestock?" [13] Jesus answered, "Everyone who drinks this water will be thirsty again, [14] but whoever drinks the water I give them will never thirst. Indeed, the water I give them will become in them a spring of water welling up to eternal life."
[15] The woman said to him, "Sir, give me this water so that I won't get thirsty and have to keep coming here to draw water." [16] He told her, "Go, call your husband and come back." [17] "I have no husband," she replied. Jesus said to her, "You are right when you say you have no husband. [18] The fact is, you have had five husbands, and the man you now have is not your husband. What you have just said is quite true."
[19] "Sir," the woman said, "I can see that you are a prophet. [20] Our ancestors worshiped on this mountain, but you Jews claim that the place where we must worship is in Jerusalem." [21] "Woman," Jesus replied, "believe me, a time is coming when you will worship the Father neither on this mountain nor in Jerusalem. [22] You Samaritans worship what you do not know; we worship what we do know, for salvation is from the Jews. [23] Yet a time is coming and has now come when the true worshipers will worship the Father in the Spirit and in truth, for they are the kind of worshipers the Father seeks. [24] God is spirit, and his worshipers must worship in the Spirit and in truth."
[25] The woman said, "I know that Messiah" (called Christ) "is coming. When he comes, he will explain everything to us." [26] Then Jesus declared, "I, the one speaking to you—I am he."

* * *

> 6:35 Then Jesus declared, "I am the bread of life. Whoever comes to me will never go hungry, and whoever believes in me will never be thirsty. ³⁶ But as I told you, you have seen me and still you do not believe. ³⁷ All those the Father gives me will come to me, and whoever comes to me I will never drive away. ³⁸ For I have come down from heaven not to do my will but to do the will of him who sent me. ³⁹ And this is the will of him who sent me, that I shall lose none of all those he has given me, but raise them up at the last day. ⁴⁰ For my Father's will is that everyone who looks to the Son and believes in him shall have eternal life, and I will raise them up at the last day."
> ⁴¹ At this the Jews there began to grumble about him because he said, "I am the bread that came down from heaven."
> ⁴² They said, "Is this not Jesus, the son of Joseph, whose father and mother we know? How can he now say, 'I came down from heaven'?"
> ⁴³ "Stop grumbling among yourselves," Jesus answered. ⁴⁴ "No one can come to me unless the Father who sent me draws them, and I will raise them up at the last day. ⁴⁵ It is written in the Prophets: 'They will all be taught by God.' Everyone who has heard the Father and learned from him comes to me. ⁴⁶ No one has seen the Father except the one who is from God; only he has seen the Father.

1. Do you notice any differences among the versions of the episode described in the Synoptics?
2. The passages from John also pertain to Jesus' identity in the eyes of others. But in these cases, Jesus responds at greater length. What do you find in the passages from John that is absent from those in the Synoptics?

13.m The Transfiguration

MATTHEW

17:1 After six days Jesus took with him Peter, James and John the brother of James, and led them up a high mountain by themselves. ² There he was transfigured before them. His face shone like the sun, and his clothes became as white as the light. ³ Just then there appeared before them Moses and Elijah, talking with Jesus.
⁴ Peter said to Jesus, "Lord, it is good for us to be here. If you wish, I will put up three shelters—one for you, one for Moses and one for Elijah." ⁵ While he was still speaking, a bright cloud covered them, and a voice from the cloud said, "This is my Son, whom I love; with him I am well pleased. Listen to him!" ⁶ When the disciples heard this, they fell facedown to the ground, terrified. ⁷ But Jesus came and touched them. "Get up," he said. "Don't be afraid."
⁸ When they looked up, they saw no one except Jesus.
⁹ As they were coming down the mountain, Jesus instructed them, "Don't tell anyone what you have seen, until the Son of Man has been raised from the dead."
¹⁰ The disciples asked him, "Why then do the teachers of the law say that Elijah must come first?" ¹¹ Jesus replied, "To be sure, Elijah comes and will restore all things. ¹² But I tell you, Elijah has already come, and they did not recognize him, but have done to him everything they wished. In the same way the Son of Man is going to suffer at their hands." ¹³ Then the disciples understood that he was talking to them about John the Baptist.

MARK

9:2 After six days Jesus took Peter, James and John with him and led them up a high mountain, where they were all alone. There he was transfigured before them. ³ His clothes became dazzling white, whiter than anyone in the world could bleach them. ⁴ And there appeared before them Elijah and Moses, who were talking with Jesus.
⁵ Peter said to Jesus, "Rabbi, it is good for us to be here. Let us put up three shelters—one for you, one for Moses and one for Elijah." ⁶ (He did not know what to say, they were so frightened.) ⁷ Then a cloud appeared and covered them, and a voice came from the cloud: "This is my Son, whom I love. Listen to him!" ⁸ Suddenly, when they looked around, they no longer saw anyone with them except Jesus.
⁹ As they were coming down the mountain, Jesus gave them orders not to tell anyone what they had seen until the Son of Man had risen from the dead. ¹⁰ They kept the matter to themselves, discussing what "rising from the dead" meant.
¹¹ And they asked him, "Why do the teachers of the law say that Elijah must come first?" ¹² Jesus replied, "To be sure, Elijah does come first, and restores all things. Why then is it written that the Son of Man must suffer much and be rejected? ¹³ But I tell you, Elijah has come, and they have done to him everything they wished, just as it is written about him."

LUKE

9:28 About eight days after Jesus said this, he took Peter, John and James with him and went up onto a mountain to pray. ²⁹ As he was praying, the appearance of his face changed, and his clothes became as bright as a flash of lightning. ³⁰ Two men, Moses and Elijah, appeared in glorious splendor, talking with Jesus. ³¹ They spoke about his departure, which he was about to bring to fulfillment at Jerusalem. ³² Peter and his companions were very sleepy, but when they became fully awake, they saw his glory and the two men standing with him. ³³ As the men were leaving Jesus, Peter said to him, "Master, it is good for us to be here. Let us put up three shelters—one for you, one for Moses and one for Elijah." (He did not know what he was saying.)
³⁴ While he was speaking, a cloud appeared and covered them, and they were afraid as they entered the cloud. ³⁵ A voice came from the cloud, saying, "This is my Son, whom I have chosen; listen to him." ³⁶ When the voice had spoken, they found that Jesus was alone. The disciples kept this to themselves and did not tell anyone at that time what they had seen.

JOHN

1. Identify the differences in the three accounts.

13.n The Son of Man Came to Serve

MATTHEW

20:20 Then the mother of Zebedee's sons came to Jesus with her sons and, kneeling down, asked a favor of him. [21] "What is it you want?" he asked. She said, "Grant that one of these two sons of mine may sit at your right and the other at your left in your kingdom."
[22] "You don't know what you are asking," Jesus said to them. "Can you drink the cup I am going to drink?" "We can," they answered. [23] Jesus said to them, "You will indeed drink from my cup, but to sit at my right or left is not for me to grant. These places belong to those for whom they have been prepared by my Father."
[24] When the ten heard about this, they were indignant with the two brothers. [25] Jesus called them together and said, "You know that the rulers of the Gentiles lord it over them, and their high officials exercise authority over them. [26] Not so with you. Instead, whoever wants to become great among you must be your servant, [27] and whoever wants to be first must be your slave— [28] just as the Son of Man did not come to be served, but to serve, and to give his life as a ransom for many."

MARK

10:35 Then James and John, the sons of Zebedee, came to him. "Teacher," they said, "we want you to do for us whatever we ask." [36] "What do you want me to do for you?" he asked. [37] They replied, "Let one of us sit at your right and the other at your left in your glory."
[38] "You don't know what you are asking," Jesus said. "Can you drink the cup I drink or be baptized with the baptism I am baptized with?" [39] "We can," they answered. Jesus said to them, "You will drink the cup I drink and be baptized with the baptism I am baptized with, [40] but to sit at my right or left is not for me to grant. These places belong to those for whom they have been prepared."
[41] When the ten heard about this, they became indignant with James and John. [42] Jesus called them together and said, "You know that those who are regarded as rulers of the Gentiles lord it over them, and their high officials exercise authority over them. [43] Not so with you. Instead, whoever wants to become great among you must be your servant, [44] and whoever wants to be first must be slave of all. [45] For even the Son of Man did not come to be served, but to serve, and to give his life as a ransom for many."

LUKE

22:24 A dispute also arose among them as to which of them was considered to be greatest. [25] Jesus said to them, "The kings of the Gentiles lord it over them; and those who exercise authority over them call themselves Benefactors. [26] But you are not to be like that. Instead, the greatest among you should be like the youngest, and the one who rules like the one who serves. [27] For who is greater, the one who is at the table or the one who serves? Is it not the one who is at the table? But I am among you as one who serves. [28] You are those who have stood by me in my trials. [29] And I confer on you a kingdom, just as my Father conferred one on me, [30] so that you may eat and drink at my table in my kingdom and sit on thrones, judging the twelve tribes of Israel.

JOHN

12:26 Whoever serves me must follow me; and where I am, my servant also will be. My Father will honor the one who serves me.

1. Identify and consider the significance of the differences among the four passages.

13.0 Priests Question the Authority of Jesus

MATTHEW
21:23 Jesus entered the temple courts, and, while he was teaching, the chief priests and the elders of the people came to him. "By what authority are you doing these things?" they asked. "And who gave you this authority?" [24] Jesus replied, "I will also ask you one question. If you answer me, I will tell you by what authority I am doing these things. [25] John's baptism—where did it come from? Was it from heaven, or of human origin?" They discussed it among themselves and said, "If we say, 'From heaven,' he will ask, 'Then why didn't you believe him?' [26] But if we say, 'Of human origin'—we are afraid of the people, for they all hold that John was a prophet." [27] So they answered Jesus, "We don't know." Then he said, "Neither will I tell you by what authority I am doing these things.

MARK
11:27 They arrived again in Jerusalem, and while Jesus was walking in the temple courts, the chief priests, the teachers of the law and the elders came to him. [28] "By what authority are you doing these things?" they asked. "And who gave you authority to do this?" [29] Jesus replied, "I will ask you one question. Answer me, and I will tell you by what authority I am doing these things. [30] John's baptism—was it from heaven, or of human origin? Tell me!" [31] They discussed it among themselves and said, "If we say, 'From heaven,' he will ask, 'Then why didn't you believe him?' [32] But if we say, 'Of human origin' …" (They feared the people, for everyone held that John really was a prophet.) [33] So they answered Jesus, "We don't know." Jesus said, "Neither will I tell you by what authority I am doing these things."

LUKE
20:1 One day as Jesus was teaching the people in the temple courts and proclaiming the good news, the chief priests and the teachers of the law, together with the elders, came up to him. [2] "Tell us by what authority you are doing these things," they said. "Who gave you this authority?" [3] He replied, "I will also ask you a question. Tell me: [4] John's baptism—was it from heaven, or of human origin?" [5] They discussed it among themselves and said, "If we say, 'From heaven,' he will ask, 'Why didn't you believe him?' [6] But if we say, 'Of human origin,' all the people will stone us, because they are persuaded that John was a prophet." [7] So they answered, "We don't know where it was from." [8] Jesus said, "Neither will I tell you by what authority I am doing these things."

JOHN
2:18 The Jews then responded to him, "What sign can you show us to prove your authority to do all this?" [19] Jesus answered them, "Destroy this temple, and I will raise it again in three days." [20] They replied, "It has taken forty-six years to build this temple, and you are going to raise it in three days?" [21] But the temple he had spoken of was his body. [22] After he was raised from the dead, his disciples recalled what he had said. Then they believed the scripture and the words that Jesus had spoken. [23] Now while he was in Jerusalem at the Passover Festival, many people saw the signs he was performing and believed in his name. [24] But Jesus would not entrust himself to them, for he knew all people. [25] He did not need any testimony about mankind, for he knew what was in each person.

1. The three accounts in the Synoptics are similar, but they do contain some differences. Identify them.
2. Note how differently Jesus answers the question in John's account.

13.p Jesus as David's Son

MATTHEW
22:41 While the Pharisees were gathered together, Jesus asked them, [42] "What do you think about the Messiah? Whose son is he?" "The son of David," they replied. [43] He said to them, "How is it then that David, speaking by the Spirit, calls him 'Lord'? For he says, [44] "'The Lord said to my Lord: "Sit at my right hand until I put your enemies under your feet."' [45] If then David calls him 'Lord,' how can he be his son?" [46] No one could say a word in reply, and from that day on no one dared to ask him any more questions.

MARK
12:35 While Jesus was teaching in the temple courts, he asked, "Why do the teachers of the law say that the Messiah is the son of David? [36] David himself, speaking by the Holy Spirit, declared: "'The Lord said to my Lord: "Sit at my right hand until I put your enemies under your feet."' [37] David himself calls him 'Lord.' How then can he be his son?" The large crowd listened to him with delight.

LUKE
20:41 Then Jesus said to them, "Why is it said that the Messiah is the son of David? [42] David himself declares in the Book of Psalms: "'The Lord said to my Lord: "Sit at my right hand [43] until I make your enemies a footstool for your feet."' [44] David calls him 'Lord.' How then can he be his son?"

JOHN
7:40 On hearing his words, some of the people said, "Surely this man is the Prophet." [41] Others said, "He is the Messiah." Still others asked, "How can the Messiah come from Galilee? [42] Does not Scripture say that the Messiah will come from David's descendants and from Bethlehem, the town where David lived?" [43] Thus the people were divided because of Jesus. [44] Some wanted to seize him, but no one laid a hand on him.

1. Note the ambiguity in all four passages.

CHAPTER 14: TRIAL, CRUCIFIXION, RESURRECTION

14.a Jesus Predicts His Death

MATTHEW
9:22 When they came together in Galilee, he said to them, "The Son of Man is going to be delivered into the hands of men. ²³ They will kill him, and on the third day he will be raised to life." And the disciples were filled with grief. * * * 16:21 From that time on Jesus began to explain to his disciples that he must go to Jerusalem and suffer many things at the hands of the elders, the chief priests and the teachers of the law, and that he must be killed and on the third day be raised to life. ²² Peter took him aside and began to rebuke him. "Never, Lord!" he said. "This shall never happen to you!" ²³ Jesus turned and said to Peter, "Get behind me, Satan! You are a stumbling block to me; you do not have in mind the concerns of God, but merely human concerns." * * * 20:17 Now Jesus was going up to Jerusalem. On the way, he took the Twelve aside and said to them, ¹⁸ "We are going up to Jerusalem, and the Son of Man will be delivered over to the chief priests and the teachers of the law. They will condemn him to death ¹⁹ and will hand him over to the Gentiles to be mocked and flogged and crucified. On the third day he will be raised to life!"
MARK
8:31 He then began to teach them that the Son of Man must suffer many things and be rejected by the elders, the chief priests and the teachers of the law, and that he must be killed and after three days rise again. ³² He spoke plainly about this, and Peter took him aside and began to rebuke him. ³³ But when Jesus turned and looked at his disciples, he rebuked Peter. "Get behind me, Satan!" he said. "You do not have in mind the concerns of God, but merely human concerns." * * * 9:30 They left that place and passed through Galilee. Jesus did not want anyone to know where they were, ³¹ because he was teaching his disciples. He said to them, "The Son of Man is going to be delivered into the hands of men. They will kill him, and after three days he will rise." ³² But they did not understand what he meant and were afraid to ask him about it. * * * 10:32 They were on their way up to Jerusalem, with Jesus leading the way, and the disciples were astonished, while those who followed were afraid. Again he took the Twelve aside and told them what was going to happen to him. ³³ "We are going up to Jerusalem," he said, "and the Son of Man will be delivered over to the chief priests and the teachers of the law. They will condemn him to death and will hand him over to the Gentiles, ³⁴ who will mock him and spit on him, flog him and kill him. Three days later he will rise."
LUKE
9:22 And he said, "The Son of Man must suffer many things and be rejected by the elders, the chief priests and the teachers of the law, and he must be killed and on the third day be raised to life." * * * 9:43 While everyone was marveling at all that Jesus did, he said to his disciples, ⁴⁴ "Listen carefully to what I am about to tell you: The Son of Man is going to be delivered into the hands of men." ⁴⁵ But they did not understand what this meant. It was hidden from them, so that they did not grasp it, and they were afraid to ask him about it.

> ***
> 18:31 Jesus took the Twelve aside and told them, "We are going up to Jerusalem, and everything that is written by the prophets about the Son of Man will be fulfilled. ³² He will be delivered over to the Gentiles. They will mock him, insult him and spit on him; ³³ they will flog him and kill him. On the third day he will rise again."
> ³⁴ The disciples did not understand any of this. Its meaning was hidden from them, and they did not know what he was talking about.

> ## JOHN
>
> 10:14 "I am the good shepherd; I know my sheep and my sheep know me— ¹⁵ just as the Father knows me and I know the Father—and I lay down my life for the sheep. ¹⁶ I have other sheep that are not of this sheep pen. I must bring them also. They too will listen to my voice, and there shall be one flock and one shepherd. ¹⁷ The reason my Father loves me is that I lay down my life—only to take it up again. ¹⁸ No one takes it from me, but I lay it down of my own accord. I have authority to lay it down and authority to take it up again. This command I received from my Father."
>
> ***
>
> 12:7 "Leave her alone," Jesus replied. "It was intended that she should save this perfume for the day of my burial. ⁸ You will always have the poor among you, but you will not always have me."
>
> ***
>
> 12:20 Now there were some Greeks among those who went up to worship at the festival. ²¹ They came to Philip, who was from Bethsaida in Galilee, with a request. "Sir," they said, "we would like to see Jesus." ²² Philip went to tell Andrew; Andrew and Philip in turn told Jesus.
>
> ²³ Jesus replied, "The hour has come for the Son of Man to be glorified. ²⁴ Very truly I tell you, unless a kernel of wheat falls to the ground and dies, it remains only a single seed. But if it dies, it produces many seeds. ²⁵ Anyone who loves their life will lose it, while anyone who hates their life in this world will keep it for eternal life. ²⁶ Whoever serves me must follow me; and where I am, my servant also will be. My Father will honor the one who serves me.
>
> ²⁷ "Now my soul is troubled, and what shall I say? 'Father, save me from this hour'? No, it was for this very reason I came to this hour. ²⁸ Father, glorify your name!" Then a voice came from heaven, "I have glorified it, and will glorify it again." ²⁹ The crowd that was there and heard it said it had thundered; others said an angel had spoken to him.
>
> ³⁰ Jesus said, "This voice was for your benefit, not mine. ³¹ Now is the time for judgment on this world; now the prince of this world will be driven out. ³² And I, when I am lifted up from the earth, will draw all people to myself." ³³ He said this to show the kind of death he was going to die.
>
> ³⁴ The crowd spoke up, "We have heard from the Law that the Messiah will remain forever, so how can you say, 'The Son of Man must be lifted up'? Who is this 'Son of Man'?" ³⁵ Then Jesus told them, "You are going to have the light just a little while longer. Walk while you have the light, before darkness overtakes you. Whoever walks in the dark does not know where they are going. ³⁶ Believe in the light while you have the light, so that you may become children of light." When he had finished speaking, Jesus left and hid himself from them.

1. In the Synoptic accounts, all of Jesus' predictions of his death were shared privately with the disciples. In John's account, the disciples are barely mentioned in this regard, while Jesus makes his prediction to others. What do you make of this?
2. Consider how the reactions of the disciples are described in the Synoptic accounts.

14.b Jesus Enters Jerusalem

MATTHEW
21:1 As they approached Jerusalem and came to Bethphage on the Mount of Olives, Jesus sent two disciples, ² saying to them, "Go to the village ahead of you, and at once you will find a donkey tied there, with her colt by her. Untie them and bring them to me. ³ If anyone says anything to you, say that the Lord needs them, and he will send them right away." ⁴ This took place to fulfill what was spoken through the prophet: ⁵ "Say to Daughter Zion, 'See, your king comes to you, gentle and riding on a donkey, and on a colt, the foal of a donkey.'" ⁶ The disciples went and did as Jesus had instructed them. ⁷ They brought the donkey and the colt and placed their cloaks on them for Jesus to sit on. ⁸ A very large crowd spread their cloaks on the road, while others cut branches from the trees and spread them on the road. ⁹ The crowds that went ahead of him and those that followed shouted, "Hosanna to the Son of David!" "Blessed is he who comes in the name of the Lord!" "Hosanna in the highest heaven!" ¹⁰ When Jesus entered Jerusalem, the whole city was stirred and asked, "Who is this?" ¹¹ The crowds answered, "This is Jesus, the prophet from Nazareth in Galilee."
MARK
11:1 As they approached Jerusalem and came to Bethphage and Bethany at the Mount of Olives, Jesus sent two of his disciples, ² saying to them, "Go to the village ahead of you, and just as you enter it, you will find a colt tied there, which no one has ever ridden. Untie it and bring it here. ³ If anyone asks you, 'Why are you doing this?' say, 'The Lord needs it and will send it back here shortly.'" ⁴ They went and found a colt outside in the street, tied at a doorway. As they untied it, ⁵ some people standing there asked, "What are you doing, untying that colt?" ⁶ They answered as Jesus had told them to, and the people let them go. ⁷ When they brought the colt to Jesus and threw their cloaks over it, he sat on it. ⁸ Many people spread their cloaks on the road, while others spread branches they had cut in the fields. ⁹ Those who went ahead and those who followed shouted, "Hosanna!" "Blessed is he who comes in the name of the Lord!" ¹⁰ "Blessed is the coming kingdom of our father David!" "Hosanna in the highest heaven!" ¹¹ Jesus entered Jerusalem and went into the temple courts. He looked around at everything, but since it was already late, he went out to Bethany with the Twelve.
LUKE
19:28 After Jesus had said this, he went on ahead, going up to Jerusalem. ²⁹ As he approached Bethphage and Bethany at the hill called the Mount of Olives, he sent two of his disciples, saying to them, ³⁰ "Go to the village ahead of you, and as you enter it, you will find a colt tied there, which no one has ever ridden. Untie it and bring it here. ³¹ If anyone asks you, 'Why are you untying it?' say, 'The Lord needs it.'" ³² Those who were sent ahead went and found it just as he had told them. ³³ As they were untying the colt, its owners asked them, "Why are you untying the colt?" ³⁴ They replied, "The Lord needs it." ³⁵ They brought it to Jesus, threw their cloaks on the colt and put Jesus on it. ³⁶ As he went along, people spread their cloaks on the road. ³⁷ When he came near the place where the road goes down the Mount of Olives, the whole crowd of disciples began joyfully to praise God in loud voices for all the miracles they had seen: ³⁸ "Blessed is the king who comes in the name of the Lord!" "Peace in heaven and glory in the highest!" ³⁹ Some of the Pharisees in the crowd said to Jesus, "Teacher, rebuke your disciples!" ⁴⁰ "I tell you," he replied, "if they keep quiet, the stones will cry out." ⁴¹ As he approached Jerusalem and saw the city, he wept over it ⁴² and said, "If you, even you, had only known on this day what would bring you peace—but now it is hidden from your eyes. ⁴³ The days will come upon you when your enemies will build an embankment against you and encircle you and hem you in on every side. ⁴⁴ They will dash you to the ground, you and the children within your walls. They will not leave one stone on another, because you did not recognize the time of God's coming to you."

JOHN

2:13 When it was almost time for the Jewish Passover, Jesus went up to Jerusalem.

* * *

12:12 The next day the great crowd that had come for the festival heard that Jesus was on his way to Jerusalem. [13] They took palm branches and went out to meet him, shouting, Hosanna!" "Blessed is he who comes in the name of the Lord!" "Blessed is the king of Israel!"
[14] Jesus found a young donkey and sat on it, as it is written: [15] "Do not be afraid, Daughter Zion; see, your king is coming, seated on a donkey's colt."
[16] At first his disciples did not understand all this. Only after Jesus was glorified did they realize that these things had been written about him and that these things had been done to him.
[17] Now the crowd that was with him when he called Lazarus from the tomb and raised him from the dead continued to spread the word. [18] Many people, because they had heard that he had performed this sign, went out to meet him. [19] So the Pharisees said to one another, "See, this is getting us nowhere. Look how the whole world has gone after him!"

1. Compare the four accounts. Are there significant differences among them?

14.c A Lament for Jerusalem

MATTHEW
23:37 "Jerusalem, Jerusalem, you who kill the prophets and stone those sent to you, how often I have longed to gather your children together, as a hen gathers her chicks under her wings, and you were not willing. 38 Look, your house is left to you desolate. 39 For I tell you, you will not see me again until you say, 'Blessed is he who comes in the name of the Lord.'"
MARK
LUKE
13:31 At that time some Pharisees came to Jesus and said to him, "Leave this place and go somewhere else. Herod wants to kill you." 32 He replied, "Go tell that fox, 'I will keep on driving out demons and healing people today and tomorrow, and on the third day I will reach my goal.' 33 In any case, I must press on today and tomorrow and the next day—for surely no prophet can die outside Jerusalem! 34 "Jerusalem, Jerusalem, you who kill the prophets and stone those sent to you, how often I have longed to gather your children together, as a hen gathers her chicks under her wings, and you were not willing. 35 Look, your house is left to you desolate. I tell you, you will not see me again until you say, 'Blessed is he who comes in the name of the Lord.'"
JOHN

1. When a similar passage is found in Matthew and Luke, but does not appear in Mark, what is its probable source?

14.d Plotting against Jesus

MATTHEW
26:1 When Jesus had finished saying all these things, he said to his disciples, ² "As you know, the Passover is two days away—and the Son of Man will be handed over to be crucified." ³ Then the chief priests and the elders of the people assembled in the palace of the high priest, whose name was Caiaphas, ⁴ and they schemed to arrest Jesus secretly and kill him. ⁵ "But not during the festival," they said, "or there may be a riot among the people."

MARK
14:1 Now the Passover and the Festival of Unleavened Bread were only two days away, and the chief priests and the teachers of the law were scheming to arrest Jesus secretly and kill him. ² "But not during the festival," they said, "or the people may riot."

LUKE
19:47 Every day he was teaching at the temple. But the chief priests, the teachers of the law and the leaders among the people were trying to kill him. ⁴⁸ Yet they could not find any way to do it, because all the people hung on his words. * * * 22:1 Now the Festival of Unleavened Bread, called the Passover, was approaching, ² and the chief priests and the teachers of the law were looking for some way to get rid of Jesus, for they were afraid of the people. ³ Then Satan entered Judas, called Iscariot, one of the Twelve. ⁴ And Judas went to the chief priests and the officers of the temple guard and discussed with them how he might betray Jesus. ⁵ They were delighted and agreed to give him money. ⁶ He consented, and watched for an opportunity to hand Jesus over to them when no crowd was present.

JOHN
11:45 Therefore many of the Jews who had come to visit Mary, and had seen what Jesus did, believed in him. ⁴⁶ But some of them went to the Pharisees and told them what Jesus had done. ⁴⁷ Then the chief priests and the Pharisees called a meeting of the Sanhedrin. "What are we accomplishing?" they asked. "Here is this man performing many signs. ⁴⁸ If we let him go on like this, everyone will believe in him, and then the Romans will come and take away both our temple and our nation." ⁴⁹ Then one of them, named Caiaphas, who was high priest that year, spoke up, "You know nothing at all! ⁵⁰ You do not realize that it is better for you that one man die for the people than that the whole nation perish." ⁵¹ He did not say this on his own, but as high priest that year he prophesied that Jesus would die for the Jewish nation, ⁵² and not only for that nation but also for the scattered children of God, to bring them together and make them one. ⁵³ So from that day on they plotted to take his life. ⁵⁴ Therefore Jesus no longer moved about publicly among the people of Judea. Instead he withdrew to a region near the wilderness, to a village called Ephraim, where he stayed with his disciples.

1. Note the different perspectives in the four accounts.

14.e Jesus Is Anointed

MATTHEW

26:6 While Jesus was in Bethany in the home of Simon the Leper, [7] a woman came to him with an alabaster jar of very expensive perfume, which she poured on his head as he was reclining at the table. [8] When the disciples saw this, they were indignant. "Why this waste?" they asked. [9] "This perfume could have been sold at a high price and the money given to the poor."
[10] Aware of this, Jesus said to them, "Why are you bothering this woman? She has done a beautiful thing to me. [11] The poor you will always have with you, but you will not always have me. [12] When she poured this perfume on my body, she did it to prepare me for burial. [13] Truly I tell you, wherever this gospel is preached throughout the world, what she has done will also be told, in memory of her."

MARK

14:3 While he was in Bethany, reclining at the table in the home of Simon the Leper, a woman came with an alabaster jar of very expensive perfume, made of pure nard. She broke the jar and poured the perfume on his head. [4] Some of those present were saying indignantly to one another, "Why this waste of perfume? [5] It could have been sold for more than a year's wages and the money given to the poor." And they rebuked her harshly.
[6] "Leave her alone," said Jesus. "Why are you bothering her? She has done a beautiful thing to me. [7] The poor you will always have with you, and you can help them any time you want. But you will not always have me. [8] She did what she could. She poured perfume on my body beforehand to prepare for my burial. [9] Truly I tell you, wherever the gospel is preached throughout the world, what she has done will also be told, in memory of her."

LUKE

7:36 When one of the Pharisees invited Jesus to have dinner with him, he went to the Pharisee's house and reclined at the table. [37] A woman in that town who lived a sinful life learned that Jesus was eating at the Pharisee's house, so she came there with an alabaster jar of perfume. [38] As she stood behind him at his feet weeping, she began to wet his feet with her tears. Then she wiped them with her hair, kissed them and poured perfume on them.
[39] When the Pharisee who had invited him saw this, he said to himself, "If this man were a prophet, he would know who is touching him and what kind of woman she is—that she is a sinner."
[40] Jesus answered him, "Simon, I have something to tell you." "Tell me, teacher," he said.
[41] "Two people owed money to a certain moneylender. One owed him five hundred denarii, and the other fifty.
[42] Neither of them had the money to pay him back, so he forgave the debts of both. Now which of them will love him more?" [43] Simon replied, "I suppose the one who had the bigger debt forgiven." "You have judged correctly," Jesus said.
[44] Then he turned toward the woman and said to Simon, "Do you see this woman? I came into your house. You did not give me any water for my feet, but she wet my feet with her tears and wiped them with her hair. [45] You did not give me a kiss, but this woman, from the time I entered, has not stopped kissing my feet. [46] You did not put oil on my head, but she has poured perfume on my feet. [47] Therefore, I tell you, her many sins have been forgiven—as her great love has shown. But whoever has been forgiven little loves little."
[48] Then Jesus said to her, "Your sins are forgiven." [49] The other guests began to say among themselves, "Who is this who even forgives sins?" [50] Jesus said to the woman, "Your faith has saved you; go in peace."

JOHN

12:1 Six days before the Passover, Jesus came to Bethany, where Lazarus lived, whom Jesus had raised from the dead. [2] Here a dinner was given in Jesus' honor. Martha served, while Lazarus was among those reclining at the table with him. [3] Then Mary took about a pint of pure nard, an expensive perfume; she poured it on Jesus' feet and wiped his feet with her hair. And the house was filled with the fragrance of the perfume.
[4] But one of his disciples, Judas Iscariot, who was later to betray him, objected, [5] "Why wasn't this perfume sold and the money given to the poor? It was worth a year's wages." [6] He did not say this because he cared about the poor but because he was a thief; as keeper of the money bag, he used to help himself to what was put into it.

> ⁷"Leave her alone," Jesus replied. "It was intended that she should save this perfume for the day of my burial. ⁸You will always have the poor among you, but you will not always have me."

1. There are small differences between the accounts of Matthew and Mark, but great differences between Mark's original and the accounts of Luke and of John. Sort out and assess the differences.
2. What are the key points that make clear this is the same episode that all four Gospels are describing?

14.f Judas Betrays Jesus

MATTHEW

26:14 Then one of the Twelve—the one called Judas Iscariot—went to the chief priests [15] and asked, "What are you willing to give me if I deliver him over to you?" So they counted out for him thirty pieces of silver. [16] From then on Judas watched for an opportunity to hand him over.

MARK

14:10 Then Judas Iscariot, one of the Twelve, went to the chief priests to betray Jesus to them. [11] They were delighted to hear this and promised to give him money. So he watched for an opportunity to hand him over.

LUKE

22:1 Now the Festival of Unleavened Bread, called the Passover, was approaching, [2] and the chief priests and the teachers of the law were looking for some way to get rid of Jesus, for they were afraid of the people. [3] Then Satan entered Judas, called Iscariot, one of the Twelve. [4] And Judas went to the chief priests and the officers of the temple guard and discussed with them how he might betray Jesus. [5] They were delighted and agreed to give him money. [6] He consented, and watched for an opportunity to hand Jesus over to them when no crowd was present.

JOHN

6:70 Then Jesus replied, "Have I not chosen you, the Twelve? Yet one of you is a devil!" [71] (He meant Judas, the son of Simon Iscariot, who, though one of the Twelve, was later to betray him.)

* * *

13:2 The evening meal was in progress, and the devil had already prompted Judas, the son of Simon Iscariot, to betray Jesus.

* * *

13:21 After he had said this, Jesus was troubled in spirit and testified, "Very truly I tell you, one of you is going to betray me." [22] His disciples stared at one another, at a loss to know which of them he meant. [23] One of them, the disciple whom Jesus loved, was reclining next to him. [24] Simon Peter motioned to this disciple and said, "Ask him which one he means."

[25] Leaning back against Jesus, he asked him, "Lord, who is it?" [26] Jesus answered, "It is the one to whom I will give this piece of bread when I have dipped it in the dish." Then, dipping the piece of bread, he gave it to Judas, the son of Simon Iscariot. [27] As soon as Judas took the bread, Satan entered into him. So Jesus told him, "What you are about to do, do quickly." [28] But no one at the meal understood why Jesus said this to him. [29] Since Judas had charge of the money, some thought Jesus was telling him to buy what was needed for the festival, or to give something to the poor. [30] As soon as Judas had taken the bread, he went out. And it was night.

1. What is a key difference between the three Synoptic accounts and that of John? Does John's account actually contradict the others?

14.g On What Day Was the Crucifixion?

MATTHEW
26:17 On the first day of the Festival of Unleavened Bread, the disciples came to Jesus and asked, "Where do you want us to make preparations for you to eat the Passover?" ¹⁸ He replied, "Go into the city to a certain man and tell him, 'The Teacher says: My appointed time is near. I am going to celebrate the Passover with my disciples at your house.'" ¹⁹ So the disciples did as Jesus had directed them and prepared the Passover. ²⁰ When evening came, Jesus was reclining at the table with the Twelve. *** 27:62 The next day, the one after Preparation Day, the chief priests and the Pharisees went to Pilate. ⁶³ "Sir," they said, "we remember that while he was still alive that deceiver said, 'After three days I will rise again.' ⁶⁴ So give the order for the tomb to be made secure until the third day. Otherwise, his disciples may come and steal the body and tell the people that he has been raised from the dead. This last deception will be worse than the first."

MARK
14:12 On the first day of the Festival of Unleavened Bread, when it was customary to sacrifice the Passover lamb, Jesus' disciples asked him, "Where do you want us to go and make preparations for you to eat the Passover?" ¹³ So he sent two of his disciples, telling them, "Go into the city, and a man carrying a jar of water will meet you. Follow him. ¹⁴ Say to the owner of the house he enters, 'The Teacher asks: Where is my guest room, where I may eat the Passover with my disciples?' ¹⁵ He will show you a large room upstairs, furnished and ready. Make preparations for us there." ¹⁶ The disciples left, went into the city and found things just as Jesus had told them. So they prepared the Passover. ¹⁷ When evening came, Jesus arrived with the Twelve. *** 15:42 It was Preparation Day (that is, the day before the Sabbath). So as evening approached, ⁴³ Joseph of Arimathea, a prominent member of the Council, who was himself waiting for the kingdom of God, went boldly to Pilate and asked for Jesus' body. ⁴⁴ Pilate was surprised to hear that he was already dead. Summoning the centurion, he asked him if Jesus had already died. ⁴⁵ When he learned from the centurion that it was so, he gave the body to Joseph. ⁴⁶ So Joseph bought some linen cloth, took down the body, wrapped it in the linen, and placed it in a tomb cut out of rock. Then he rolled a stone against the entrance of the tomb. ⁴⁷ Mary Magdalene and Mary the mother of Joseph saw where he was laid.

LUKE
22:7 Then came the day of Unleavened Bread on which the Passover lamb had to be sacrificed. ⁸ Jesus sent Peter and John, saying, "Go and make preparations for us to eat the Passover." ⁹ "Where do you want us to prepare for it?" they asked. ¹⁰ He replied, "As you enter the city, a man carrying a jar of water will meet you. Follow him to the house that he enters, ¹¹ and say to the owner of the house, 'The Teacher asks: Where is the guest room, where I may eat the Passover with my disciples?' ¹² He will show you a large room upstairs, all furnished. Make preparations there." ¹³ They left and found things just as Jesus had told them. So they prepared the Passover. ¹⁴ When the hour came, Jesus and his apostles reclined at the table. ¹⁵ And he said to them, "I have eagerly desired to eat this Passover with you before I suffer. ¹⁶ For I tell you, I will not eat it again until it finds fulfillment in the kingdom of God." *** 23:50 Now there was a man named Joseph, a member of the Council, a good and upright man, ⁵¹ who had not consented to their decision and action. He came from the Judean town of Arimathea, and he himself was waiting for the kingdom of God. ⁵² Going to Pilate, he asked for Jesus' body. ⁵³ Then he took it down, wrapped it in linen cloth and placed it in a tomb cut in the rock, one in which no one had yet been laid. ⁵⁴ It was Preparation Day, and the Sabbath was about to begin.

JOHN
19:13 When Pilate heard this, he brought Jesus out and sat down on the judge's seat at a place known as the Stone Pavement (which in Aramaic is Gabbatha). ¹⁴ It was the day of Preparation of the Passover; it was about noon. "Here is your king," Pilate said to the Jews. * * * 19:30 When he had received the drink, Jesus said, "It is finished." With that, he bowed his head and gave up his spirit. ³¹ Now it was the day of Preparation, and the next day was to be a special Sabbath. Because the Jews did not want the bodies left on the crosses during the Sabbath, they asked Pilate to have the legs broken and the bodies taken down. * * * 19:38 Later, Joseph of Arimathea asked Pilate for the body of Jesus. …⁴¹ At the place where Jesus was crucified, there was a garden, and in the garden a new tomb, in which no one had ever been laid. ⁴² Because it was the Jewish day of Preparation and since the tomb was nearby, they laid Jesus there.

1. Reading each account carefully, figure out on which day (Preparation Day or Passover) Jesus was crucified. The four accounts do not all agree. Remember that in Jewish culture, each "day" started at sundown.
2. Did the writer of the Gospel who said the Crucifixion occurred on Preparation Day make a mistake? Or was he correct and the other three in error? Or was this historical detail changed for some reason?

14.h The Last Supper

MATTHEW

26:17 On the first day of the Festival of Unleavened Bread, the disciples came to Jesus and asked, "Where do you want us to make preparations for you to eat the Passover?"
[18] He replied, "Go into the city to a certain man and tell him, 'The Teacher says: My appointed time is near. I am going to celebrate the Passover with my disciples at your house.'" [19] So the disciples did as Jesus had directed them and prepared the Passover.
[20] When evening came, Jesus was reclining at the table with the Twelve. [21] And while they were eating, he said, "Truly I tell you, one of you will betray me." [22] They were very sad and began to say to him one after the other, "Surely you don't mean me, Lord?"
[23] Jesus replied, "The one who has dipped his hand into the bowl with me will betray me. [24] The Son of Man will go just as it is written about him. But woe to that man who betrays the Son of Man! It would be better for him if he had not been born."
[25] Then Judas, the one who would betray him, said, "Surely you don't mean me, Rabbi?" Jesus answered, "You have said so."
[26] While they were eating, Jesus took bread, and when he had given thanks, he broke it and gave it to his disciples, saying, "Take and eat; this is my body."
[27] Then he took a cup, and when he had given thanks, he gave it to them, saying, "Drink from it, all of you. [28] This is my blood of the covenant, which is poured out for many for the forgiveness of sins. [29] I tell you, I will not drink from this fruit of the vine from now on until that day when I drink it new with you in my Father's kingdom."
[30] When they had sung a hymn, they went out to the Mount of Olives.

MARK

14:12 On the first day of the Festival of Unleavened Bread, when it was customary to sacrifice the Passover lamb, Jesus' disciples asked him, "Where do you want us to go and make preparations for you to eat the Passover?"
[13] So he sent two of his disciples, telling them, "Go into the city, and a man carrying a jar of water will meet you. Follow him. [14] Say to the owner of the house he enters, 'The Teacher asks: Where is my guest room, where I may eat the Passover with my disciples?' [15] He will show you a large room upstairs, furnished and ready. Make preparations for us there." [16] The disciples left, went into the city and found things just as Jesus had told them. So they prepared the Passover.
[17] When evening came, Jesus arrived with the Twelve. [18] While they were reclining at the table eating, he said, "Truly I tell you, one of you will betray me—one who is eating with me." [19] They were saddened, and one by one they said to him, "Surely you don't mean me?"
[20] "It is one of the Twelve," he replied, "one who dips bread into the bowl with me. [21] The Son of Man will go just as it is written about him. But woe to that man who betrays the Son of Man! It would be better for him if he had not been born."
[22] While they were eating, Jesus took bread, and when he had given thanks, he broke it and gave it to his disciples, saying, "Take it; this is my body."
[23] Then he took a cup, and when he had given thanks, he gave it to them, and they all drank from it. [24] "This is my blood of the covenant, which is poured out for many," he said to them. [25] "Truly I tell you, I will not drink again from the fruit of the vine until that day when I drink it new in the kingdom of God."
[26] When they had sung a hymn, they went out to the Mount of Olives.

LUKE

22:7 Then came the day of Unleavened Bread on which the Passover lamb had to be sacrificed. [8] Jesus sent Peter and John, saying, "Go and make preparations for us to eat the Passover." [9] "Where do you want us to prepare for it?" they asked.
[10] He replied, "As you enter the city, a man carrying a jar of water will meet you. Follow him to the house that he enters, [11] and say to the owner of the house, 'The Teacher asks: Where is the guest room, where I may eat the

Passover with my disciples?' ¹² He will show you a large room upstairs, all furnished. Make preparations there."
¹³ They left and found things just as Jesus had told them. So they prepared the Passover.
¹⁴ When the hour came, Jesus and his apostles reclined at the table. ¹⁵ And he said to them, "I have eagerly desired to eat this Passover with you before I suffer. ¹⁶ For I tell you, I will not eat it again until it finds fulfillment in the kingdom of God."
¹⁷ After taking the cup, he gave thanks and said, "Take this and divide it among you. ¹⁸ For I tell you I will not drink again from the fruit of the vine until the kingdom of God comes."
¹⁹ And he took bread, gave thanks and broke it, and gave it to them, saying, "This is my body given for you; do this in remembrance of me."
²⁰ In the same way, after the supper he took the cup, saying, "This cup is the new covenant in my blood, which is poured out for you. ²¹ But the hand of him who is going to betray me is with mine on the table. ²² The Son of Man will go as it has been decreed. But woe to that man who betrays him!" ²³ They began to question among themselves which of them it might be who would do this.

JOHN

6:47 Very truly I tell you, the one who believes has eternal life. ⁴⁸ I am the bread of life. ⁴⁹ Your ancestors ate the manna in the wilderness, yet they died. ⁵⁰ But here is the bread that comes down from heaven, which anyone may eat and not die. ⁵¹ I am the living bread that came down from heaven. Whoever eats this bread will live forever. This bread is my flesh, which I will give for the life of the world."
⁵² Then the Jews began to argue sharply among themselves, "How can this man give us his flesh to eat?"
⁵³ Jesus said to them, "Very truly I tell you, unless you eat the flesh of the Son of Man and drink his blood, you have no life in you. ⁵⁴ Whoever eats my flesh and drinks my blood has eternal life, and I will raise them up at the last day. ⁵⁵ For my flesh is real food and my blood is real drink. ⁵⁶ Whoever eats my flesh and drinks my blood remains in me, and I in them. ⁵⁷ Just as the living Father sent me and I live because of the Father, so the one who feeds on me will live because of me. ⁵⁸ This is the bread that came down from heaven. Your ancestors ate manna and died, but whoever feeds on this bread will live forever." ⁵⁹ He said this while teaching in the synagogue in Capernaum.

* * *

13:1 It was just before the Passover Festival. Jesus knew that the hour had come for him to leave this world and go to the Father. Having loved his own who were in the world, he loved them to the end.
² The evening meal was in progress, and the devil had already prompted Judas, the son of Simon Iscariot, to betray Jesus. ³ Jesus knew that the Father had put all things under his power, and that he had come from God and was returning to God; ⁴ so he got up from the meal, took off his outer clothing, and wrapped a towel around his waist.
⁵ After that, he poured water into a basin and began to wash his disciples' feet, drying them with the towel that was wrapped around him.
⁶ He came to Simon Peter, who said to him, "Lord, are you going to wash my feet?" ⁷ Jesus replied, "You do not realize now what I am doing, but later you will understand." ⁸ "No," said Peter, "you shall never wash my feet." Jesus answered, "Unless I wash you, you have no part with me." ⁹ "Then, Lord," Simon Peter replied, "not just my feet but my hands and my head as well!"
¹⁰ Jesus answered, "Those who have had a bath need only to wash their feet; their whole body is clean. And you are clean, though not every one of you." ¹¹ For he knew who was going to betray him, and that was why he said not every one was clean.
¹² When he had finished washing their feet, he put on his clothes and returned to his place. "Do you understand what I have done for you?" he asked them. ¹³ "You call me 'Teacher' and 'Lord,' and rightly so, for that is what I am. ¹⁴ Now that I, your Lord and Teacher, have washed your feet, you also should wash one another's feet. ¹⁵ I have set you an example that you should do as I have done for you. ¹⁶ Very truly I tell you, no servant is greater than his master, nor is a messenger greater than the one who sent him. ¹⁷ Now that you know these things, you will be blessed if you do them.
¹⁸ "I am not referring to all of you; I know those I have chosen. But this is to fulfill this passage of Scripture: 'He who shared my bread has turned against me.'
¹⁹ "I am telling you now before it happens, so that when it does happen you will believe that I am who I am. ²⁰ Very truly I tell you, whoever accepts anyone I send accepts me; and whoever accepts me accepts the one who sent me."
²¹ After he had said this, Jesus was troubled in spirit and testified, "Very truly I tell you, one of you is going to betray me." ²² His disciples stared at one another, at a loss to know which of them he meant. ²³ One of them, the

disciple whom Jesus loved, was reclining next to him. ²⁴ Simon Peter motioned to this disciple and said, "Ask him which one he means."

²⁵ Leaning back against Jesus, he asked him, "Lord, who is it?" ²⁶ Jesus answered, "It is the one to whom I will give this piece of bread when I have dipped it in the dish." Then, dipping the piece of bread, he gave it to Judas, the son of Simon Iscariot. ²⁷ As soon as Judas took the bread, Satan entered into him.

So Jesus told him, "What you are about to do, do quickly." ²⁸ But no one at the meal understood why Jesus said this to him. ²⁹ Since Judas had charge of the money, some thought Jesus was telling him to buy what was needed for the festival, or to give something to the poor. ³⁰ As soon as Judas had taken the bread, he went out. And it was night.

³¹ When he was gone, Jesus said, "Now the Son of Man is glorified and God is glorified in him. ³² If God is glorified in him, God will glorify the Son in himself, and will glorify him at once.

³³ "My children, I will be with you only a little longer. You will look for me, and just as I told the Jews, so I tell you now: Where I am going, you cannot come.

³⁴ "A new command I give you: Love one another. As I have loved you, so you must love one another. ³⁵ By this everyone will know that you are my disciples, if you love one another."

³⁶ Simon Peter asked him, "Lord, where are you going?" Jesus replied, "Where I am going, you cannot follow now, but you will follow later." ³⁷ Peter asked, "Lord, why can't I follow you now? I will lay down my life for you."

³⁸ Then Jesus answered, "Will you really lay down your life for me? Very truly I tell you, before the rooster crows, you will disown me three times!

* * *

14:1 "Do not let your hearts be troubled. You believe in God; believe also in me. ² My Father's house has many rooms; if that were not so, would I have told you that I am going there to prepare a place for you? ³ And if I go and prepare a place for you, I will come back and take you to be with me that you also may be where I am. ⁴ You know the way to the place where I am going."

⁵ Thomas said to him, "Lord, we don't know where you are going, so how can we know the way?" ⁶ Jesus answered, "I am the way and the truth and the life. No one comes to the Father except through me. ⁷ If you really know me, you will know my Father as well. From now on, you do know him and have seen him."

⁸ Philip said, "Lord, show us the Father and that will be enough for us." ⁹ Jesus answered: "Don't you know me, Philip, even after I have been among you such a long time? Anyone who has seen me has seen the Father. How can you say, 'Show us the Father'? ¹⁰ Don't you believe that I am in the Father, and that the Father is in me? The words I say to you I do not speak on my own authority. Rather, it is the Father, living in me, who is doing his work.

¹¹ Believe me when I say that I am in the Father and the Father is in me; or at least believe on the evidence of the works themselves. ¹² Very truly I tell you, whoever believes in me will do the works I have been doing, and they will do even greater things than these, because I am going to the Father. ¹³ And I will do whatever you ask in my name, so that the Father may be glorified in the Son. ¹⁴ You may ask me for anything in my name, and I will do it.

¹⁵ "If you love me, keep my commands. ¹⁶ And I will ask the Father, and he will give you another advocate to help you and be with you forever— ¹⁷ the Spirit of truth. The world cannot accept him, because it neither sees him nor knows him. But you know him, for he lives with you and will be in you. ¹⁸ I will not leave you as orphans; I will come to you. ¹⁹ Before long, the world will not see me anymore, but you will see me. Because I live, you also will live. ²⁰ On that day you will realize that I am in my Father, and you are in me, and I am in you. ²¹ Whoever has my commands and keeps them is the one who loves me. The one who loves me will be loved by my Father, and I too will love them and show myself to them."

²² Then Judas (not Judas Iscariot) said, "But, Lord, why do you intend to show yourself to us and not to the world?"

²³ Jesus replied, "Anyone who loves me will obey my teaching. My Father will love them, and we will come to them and make our home with them. ²⁴ Anyone who does not love me will not obey my teaching. These words you hear are not my own; they belong to the Father who sent me.

²⁵ "All this I have spoken while still with you. ²⁶ But the Advocate, the Holy Spirit, whom the Father will send in my name, will teach you all things and will remind you of everything I have said to you. ²⁷ Peace I leave with you; my peace I give you. I do not give to you as the world gives. Do not let your hearts be troubled and do not be afraid.

²⁸ "You heard me say, 'I am going away and I am coming back to you.' If you loved me, you would be glad that I am going to the Father, for the Father is greater than I. ²⁹ I have told you now before it happens, so that when it does happen you will believe. ³⁰ I will not say much more to you, for the prince of this world is coming. He has no hold over me, ³¹ but he comes so that the world may learn that I love the Father and do exactly what my Father has commanded me.

> "Come now; let us leave."

1. The accounts in the Synoptics vary a bit from each other, but are much the same. Can you identify the differences among them?
2. The account from John 13-14 is much more detailed. What passages are essentially the same as those in the Synoptics?
3. Which passages from John add things that do not appear in the Synoptics? What do you make of the omission of these passages in the other, earlier accounts?
4. The passage from John 6 occurs well before the time of the Last Supper, yet it contains a number of references to it, ahead of the event. What do you make of this?
5. Compare the accounts of the first Eucharist – the sharing of bread and wine as symbols of Christ's body and blood. What do you make of the account in John, as compared with that in the Synoptics?

14.i Jesus Predicts the Apostles' Denials

MATTHEW
26:31 Then Jesus told them, "This very night you will all fall away on account of me, for it is written: "'I will strike the shepherd, and the sheep of the flock will be scattered.' ³² But after I have risen, I will go ahead of you into Galilee." ³³ Peter replied, "Even if all fall away on account of you, I never will." ³⁴ "Truly I tell you," Jesus answered, "this very night, before the rooster crows, you will disown me three times." ³⁵ But Peter declared, "Even if I have to die with you, I will never disown you." And all the other disciples said the same.

MARK
14:27 "You will all fall away," Jesus told them, "for it is written: "'I will strike the shepherd, and the sheep will be scattered.' ²⁸ But after I have risen, I will go ahead of you into Galilee." ²⁹ Peter declared, "Even if all fall away, I will not." ³⁰ "Truly I tell you," Jesus answered, "today—yes, tonight—before the rooster crows twice you yourself will disown me three times." ³¹ But Peter insisted emphatically, "Even if I have to die with you, I will never disown you." And all the others said the same.

LUKE
22:31 "Simon, Simon, Satan has asked to sift all of you as wheat. ³² But I have prayed for you, Simon, that your faith may not fail. And when you have turned back, strengthen your brothers." ³³ But he replied, "Lord, I am ready to go with you to prison and to death." ³⁴ Jesus answered, "I tell you, Peter, before the rooster crows today, you will deny three times that you know me."

JOHN
13:36 Simon Peter asked him, "Lord, where are you going?" Jesus replied, "Where I am going, you cannot follow now, but you will follow later." ³⁷ Peter asked, "Lord, why can't I follow you now? I will lay down my life for you." ³⁸ Then Jesus answered, "Will you really lay down your life for me? Very truly I tell you, before the rooster crows, you will disown me three times!

1. This is one of the few occasions on which all four Gospels report an episode in much the same way. Can you find any notable differences among them?

14.j Jesus Prays in Gethsemane

MATTHEW

26:36 Then Jesus went with his disciples to a place called Gethsemane, and he said to them, "Sit here while I go over there and pray." ³⁷ He took Peter and the two sons of Zebedee along with him, and he began to be sorrowful and troubled. ³⁸ Then he said to them, "My soul is overwhelmed with sorrow to the point of death. Stay here and keep watch with me."
³⁹ Going a little farther, he fell with his face to the ground and prayed, "My Father, if it is possible, may this cup be taken from me. Yet not as I will, but as you will."
⁴⁰ Then he returned to his disciples and found them sleeping. "Couldn't you men keep watch with me for one hour?" he asked Peter. ⁴¹ "Watch and pray so that you will not fall into temptation. The spirit is willing, but the flesh is weak."
⁴² He went away a second time and prayed, "My Father, if it is not possible for this cup to be taken away unless I drink it, may your will be done."
⁴³ When he came back, he again found them sleeping, because their eyes were heavy. ⁴⁴ So he left them and went away once more and prayed the third time, saying the same thing.
⁴⁵ Then he returned to the disciples and said to them, "Are you still sleeping and resting? Look, the hour has come, and the Son of Man is delivered into the hands of sinners. ⁴⁶ Rise! Let us go! Here comes my betrayer!"

MARK

14:32 They went to a place called Gethsemane, and Jesus said to his disciples, "Sit here while I pray." ³³ He took Peter, James and John along with him, and he began to be deeply distressed and troubled. ³⁴ "My soul is overwhelmed with sorrow to the point of death," he said to them. "Stay here and keep watch."
³⁵ Going a little farther, he fell to the ground and prayed that if possible the hour might pass from him. ³⁶ *"Abba*, Father," he said, "everything is possible for you. Take this cup from me. Yet not what I will, but what you will."
³⁷ Then he returned to his disciples and found them sleeping. "Simon," he said to Peter, "are you asleep? Couldn't you keep watch for one hour? ³⁸ Watch and pray so that you will not fall into temptation. The spirit is willing, but the flesh is weak."
³⁹ Once more he went away and prayed the same thing. ⁴⁰ When he came back, he again found them sleeping, because their eyes were heavy. They did not know what to say to him.
⁴¹ Returning the third time, he said to them, "Are you still sleeping and resting? Enough! The hour has come. Look, the Son of Man is delivered into the hands of sinners. ⁴² Rise! Let us go! Here comes my betrayer!"

LUKE

22:39 Jesus went out as usual to the Mount of Olives, and his disciples followed him. ⁴⁰ On reaching the place, he said to them, "Pray that you will not fall into temptation." ⁴¹ He withdrew about a stone's throw beyond them, knelt down and prayed, ⁴² "Father, if you are willing, take this cup from me; yet not my will, but yours be done." ⁴³ An angel from heaven appeared to him and strengthened him. ⁴⁴ And being in anguish, he prayed more earnestly, and his sweat was like drops of blood falling to the ground.
⁴⁵ When he rose from prayer and went back to the disciples, he found them asleep, exhausted from sorrow. ⁴⁶ "Why are you sleeping?" he asked them. "Get up and pray so that you will not fall into temptation."

JOHN

18:1 When he had finished praying, Jesus left with his disciples and crossed the Kidron Valley. On the other side there was a garden, and he and his disciples went into it. ² Now Judas, who betrayed him, knew the place, because Jesus had often met there with his disciples. ³ So Judas came to the garden, guiding a detachment of soldiers and some officials from the chief priests and the Pharisees. They were carrying torches, lanterns and weapons.

1. Matthew and Mark give much the same account; compare theirs with that of Luke.
2. Note that John is quite brief in his account, by comparison.

3. How did Matthew, Mark, and Luke know what Jesus said in his prayers?

14.k Jesus Is Arrested

MATTHEW
26:47 While he was still speaking, Judas, one of the Twelve, arrived. With him was a large crowd armed with swords and clubs, sent from the chief priests and the elders of the people. [48] Now the betrayer had arranged a signal with them: "The one I kiss is the man; arrest him." [49] Going at once to Jesus, Judas said, "Greetings, Rabbi!" and kissed him. [50] Jesus replied, "Do what you came for, friend." Then the men stepped forward, seized Jesus and arrested him. [51] With that, one of Jesus' companions reached for his sword, drew it out and struck the servant of the high priest, cutting off his ear. [52] "Put your sword back in its place," Jesus said to him, "for all who draw the sword will die by the sword. [53] Do you think I cannot call on my Father, and he will at once put at my disposal more than twelve legions of angels? [54] But how then would the Scriptures be fulfilled that say it must happen in this way?" [55] In that hour Jesus said to the crowd, "Am I leading a rebellion, that you have come out with swords and clubs to capture me? Every day I sat in the temple courts teaching, and you did not arrest me. [56] But this has all taken place that the writings of the prophets might be fulfilled." Then all the disciples deserted him and fled.

MARK
14:43 Just as he was speaking, Judas, one of the Twelve, appeared. With him was a crowd armed with swords and clubs, sent from the chief priests, the teachers of the law, and the elders. [44] Now the betrayer had arranged a signal with them: "The one I kiss is the man; arrest him and lead him away under guard." [45] Going at once to Jesus, Judas said, "Rabbi!" and kissed him. [46] The men seized Jesus and arrested him. [47] Then one of those standing near drew his sword and struck the servant of the high priest, cutting off his ear. [48] "Am I leading a rebellion," said Jesus, "that you have come out with swords and clubs to capture me? [49] Every day I was with you, teaching in the temple courts, and you did not arrest me. But the Scriptures must be fulfilled." [50] Then everyone deserted him and fled. [51] A young man, wearing nothing but a linen garment, was following Jesus. When they seized him, [52] he fled naked, leaving his garment behind.

LUKE
22:35 Then Jesus asked them, "When I sent you without purse, bag or sandals, did you lack anything?" "Nothing," they answered. He said to them, "But now if you have a purse, take it, and also a bag; and if you don't have a sword, sell your cloak and buy one. [37] It is written: 'And he was numbered with the transgressors'; and I tell you that this must be fulfilled in me. Yes, what is written about me is reaching its fulfillment." The disciples said, "See, Lord, here are two swords." "That's enough!" he replied. *** 22:47 While he was still speaking a crowd came up, and the man who was called Judas, one of the Twelve, was leading them. He approached Jesus to kiss him, [48] but Jesus asked him, "Judas, are you betraying the Son of Man with a kiss?" [49] When Jesus' followers saw what was going to happen, they said, "Lord, should we strike with our swords?" [50] And one of them struck the servant of the high priest, cutting off his right ear. [51] But Jesus answered, "No more of this!" And he touched the man's ear and healed him. [52] Then Jesus said to the chief priests, the officers of the temple guard, and the elders, who had come for him, "Am I leading a rebellion, that you have come with swords and clubs? [53] Every day I was with you in the temple courts, and you did not lay a hand on me. But this is your hour—when darkness reigns."

JOHN
18:1 When he had finished praying, Jesus left with his disciples and crossed the Kidron Valley. On the other side there was a garden, and he and his disciples went into it. [2] Now Judas, who betrayed him, knew the place, because Jesus had often met there with his disciples. [3] So Judas came to the garden, guiding a detachment of soldiers and some officials from the chief priests and the Pharisees.

> They were carrying torches, lanterns and weapons.
> ⁴ Jesus, knowing all that was going to happen to him, went out and asked them, "Who is it you want?" ⁵ "Jesus of Nazareth," they replied. "I am he," Jesus said. (And Judas the traitor was standing there with them.) ⁶ When Jesus said, "I am he," they drew back and fell to the ground.
> ⁷ Again he asked them, "Who is it you want?" "Jesus of Nazareth," they said. ⁸ Jesus answered, "I told you that I am he. If you are looking for me, then let these men go." ⁹ This happened so that the words he had spoken would be fulfilled: "I have not lost one of those you gave me."
> ¹⁰ Then Simon Peter, who had a sword, drew it and struck the high priest's servant, cutting off his right ear. (The servant's name was Malchus.) ¹¹ Jesus commanded Peter, "Put your sword away! Shall I not drink the cup the Father has given me?"
> ¹² Then the detachment of soldiers with its commander and the Jewish officials arrested Jesus. They bound him
> ¹³ and brought him first to Annas, who was the father-in-law of Caiaphas, the high priest that year. ¹⁴ Caiaphas was the one who had advised the Jewish leaders that it would be good if one man died for the people.

1. Compare the four versions of this episode. It is particularly interesting to note the differences in the matter of the servant's ear.
2. Note the anomalous bit in Mark about the young man running away. What do you make of this? Note that the other three omit this detail, though it appears in the earliest Gospel.

14.1 Jesus Before the Sanhedrin

MATTHEW

26:57 Those who had arrested Jesus took him to Caiaphas the high priest, where the teachers of the law and the elders had assembled. [58] But Peter followed him at a distance, right up to the courtyard of the high priest. He entered and sat down with the guards to see the outcome.
[59] The chief priests and the whole Sanhedrin were looking for false evidence against Jesus so that they could put him to death. [60] But they did not find any, though many false witnesses came forward.
Finally two came forward [61] and declared, "This fellow said, 'I am able to destroy the temple of God and rebuild it in three days.'" [62] Then the high priest stood up and said to Jesus, "Are you not going to answer? What is this testimony that these men are bringing against you?" [63] But Jesus remained silent.
The high priest said to him, "I charge you under oath by the living God: Tell us if you are the Messiah, the Son of God." [64] "You have said so," Jesus replied. "But I say to all of you: From now on you will see the Son of Man sitting at the right hand of the Mighty One and coming on the clouds of heaven."
[65] Then the high priest tore his clothes and said, "He has spoken blasphemy! Why do we need any more witnesses? Look, now you have heard the blasphemy. [66] What do you think?" "He is worthy of death," they answered. [67] Then they spit in his face and struck him with their fists. Others slapped him [68] and said, "Prophesy to us, Messiah. Who hit you?"

MARK

14:53 They took Jesus to the high priest, and all the chief priests, the elders and the teachers of the law came together. [54] Peter followed him at a distance, right into the courtyard of the high priest. There he sat with the guards and warmed himself at the fire.
[55] The chief priests and the whole Sanhedrin were looking for evidence against Jesus so that they could put him to death, but they did not find any. [56] Many testified falsely against him, but their statements did not agree.
[57] Then some stood up and gave this false testimony against him: [58] "We heard him say, 'I will destroy this temple made with human hands and in three days will build another, not made with hands.'" [59] Yet even then their testimony did not agree. [60] Then the high priest stood up before them and asked Jesus, "Are you not going to answer? What is this testimony that these men are bringing against you?" [61] But Jesus remained silent and gave no answer.
Again the high priest asked him, "Are you the Messiah, the Son of the Blessed One?" [62] "I am," said Jesus. "And you will see the Son of Man sitting at the right hand of the Mighty One and coming on the clouds of heaven."
[63] The high priest tore his clothes. "Why do we need any more witnesses?" he asked. [64] "You have heard the blasphemy. What do you think?" They all condemned him as worthy of death. [65] Then some began to spit at him; they blindfolded him, struck him with their fists, and said, "Prophesy!" And the guards took him and beat him.

LUKE

22:54 Then seizing him, they led him away and took him into the house of the high priest. Peter followed at a distance.

* * *

22:63 The men who were guarding Jesus began mocking and beating him. [64] They blindfolded him and demanded, "Prophesy! Who hit you?" [65] And they said many other insulting things to him.
[66] At daybreak the council of the elders of the people, both the chief priests and the teachers of the law, met together, and Jesus was led before them. [67] "If you are the Messiah," they said, "tell us." Jesus answered, "If I tell you, you will not believe me, [68] and if I asked you, you would not answer. [69] But from now on, the Son of Man will be seated at the right hand of the mighty God."
[70] They all asked, "Are you then the Son of God?" He replied, "You say that I am." [71] Then they said, "Why do we need any more testimony? We have heard it from his own lips."

JOHN

18:12 Then the detachment of soldiers with its commander and the Jewish officials arrested Jesus. They bound him [13] and brought him first to Annas, who was the father-in-law of Caiaphas, the high priest that year. [14] Caiaphas was the one who had advised the Jewish leaders that it would be good if one man died for the people.

* * *

18:19 Meanwhile, the high priest questioned Jesus about his disciples and his teaching. [20] "I have spoken openly to the world," Jesus replied. "I always taught in synagogues or at the temple, where all the Jews come together. I said nothing in secret. [21] Why question me? Ask those who heard me. Surely they know what I said."

[22] When Jesus said this, one of the officials nearby slapped him in the face. "Is this the way you answer the high priest?" he demanded. [23] "If I said something wrong," Jesus replied, "testify as to what is wrong. But if I spoke the truth, why did you strike me?" [24] Then Annas sent him bound to Caiaphas the high priest.

1. Who do you suppose witnessed and recorded the Sanhedrin trial? Peter was nearby, but would probably not have heard it all. Some scholars have suggested that the risen Lazarus was a junior priest in the temple and was present; read how Lazarus is identified in John's Gospel.
2. Compare the four reports of the words of Jesus during the trial.
3. Where do the four Gospels say that this episode took place?

14.m Peter Denies Jesus

MATTHEW

26:69 Now Peter was sitting out in the courtyard, and a servant girl came to him. "You also were with Jesus of Galilee," she said. [70] But he denied it before them all. "I don't know what you're talking about," he said.
[71] Then he went out to the gateway, where another servant girl saw him and said to the people there, "This fellow was with Jesus of Nazareth." [72] He denied it again, with an oath: "I don't know the man!"
[73] After a little while, those standing there went up to Peter and said, "Surely you are one of them; your accent gives you away." [74] Then he began to call down curses, and he swore to them, "I don't know the man!"
Immediately a rooster crowed. [75] Then Peter remembered the word Jesus had spoken: "Before the rooster crows, you will disown me three times." And he went outside and wept bitterly.

MARK

14:66 While Peter was below in the courtyard, one of the servant girls of the high priest came by. [67] When she saw Peter warming himself, she looked closely at him. "You also were with that Nazarene, Jesus," she said. [68] But he denied it. "I don't know or understand what you're talking about," he said, and went out into the entryway.
[69] When the servant girl saw him there, she said again to those standing around, "This fellow is one of them."
[70] Again he denied it.
After a little while, those standing near said to Peter, "Surely you are one of them, for you are a Galilean." [71] He began to call down curses, and he swore to them, "I don't know this man you're talking about."
[72] Immediately the rooster crowed the second time. Then Peter remembered the word Jesus had spoken to him: "Before the rooster crows twice you will disown me three times." And he broke down and wept.

LUKE

22:54 Then seizing him, they led him away and took him into the house of the high priest. Peter followed at a distance. [55] And when some there had kindled a fire in the middle of the courtyard and had sat down together, Peter sat down with them. [56] A servant girl saw him seated there in the firelight. She looked closely at him and said, "This man was with him." [57] But he denied it. "Woman, I don't know him," he said.
[58] A little later someone else saw him and said, "You also are one of them." "Man, I am not!" Peter replied.
[59] About an hour later another asserted, "Certainly this fellow was with him, for he is a Galilean." [60] Peter replied, "Man, I don't know what you're talking about!" Just as he was speaking, the rooster crowed. [61] The Lord turned and looked straight at Peter. Then Peter remembered the word the Lord had spoken to him: "Before the rooster crows today, you will disown me three times." [62] And he went outside and wept bitterly.

JOHN

18:15 Simon Peter and another disciple were following Jesus. Because this disciple was known to the high priest, he went with Jesus into the high priest's courtyard, [16] but Peter had to wait outside at the door. The other disciple, who was known to the high priest, came back, spoke to the servant girl on duty there and brought Peter in.
[17] "You aren't one of this man's disciples too, are you?" she asked Peter. He replied, "I am not." [18] It was cold, and the servants and officials stood around a fire they had made to keep warm. Peter also was standing with them, warming himself.

* * *

18:25 Meanwhile, Simon Peter was still standing there warming himself. So they asked him, "You aren't one of his disciples too, are you?" He denied it, saying, "I am not."
[26] One of the high priest's servants, a relative of the man whose ear Peter had cut off, challenged him, "Didn't I see you with him in the garden?" [27] Again Peter denied it, and at that moment a rooster began to crow.

1. Compare the four versions of this episode.

14.n Jesus Before Pilate

MATTHEW

27:1 Early in the morning, all the chief priests and the elders of the people made their plans how to have Jesus executed. [2] So they bound him, led him away and handed him over to Pilate the governor.

*　*　*

27:11 Meanwhile Jesus stood before the governor, and the governor asked him, "Are you the king of the Jews?" "You have said so," Jesus replied. [12] When he was accused by the chief priests and the elders, he gave no answer. [13] Then Pilate asked him, "Don't you hear the testimony they are bringing against you?" [14] But Jesus made no reply, not even to a single charge—to the great amazement of the governor.
[15] Now it was the governor's custom at the festival to release a prisoner chosen by the crowd. [16] At that time they had a well-known prisoner whose name was Jesus Barabbas. [17] So when the crowd had gathered, Pilate asked them, "Which one do you want me to release to you: Jesus Barabbas, or Jesus who is called the Messiah?" [18] For he knew it was out of self-interest that they had handed Jesus over to him.
[19] While Pilate was sitting on the judge's seat, his wife sent him this message: "Don't have anything to do with that innocent man, for I have suffered a great deal today in a dream because of him."
[20] But the chief priests and the elders persuaded the crowd to ask for Barabbas and to have Jesus executed. [21] "Which of the two do you want me to release to you?" asked the governor. "Barabbas," they answered.
[22] "What shall I do, then, with Jesus who is called the Messiah?" Pilate asked. They all answered, "Crucify him!"
[23] "Why? What crime has he committed?" asked Pilate. But they shouted all the louder, "Crucify him!"
[24] When Pilate saw that he was getting nowhere, but that instead an uproar was starting, he took water and washed his hands in front of the crowd. "I am innocent of this man's blood," he said. "It is your responsibility!" [25] All the people answered, "His blood is on us and on our children!"
[26] Then he released Barabbas to them. But he had Jesus flogged, and handed him over to be crucified.

MARK

15:1 Very early in the morning, the chief priests, with the elders, the teachers of the law and the whole Sanhedrin, made their plans. So they bound Jesus, led him away and handed him over to Pilate.
[2] "Are you the king of the Jews?" asked Pilate. "You have said so," Jesus replied.
[3] The chief priests accused him of many things. [4] So again Pilate asked him, "Aren't you going to answer? See how many things they are accusing you of." [5] But Jesus still made no reply, and Pilate was amazed.
[6] Now it was the custom at the festival to release a prisoner whom the people requested. [7] A man called Barabbas was in prison with the insurrectionists who had committed murder in the uprising. [8] The crowd came up and asked Pilate to do for them what he usually did.
[9] "Do you want me to release to you the king of the Jews?" asked Pilate, [10] knowing it was out of self-interest that the chief priests had handed Jesus over to him. [11] But the chief priests stirred up the crowd to have Pilate release Barabbas instead.
[12] "What shall I do, then, with the one you call the king of the Jews?" Pilate asked them. [13] "Crucify him!" they shouted. [14] "Why? What crime has he committed?" asked Pilate. But they shouted all the louder, "Crucify him!"
[15] Wanting to satisfy the crowd, Pilate released Barabbas to them. He had Jesus flogged, and handed him over to be crucified.

LUKE

23:1 Then the whole assembly rose and led him off to Pilate. [2] And they began to accuse him, saying, "We have found this man subverting our nation. He opposes payment of taxes to Caesar and claims to be Messiah, a king."
[3] So Pilate asked Jesus, "Are you the king of the Jews?" "You have said so," Jesus replied.
[4] Then Pilate announced to the chief priests and the crowd, "I find no basis for a charge against this man." [5] But they insisted, "He stirs up the people all over Judea by his teaching. He started in Galilee and has come all the way here."
[6] On hearing this, Pilate asked if the man was a Galilean. [7] When he learned that Jesus was under Herod's

jurisdiction, he sent him to Herod, who was also in Jerusalem at that time.
⁸ When Herod saw Jesus, he was greatly pleased, because for a long time he had been wanting to see him. From what he had heard about him, he hoped to see him perform a sign of some sort. ⁹ He plied him with many questions, but Jesus gave him no answer. ¹⁰ The chief priests and the teachers of the law were standing there, vehemently accusing him. ¹¹ Then Herod and his soldiers ridiculed and mocked him. Dressing him in an elegant robe, they sent him back to Pilate. ¹² That day Herod and Pilate became friends—before this they had been enemies.
¹³ Pilate called together the chief priests, the rulers and the people, ¹⁴ and said to them, "You brought me this man as one who was inciting the people to rebellion. I have examined him in your presence and have found no basis for your charges against him. ¹⁵ Neither has Herod, for he sent him back to us; as you can see, he has done nothing to deserve death. ¹⁶ Therefore, I will punish him and then release him." [17]
¹⁸ But the whole crowd shouted, "Away with this man! Release Barabbas to us!" ¹⁹ (Barabbas had been thrown into prison for an insurrection in the city, and for murder.)
²⁰ Wanting to release Jesus, Pilate appealed to them again. ²¹ But they kept shouting, "Crucify him! Crucify him!"
²² For the third time he spoke to them: "Why? What crime has this man committed? I have found in him no grounds for the death penalty. Therefore I will have him punished and then release him."
²³ But with loud shouts they insistently demanded that he be crucified, and their shouts prevailed. ²⁴ So Pilate decided to grant their demand. ²⁵ He released the man who had been thrown into prison for insurrection and murder, the one they asked for, and surrendered Jesus to their will.

JOHN

18:28 Then the Jewish leaders took Jesus from Caiaphas to the palace of the Roman governor. By now it was early morning, and to avoid ceremonial uncleanness they did not enter the palace, because they wanted to be able to eat the Passover. ²⁹ So Pilate came out to them and asked, "What charges are you bringing against this man?"
³⁰ "If he were not a criminal," they replied, "we would not have handed him over to you." ³¹ Pilate said, "Take him yourselves and judge him by your own law." "But we have no right to execute anyone," they objected. ³² This took place to fulfill what Jesus had said about the kind of death he was going to die.
³³ Pilate then went back inside the palace, summoned Jesus and asked him, "Are you the king of the Jews?" ³⁴ "Is that your own idea," Jesus asked, "or did others talk to you about me?" ³⁵ "Am I a Jew?" Pilate replied. "Your own people and chief priests handed you over to me. What is it you have done?"
³⁶ Jesus said, "My kingdom is not of this world. If it were, my servants would fight to prevent my arrest by the Jewish leaders. But now my kingdom is from another place."
³⁷ "You are a king, then!" said Pilate. Jesus answered, "You say that I am a king. In fact, the reason I was born and came into the world is to testify to the truth. Everyone on the side of truth listens to me."
³⁸ "What is truth?" retorted Pilate. With this he went out again to the Jews gathered there and said, "I find no basis for a charge against him. ³⁹ But it is your custom for me to release to you one prisoner at the time of the Passover. Do you want me to release 'the king of the Jews'?" ⁴⁰ They shouted back, "No, not him! Give us Barabbas!" Now Barabbas had taken part in an uprising.
19:1 Then Pilate took Jesus and had him flogged. ² The soldiers twisted together a crown of thorns and put it on his head. They clothed him in a purple robe ³ and went up to him again and again, saying, "Hail, king of the Jews!" And they slapped him in the face.
⁴ Once more Pilate came out and said to the Jews gathered there, "Look, I am bringing him out to you to let you know that I find no basis for a charge against him." ⁵ When Jesus came out wearing the crown of thorns and the purple robe, Pilate said to them, "Here is the man!"
⁶ As soon as the chief priests and their officials saw him, they shouted, "Crucify! Crucify!" But Pilate answered, "You take him and crucify him. As for me, I find no basis for a charge against him."
⁷ The Jewish leaders insisted, "We have a law, and according to that law he must die, because he claimed to be the Son of God."
⁸ When Pilate heard this, he was even more afraid, ⁹ and he went back inside the palace. "Where do you come from?" he asked Jesus, but Jesus gave him no answer. ¹⁰ "Do you refuse to speak to me?" Pilate said. "Don't you realize I have power either to free you or to crucify you?" ¹¹ Jesus answered, "You would have no power over me if it were not given to you from above. Therefore the one who handed me over to you is guilty of a greater sin."
¹² From then on, Pilate tried to set Jesus free, but the Jewish leaders kept shouting, "If you let this man go, you are no friend of Caesar. Anyone who claims to be a king opposes Caesar." ¹³ When Pilate heard this, he brought Jesus

> out and sat down on the judge's seat at a place known as the Stone Pavement (which in Aramaic is Gabbatha). ¹⁴ It was the day of Preparation of the Passover; it was about noon.
> "Here is your king," Pilate said to the Jews. ¹⁵ But they shouted, "Take him away! Take him away! Crucify him!" "Shall I crucify your king?" Pilate asked. "We have no king but Caesar," the chief priests answered. ¹⁶ Finally Pilate handed him over to them to be crucified.

1. How do you suppose the dialogues between Jesus and Pilate were recorded and made it into the Gospels (in their several versions)?
2. Note Matthew 27:24-25 concerning responsibility for Jesus' death. This exchange does not appear in the other three Gospels. What do you make of it?
3. Compare the words of Jesus as reported in the four Gospel accounts.
4. Only Luke reports that Pilate suspended the trial and sent Jesus to Herod, only to have Herod send him back, all in the same day. What do you make of this? Does it seem plausible.?

14.0 Jesus is Crucified

MATTHEW
27:27 Then the governor's soldiers took Jesus into the Praetorium and gathered the whole company of soldiers around him. ²⁸ They stripped him and put a scarlet robe on him, ²⁹ and then twisted together a crown of thorns and set it on his head. They put a staff in his right hand. Then they knelt in front of him and mocked him. "Hail, king of the Jews!" they said. ³⁰ They spit on him, and took the staff and struck him on the head again and again. ³¹ After they had mocked him, they took off the robe and put his own clothes on him. Then they led him away to crucify him. ³² As they were going out, they met a man from Cyrene, named Simon, and they forced him to carry the cross. ³³ They came to a place called Golgotha (which means "the place of the skull"). ³⁴ There they offered Jesus wine to drink, mixed with gall; but after tasting it, he refused to drink it. ³⁵ When they had crucified him, they divided up his clothes by casting lots. ³⁶ And sitting down, they kept watch over him there. ³⁷ Above his head they placed the written charge against him: THIS IS JESUS, THE KING OF THE JEWS. ³⁸ Two rebels were crucified with him, one on his right and one on his left. ³⁹ Those who passed by hurled insults at him, shaking their heads ⁴⁰ and saying, "You who are going to destroy the temple and build it in three days, save yourself! Come down from the cross, if you are the Son of God!" ⁴¹ In the same way the chief priests, the teachers of the law and the elders mocked him. ⁴² "He saved others," they said, "but he can't save himself! He's the king of Israel! Let him come down now from the cross, and we will believe in him. ⁴³ He trusts in God. Let God rescue him now if he wants him, for he said, 'I am the Son of God.'" ⁴⁴ In the same way the rebels who were crucified with him also heaped insults on him.

MARK
15:16 The soldiers led Jesus away into the palace (that is, the Praetorium) and called together the whole company of soldiers. ¹⁷ They put a purple robe on him, then twisted together a crown of thorns and set it on him. ¹⁸ And they began to call out to him, "Hail, king of the Jews!" ¹⁹ Again and again they struck him on the head with a staff and spit on him. Falling on their knees, they paid homage to him. ²⁰ And when they had mocked him, they took off the purple robe and put his own clothes on him. Then they led him out to crucify him. ²¹ A certain man from Cyrene, Simon, the father of Alexander and Rufus, was passing by on his way in from the country, and they forced him to carry the cross. ²² They brought Jesus to the place called Golgotha (which means "the place of the skull"). ²³ Then they offered him wine mixed with myrrh, but he did not take it. ²⁴ And they crucified him. Dividing up his clothes, they cast lots to see what each would get. ²⁵ It was nine in the morning when they crucified him. ²⁶ The written notice of the charge against him read: THE KING OF THE JEWS. ²⁷ They crucified two rebels with him, one on his right and one on his left. [28] ²⁹ Those who passed by hurled insults at him, shaking their heads and saying, "So! You who are going to destroy the temple and build it in three days, ³⁰ come down from the cross and save yourself!" ³¹ In the same way the chief priests and the teachers of the law mocked him among themselves. "He saved others," they said, "but he can't save himself! ³² Let this Messiah, this king of Israel, come down now from the cross, that we may see and believe." Those crucified with him also heaped insults on him.

LUKE
23:26 As the soldiers led him away, they seized Simon from Cyrene, who was on his way in from the country, and put the cross on him and made him carry it behind Jesus. ²⁷ A large number of people followed him, including women who mourned and wailed for him. ²⁸ Jesus turned and said to them, "Daughters of Jerusalem, do not weep for me; weep for yourselves and for your children. ²⁹ For the time will come when you will say, 'Blessed are the childless women, the wombs that never bore and the breasts that never nursed!' ³⁰ Then "'they will say to the mountains, "Fall on us!" and to the hills, "Cover us!"' ³¹ For if people do these things when the tree is green, what will happen when it is dry?" ³² Two other men, both criminals, were also led out with him to be executed. ³³ When they came to the place called the Skull, they crucified him there, along with the criminals—one on his right, the other on his left. ³⁴ Jesus said,

"Father, forgive them, for they do not know what they are doing." And they divided up his clothes by casting lots. ³⁵ The people stood watching, and the rulers even sneered at him. They said, "He saved others; let him save himself if he is God's Messiah, the Chosen One."
³⁶ The soldiers also came up and mocked him. They offered him wine vinegar ³⁷ and said, "If you are the king of the Jews, save yourself."
³⁸ There was a written notice above him, which read: THIS IS THE KING OF THE JEWS.
³⁹ One of the criminals who hung there hurled insults at him: "Aren't you the Messiah? Save yourself and us!" ⁴⁰ But the other criminal rebuked him. "Don't you fear God," he said, "since you are under the same sentence? ⁴¹ We are punished justly, for we are getting what our deeds deserve. But this man has done nothing wrong."
⁴² Then he said, "Jesus, remember me when you come into your kingdom." ⁴³ Jesus answered him, "Truly I tell you, today you will be with me in paradise."

JOHN

19:16 So the soldiers took charge of Jesus. ¹⁷ Carrying his own cross, he went out to the place of the Skull (which in Aramaic is called Golgotha). ¹⁸ There they crucified him, and with him two others—one on each side and Jesus in the middle.
¹⁹ Pilate had a notice prepared and fastened to the cross. It read: JESUS OF NAZARETH, THE KING OF THE JEWS. ²⁰ Many of the Jews read this sign, for the place where Jesus was crucified was near the city, and the sign was written in Aramaic, Latin and Greek. ²¹ The chief priests of the Jews protested to Pilate, "Do not write 'The King of the Jews,' but that this man claimed to be king of the Jews." ²² Pilate answered, "What I have written, I have written."
²³ When the soldiers crucified Jesus, they took his clothes, dividing them into four shares, one for each of them, with the undergarment remaining. This garment was seamless, woven in one piece from top to bottom. ²⁴ "Let's not tear it," they said to one another. "Let's decide by lot who will get it." This happened that the scripture might be fulfilled that said, "They divided my clothes among them and cast lots for my garment." So this is what the soldiers did.
²⁵ Near the cross of Jesus stood his mother, his mother's sister, Mary the wife of Clopas, and Mary Magdalene.
²⁶ When Jesus saw his mother there, and the disciple whom he loved standing nearby, he said to her, "Woman, here is your son," ²⁷ and to the disciple, "Here is your mother." From that time on, this disciple took her into his home.

1. Compare the four accounts. Note particularly the words attributed to Jesus in each (if any), and to the men crucified with him.

14.p The Death of Jesus

MATTHEW

27:45 From noon until three in the afternoon darkness came over all the land. [46] About three in the afternoon Jesus cried out in a loud voice, *"Eli, Eli, lema sabachthani?"* (which means "My God, my God, why have you forsaken me?"). [47] When some of those standing there heard this, they said, "He's calling Elijah."
[48] Immediately one of them ran and got a sponge. He filled it with wine vinegar, put it on a staff, and offered it to Jesus to drink. [49] The rest said, "Now leave him alone. Let's see if Elijah comes to save him."
[50] And when Jesus had cried out again in a loud voice, he gave up his spirit.
[51] At that moment the curtain of the temple was torn in two from top to bottom. The earth shook, the rocks split
[52] and the tombs broke open. The bodies of many holy people who had died were raised to life. [53] They came out of the tombs after Jesus' resurrection and went into the holy city and appeared to many people.
[54] When the centurion and those with him who were guarding Jesus saw the earthquake and all that had happened, they were terrified, and exclaimed, "Surely he was the Son of God!"
[55] Many women were there, watching from a distance. They had followed Jesus from Galilee to care for his needs.
[56] Among them were Mary Magdalene, Mary the mother of James and Joseph, and the mother of Zebedee's sons.

MARK

15:33 At noon, darkness came over the whole land until three in the afternoon. [34] And at three in the afternoon Jesus cried out in a loud voice, *"Eloi, Eloi, lema sabachthani?"* (which means "My God, my God, why have you forsaken me?"). [35] When some of those standing near heard this, they said, "Listen, he's calling Elijah."
[36] Someone ran, filled a sponge with wine vinegar, put it on a staff, and offered it to Jesus to drink. "Now leave him alone. Let's see if Elijah comes to take him down," he said.
[37] With a loud cry, Jesus breathed his last.
[38] The curtain of the temple was torn in two from top to bottom. [39] And when the centurion, who stood there in front of Jesus, saw how he died, he said, "Surely this man was the Son of God!"
[40] Some women were watching from a distance. Among them were Mary Magdalene, Mary the mother of James the younger and of Joseph, and Salome. [41] In Galilee these women had followed him and cared for his needs. Many other women who had come up with him to Jerusalem were also there.

LUKE

23:44 It was now about noon, and darkness came over the whole land until three in the afternoon, [45] for the sun stopped shining. And the curtain of the temple was torn in two. [46] Jesus called out with a loud voice, "Father, into your hands I commit my spirit." When he had said this, he breathed his last.
[47] The centurion, seeing what had happened, praised God and said, "Surely this was a righteous man." [48] When all the people who had gathered to witness this sight saw what took place, they beat their breasts and went away. [49] But all those who knew him, including the women who had followed him from Galilee, stood at a distance, watching these things.

JOHN

19:28 Later, knowing that everything had now been finished, and so that Scripture would be fulfilled, Jesus said, "I am thirsty." [29] A jar of wine vinegar was there, so they soaked a sponge in it, put the sponge on a stalk of the hyssop plant, and lifted it to Jesus' lips. [30] When he had received the drink, Jesus said, "It is finished." With that, he bowed his head and gave up his spirit.
[31] Now it was the day of Preparation, and the next day was to be a special Sabbath. Because the Jewish leaders did not want the bodies left on the crosses during the Sabbath, they asked Pilate to have the legs broken and the bodies taken down. [32] The soldiers therefore came and broke the legs of the first man who had been crucified with Jesus, and then those of the other. [33] But when they came to Jesus and found that he was already dead, they did not break his legs.
[34] Instead, one of the soldiers pierced Jesus' side with a spear, bringing a sudden flow of blood and water. [35] The man

who saw it has given testimony, and his testimony is true. He knows that he tells the truth, and he testifies so that you also may believe. ³⁶ These things happened so that the scripture would be fulfilled: "Not one of his bones will be broken," ³⁷ and, as another scripture says, "They will look on the one they have pierced."

1. Compare each account's report of Jesus' last words; of the centurion's words.
2. According to the four accounts, who among Jesus' family and followers were on the scene?
3. Note John 19:35. Who was this man? What do you suppose his "testimony" is? Is it a document we know of?

14.q The Burial of Jesus

MATTHEW
27:57 As evening approached, there came a rich man from Arimathea, named Joseph, who had himself become a disciple of Jesus. [58] Going to Pilate, he asked for Jesus' body, and Pilate ordered that it be given to him. [59] Joseph took the body, wrapped it in a clean linen cloth, [60] and placed it in his own new tomb that he had cut out of the rock. He rolled a big stone in front of the entrance to the tomb and went away. [61] Mary Magdalene and the other Mary were sitting there opposite the tomb. [62] The next day, the one after Preparation Day, the chief priests and the Pharisees went to Pilate. [63] "Sir," they said, "we remember that while he was still alive that deceiver said, 'After three days I will rise again.' [64] So give the order for the tomb to be made secure until the third day. Otherwise, his disciples may come and steal the body and tell the people that he has been raised from the dead. This last deception will be worse than the first." [65] "Take a guard," Pilate answered. "Go, make the tomb as secure as you know how." [66] So they went and made the tomb secure by putting a seal on the stone and posting the guard.

MARK
15:42 It was Preparation Day (that is, the day before the Sabbath). So as evening approached, [43] Joseph of Arimathea, a prominent member of the Council, who was himself waiting for the kingdom of God, went boldly to Pilate and asked for Jesus' body. [44] Pilate was surprised to hear that he was already dead. Summoning the centurion, he asked him if Jesus had already died. [45] When he learned from the centurion that it was so, he gave the body to Joseph. [46] So Joseph bought some linen cloth, took down the body, wrapped it in the linen, and placed it in a tomb cut out of rock. Then he rolled a stone against the entrance of the tomb. [47] Mary Magdalene and Mary the mother of Joseph saw where he was laid.

LUKE
23:50 Now there was a man named Joseph, a member of the Council, a good and upright man, [51] who had not consented to their decision and action. He came from the Judean town of Arimathea, and he himself was waiting for the kingdom of God. [52] Going to Pilate, he asked for Jesus' body. [53] Then he took it down, wrapped it in linen cloth and placed it in a tomb cut in the rock, one in which no one had yet been laid. [54] It was Preparation Day, and the Sabbath was about to begin. [55] The women who had come with Jesus from Galilee followed Joseph and saw the tomb and how his body was laid in it. [56] Then they went home and prepared spices and perfumes. But they rested on the Sabbath in obedience to the commandment.

JOHN
19:38 Later, Joseph of Arimathea asked Pilate for the body of Jesus. Now Joseph was a disciple of Jesus, but secretly because he feared the Jewish leaders. With Pilate's permission, he came and took the body away. [39] He was accompanied by Nicodemus, the man who earlier had visited Jesus at night. Nicodemus brought a mixture of myrrh and aloes, about seventy-five pounds. [40] Taking Jesus' body, the two of them wrapped it, with the spices, in strips of linen. This was in accordance with Jewish burial customs. [41] At the place where Jesus was crucified, there was a garden, and in the garden a new tomb, in which no one had ever been laid. [42] Because it was the Jewish day of Preparation and since the tomb was nearby, they laid Jesus there.

1. Note how closely the Synoptic accounts resemble each other. Then consider John's account.

14.r The Empty Tomb

MATTHEW

28:1 After the Sabbath, at dawn on the first day of the week, Mary Magdalene and the other Mary went to look at the tomb.
² There was a violent earthquake, for an angel of the Lord came down from heaven and, going to the tomb, rolled back the stone and sat on it. ³ His appearance was like lightning, and his clothes were white as snow. ⁴ The guards were so afraid of him that they shook and became like dead men.
⁵ The angel said to the women, "Do not be afraid, for I know that you are looking for Jesus, who was crucified. ⁶ He is not here; he has risen, just as he said. Come and see the place where he lay. ⁷ Then go quickly and tell his disciples: 'He has risen from the dead and is going ahead of you into Galilee. There you will see him.' Now I have told you."
⁸ So the women hurried away from the tomb, afraid yet filled with joy, and ran to tell his disciples. ⁹ Suddenly Jesus met them. "Greetings," he said. They came to him, clasped his feet and worshiped him. ¹⁰ Then Jesus said to them, "Do not be afraid. Go and tell my brothers to go to Galilee; there they will see me."
¹¹ While the women were on their way, some of the guards went into the city and reported to the chief priests everything that had happened. ¹² When the chief priests had met with the elders and devised a plan, they gave the soldiers a large sum of money, ¹³ telling them, "You are to say, 'His disciples came during the night and stole him away while we were asleep.' ¹⁴ If this report gets to the governor, we will satisfy him and keep you out of trouble."
¹⁵ So the soldiers took the money and did as they were instructed. And this story has been widely circulated among the Jews to this very day.

MARK

16:1 When the Sabbath was over, Mary Magdalene, Mary the mother of James, and Salome bought spices so that they might go to anoint Jesus' body. ² Very early on the first day of the week, just after sunrise, they were on their way to the tomb ³ and they asked each other, "Who will roll the stone away from the entrance of the tomb?"
⁴ But when they looked up, they saw that the stone, which was very large, had been rolled away. ⁵ As they entered the tomb, they saw a young man dressed in a white robe sitting on the right side, and they were alarmed.
⁶ "Don't be alarmed," he said. "You are looking for Jesus the Nazarene, who was crucified. He has risen! He is not here. See the place where they laid him. ⁷ But go, tell his disciples and Peter, 'He is going ahead of you into Galilee. There you will see him, just as he told you.'"
⁸ Trembling and bewildered, the women went out and fled from the tomb. They said nothing to anyone, because they were afraid.

LUKE

24:1 On the first day of the week, very early in the morning, the women took the spices they had prepared and went to the tomb. ² They found the stone rolled away from the tomb, ³ but when they entered, they did not find the body of the Lord Jesus.
⁴ While they were wondering about this, suddenly two men in clothes that gleamed like lightning stood beside them.
⁵ In their fright the women bowed down with their faces to the ground, but the men said to them, "Why do you look for the living among the dead? ⁶ He is not here; he has risen! Remember how he told you, while he was still with you in Galilee: ⁷ 'The Son of Man must be delivered over to the hands of sinners, be crucified and on the third day be raised again.' " ⁸ Then they remembered his words.
⁹ When they came back from the tomb, they told all these things to the Eleven and to all the others. ¹⁰ It was Mary Magdalene, Joanna, Mary the mother of James, and the others with them who told this to the apostles. ¹¹ But they did not believe the women, because their words seemed to them like nonsense. ¹² Peter, however, got up and ran to the tomb. Bending over, he saw the strips of linen lying by themselves, and he went away, wondering to himself what had happened.

JOHN

20:1 Early on the first day of the week, while it was still dark, Mary Magdalene went to the tomb and saw that the stone had been removed from the entrance. ² So she came running to Simon Peter and the other disciple, the one Jesus loved, and said, "They have taken the Lord out of the tomb, and we don't know where they have put him!" ³ So Peter and the other disciple started for the tomb. ⁴ Both were running, but the other disciple outran Peter and reached the tomb first. ⁵ He bent over and looked in at the strips of linen lying there but did not go in. ⁶ Then Simon Peter came along behind him and went straight into the tomb. He saw the strips of linen lying there, ⁷ as well as the cloth that had been wrapped around Jesus' head. The cloth was still lying in its place, separate from the linen. ⁸ Finally the other disciple, who had reached the tomb first, also went inside. He saw and believed. ⁹ (They still did not understand from Scripture that Jesus had to rise from the dead.) ¹⁰ Then the disciples went back to where they were staying.

1. Compare the four accounts, specifically:
    a. Who went to the tomb first thing in the morning?
    b. What did they find?
    c. Whom did they encounter there? What were they told to do?
    d. What did they do then?
    e. What did the disciples do when they heard about the empty tomb?
2. In John's account, "the other disciple, the one Jesus loved" ran to the tomb with Peter. Does this connect with John 19:35?
3. Originally, Mark's Gospel appears to have ended abruptly at this point (Mark 16:8). If the first Gospel in fact ended here, what elements of the story as we know it did Mark omit? Why would he have done so?
4. In considering the abrupt ending of Mark, don't neglect simple possibilities such as a key early manuscript losing its last pages, or Mark being interrupted and never finishing his account. But the phrase "they said nothing to anyone" echoes Jesus' instructions to the healed leper in Mark 1:44; does that put any different light on the question?

14.s The Post-Resurrection Appearances

MATTHEW
28:16 Then the eleven disciples went to Galilee, to the mountain where Jesus had told them to go. [17] When they saw him, they worshiped him; but some doubted. [18] Then Jesus came to them and said, "All authority in heaven and on earth has been given to me. [19] Therefore go and make disciples of all nations, baptizing them in the name of the Father and of the Son and of the Holy Spirit, [20] and teaching them to obey everything I have commanded you. And surely I am with you always, to the very end of the age."

MARK
16:9 (the following passage is absent from the earliest manuscripts) When Jesus rose early on the first day of the week, he appeared first to Mary Magdalene, out of whom he had driven seven demons. [10] She went and told those who had been with him and who were mourning and weeping. [11] When they heard that Jesus was alive and that she had seen him, they did not believe it. [12] Afterward Jesus appeared in a different form to two of them while they were walking in the country. [13] These returned and reported it to the rest; but they did not believe them either. [14] Later Jesus appeared to the Eleven as they were eating; he rebuked them for their lack of faith and their stubborn refusal to believe those who had seen him after he had risen. [15] He said to them, "Go into all the world and preach the gospel to all creation. [16] Whoever believes and is baptized will be saved, but whoever does not believe will be condemned. [17] And these signs will accompany those who believe: In my name they will drive out demons; they will speak in new tongues; [18] they will pick up snakes with their hands; and when they drink deadly poison, it will not hurt them at all; they will place their hands on sick people, and they will get well." [19] After the Lord Jesus had spoken to them, he was taken up into heaven and he sat at the right hand of God. [20] Then the disciples went out and preached everywhere, and the Lord worked with them and confirmed his word by the signs that accompanied it.

LUKE
24:13 Now that same day two of them were going to a village called Emmaus, about seven miles from Jerusalem. [14] They were talking with each other about everything that had happened. [15] As they talked and discussed these things with each other, Jesus himself came up and walked along with them; [16] but they were kept from recognizing him. [17] He asked them, "What are you discussing together as you walk along?" They stood still, their faces downcast. [18] One of them, named Cleopas, asked him, "Are you the only one visiting Jerusalem who does not know the things that have happened there in these days?" [19] "What things?" he asked. "About Jesus of Nazareth," they replied. "He was a prophet, powerful in word and deed before God and all the people. [20] The chief priests and our rulers handed him over to be sentenced to death, and they crucified him; [21] but we had hoped that he was the one who was going to redeem Israel. And what is more, it is the third day since all this took place. [22] In addition, some of our women amazed us. They went to the tomb early this morning [23] but didn't find his body. They came and told us that they had seen a vision of angels, who said he was alive. [24] Then some of our companions went to the tomb and found it just as the women had said, but they did not see Jesus." [25] He said to them, "How foolish you are, and how slow to believe all that the prophets have spoken! [26] Did not the Messiah have to suffer these things and then enter his glory?" [27] And beginning with Moses and all the Prophets, he explained to them what was said in all the Scriptures concerning himself. [28] As they approached the village to which they were going, Jesus continued on as if he were going farther. [29] But they urged him strongly, "Stay with us, for it is nearly evening; the day is almost over." So he went in to stay with them. [30] When he was at the table with them, he took bread, gave thanks, broke it and began to give it to them. [31] Then their eyes were opened and they recognized him, and he disappeared from their sight. [32] They asked each other, "Were not our hearts burning within us while he talked with us on the road and opened the Scriptures to us?"

³³ They got up and returned at once to Jerusalem. There they found the Eleven and those with them, assembled together ³⁴ and saying, "It is true! The Lord has risen and has appeared to Simon." ³⁵ Then the two told what had happened on the way, and how Jesus was recognized by them when he broke the bread.

³⁶ While they were still talking about this, Jesus himself stood among them and said to them, "Peace be with you."

³⁷ They were startled and frightened, thinking they saw a ghost. ³⁸ He said to them, "Why are you troubled, and why do doubts rise in your minds? ³⁹ Look at my hands and my feet. It is I myself! Touch me and see; a ghost does not have flesh and bones, as you see I have."

⁴⁰ When he had said this, he showed them his hands and feet. ⁴¹ And while they still did not believe it because of joy and amazement, he asked them, "Do you have anything here to eat?" ⁴² They gave him a piece of broiled fish, ⁴³ and he took it and ate it in their presence.

⁴⁴ He said to them, "This is what I told you while I was still with you: Everything must be fulfilled that is written about me in the Law of Moses, the Prophets and the Psalms."

⁴⁵ Then he opened their minds so they could understand the Scriptures. ⁴⁶ He told them, "This is what is written: The Messiah will suffer and rise from the dead on the third day, ⁴⁷ and repentance for the forgiveness of sins will be preached in his name to all nations, beginning at Jerusalem. ⁴⁸ You are witnesses of these things. ⁴⁹ I am going to send you what my Father has promised; but stay in the city until you have been clothed with power from on high."

⁵⁰ When he had led them out to the vicinity of Bethany, he lifted up his hands and blessed them. ⁵¹ While he was blessing them, he left them and was taken up into heaven. ⁵² Then they worshiped him and returned to Jerusalem with great joy. ⁵³ And they stayed continually at the temple, praising God.

* * *

Acts 1:1 In my former book, Theophilus, I wrote about all that Jesus began to do and to teach ² until the day he was taken up to heaven, after giving instructions through the Holy Spirit to the apostles he had chosen. ³ After his suffering, he presented himself to them and gave many convincing proofs that he was alive. He appeared to them over a period of forty days and spoke about the kingdom of God. ⁴ On one occasion, while he was eating with them, he gave them this command: "Do not leave Jerusalem, but wait for the gift my Father promised, which you have heard me speak about. ⁵ For John baptized with water, but in a few days you will be baptized with the Holy Spirit."

⁶ Then they gathered around him and asked him, "Lord, are you at this time going to restore the kingdom to Israel?"

⁷ He said to them: "It is not for you to know the times or dates the Father has set by his own authority. ⁸ But you will receive power when the Holy Spirit comes on you; and you will be my witnesses in Jerusalem, and in all Judea and Samaria, and to the ends of the earth."

⁹ After he said this, he was taken up before their very eyes, and a cloud hid him from their sight.

¹⁰ They were looking intently up into the sky as he was going, when suddenly two men dressed in white stood beside them. ¹¹ "Men of Galilee," they said, "why do you stand here looking into the sky? This same Jesus, who has been taken from you into heaven, will come back in the same way you have seen him go into heaven."

JOHN

20:11 Now Mary stood outside the tomb crying. As she wept, she bent over to look into the tomb ¹² and saw two angels in white, seated where Jesus' body had been, one at the head and the other at the foot.

¹³ They asked her, "Woman, why are you crying?" "They have taken my Lord away," she said, "and I don't know where they have put him." ¹⁴ At this, she turned around and saw Jesus standing there, but she did not realize that it was Jesus.

¹⁵ He asked her, "Woman, why are you crying? Who is it you are looking for?" Thinking he was the gardener, she said, "Sir, if you have carried him away, tell me where you have put him, and I will get him."

¹⁶ Jesus said to her, "Mary." She turned toward him and cried out in Aramaic, "Rabboni!" (which means "Teacher").

¹⁷ Jesus said, "Do not hold on to me, for I have not yet ascended to the Father. Go instead to my brothers and tell them, 'I am ascending to my Father and your Father, to my God and your God.'"

¹⁸ Mary Magdalene went to the disciples with the news: "I have seen the Lord!" And she told them that he had said these things to her.

¹⁹ On the evening of that first day of the week, when the disciples were together, with the doors locked for fear of the Jewish leaders, Jesus came and stood among them and said, "Peace be with you!" ²⁰ After he said this, he showed them his hands and side. The disciples were overjoyed when they saw the Lord.

²¹ Again Jesus said, "Peace be with you! As the Father has sent me, I am sending you." ²² And with that he breathed on them and said, "Receive the Holy Spirit. ²³ If you forgive anyone's sins, their sins are forgiven; if you do not

forgive them, they are not forgiven."

²⁴ Now Thomas (also known as Didymus), one of the Twelve, was not with the disciples when Jesus came. ²⁵ So the other disciples told him, "We have seen the Lord!" But he said to them, "Unless I see the nail marks in his hands and put my finger where the nails were, and put my hand into his side, I will not believe."

²⁶ A week later his disciples were in the house again, and Thomas was with them. Though the doors were locked, Jesus came and stood among them and said, "Peace be with you!" ²⁷ Then he said to Thomas, "Put your finger here; see my hands. Reach out your hand and put it into my side. Stop doubting and believe." ²⁸ Thomas said to him, "My Lord and my God!" ²⁹ Then Jesus told him, "Because you have seen me, you have believed; blessed are those who have not seen and yet have believed."

³⁰ Jesus performed many other signs in the presence of his disciples, which are not recorded in this book. ³¹ But these are written that you may believe that Jesus is the Messiah, the Son of God, and that by believing you may have life in his name.

21:1 Afterward Jesus appeared again to his disciples, by the Sea of Galilee. It happened this way: ² Simon Peter, Thomas (also known as Didymus), Nathanael from Cana in Galilee, the sons of Zebedee, and two other disciples were together. ³ "I'm going out to fish," Simon Peter told them, and they said, "We'll go with you." So they went out and got into the boat, but that night they caught nothing.

⁴ Early in the morning, Jesus stood on the shore, but the disciples did not realize that it was Jesus. ⁵ He called out to them, "Friends, haven't you any fish?" "No," they answered. ⁶ He said, "Throw your net on the right side of the boat and you will find some." When they did, they were unable to haul the net in because of the large number of fish.

⁷ Then the disciple whom Jesus loved said to Peter, "It is the Lord!" As soon as Simon Peter heard him say, "It is the Lord," he wrapped his outer garment around him (for he had taken it off) and jumped into the water. ⁸ The other disciples followed in the boat, towing the net full of fish, for they were not far from shore, about a hundred yards.

⁹ When they landed, they saw a fire of burning coals there with fish on it, and some bread.

¹⁰ Jesus said to them, "Bring some of the fish you have just caught." ¹¹ So Simon Peter climbed back into the boat and dragged the net ashore. It was full of large fish, 153, but even with so many the net was not torn. ¹² Jesus said to them, "Come and have breakfast." None of the disciples dared ask him, "Who are you?" They knew it was the Lord.

¹³ Jesus came, took the bread and gave it to them, and did the same with the fish. ¹⁴ This was now the third time Jesus appeared to his disciples after he was raised from the dead.

¹⁵ When they had finished eating, Jesus said to Simon Peter, "Simon son of John, do you love me more than these?" "Yes, Lord," he said, "you know that I love you." Jesus said, "Feed my lambs."

¹⁶ Again Jesus said, "Simon son of John, do you love me?" He answered, "Yes, Lord, you know that I love you." Jesus said, "Take care of my sheep."

¹⁷ The third time he said to him, "Simon son of John, do you love me?" Peter was hurt because Jesus asked him the third time, "Do you love me?" He said, "Lord, you know all things; you know that I love you." Jesus said, "Feed my sheep.

¹⁸ Very truly I tell you, when you were younger you dressed yourself and went where you wanted; but when you are old you will stretch out your hands, and someone else will dress you and lead you where you do not want to go."

¹⁹ Jesus said this to indicate the kind of death by which Peter would glorify God. Then he said to him, "Follow me!"

²⁰ Peter turned and saw that the disciple whom Jesus loved was following them. (This was the one who had leaned back against Jesus at the supper and had said, "Lord, who is going to betray you?") ²¹ When Peter saw him, he asked, "Lord, what about him?"

²² Jesus answered, "If I want him to remain alive until I return, what is that to you? You must follow me." ²³ Because of this, the rumor spread among the believers that this disciple would not die. But Jesus did not say that he would not die; he only said, "If I want him to remain alive until I return, what is that to you?"

²⁴ This is the disciple who testifies to these things and who wrote them down. We know that his testimony is true.

²⁵ Jesus did many other things as well. If every one of them were written down, I suppose that even the whole world would not have room for the books that would be written.

1. Note the wide divergences in the four sets of post-Resurrection appearances of Jesus:
    a. How long after the Resurrection did Jesus' appearances continue, in each account?
    b. To whom did Jesus appear in each?
    c. Where (Jerusalem, Galilee, elsewhere) did each appearance take place?

      d. What messages or commands did Jesus convey in each?
2. Why do you suppose verses 9-20 were added to Mark 16 at a later date (probably in the 2nd or 3rd century)?
3. John 20:30-31 reads as if it were originally the end of this Gospel, yet there then follows another chapter (which itself is reminiscent of Luke 5:1-10). What do you make of this ending to John?
4. How many versions of the Great Commission can you identify?
5. Among all of the facts of Jesus' time on earth, it would seem that the post-Resurrection appearances would have been the most carefully recorded. Yet the four Gospels vary widely. What are we to make of this?
6. Paul has a pertinent passage in 1 Corinthians 15 that should be considered in any comparison of scriptural descriptions of the post-Resurrection appearances of Jesus. Keep in mind that Paul wrote this in about 54-55 A.D. – before any of the Gospels were written – and was reporting what he had heard directly from the apostles and others in Jerusalem who personally attested to having seen the risen Christ:

> 15:3 For what I received I passed on to you as of first importance: that Christ died for our sins according to the Scriptures, ^{4} that he was buried, that he was raised on the third day according to the Scriptures, ^{5} and that he appeared to Cephas, and then to the Twelve. ^{6} After that, he appeared to more than five hundred of the brothers and sisters at the same time, most of whom are still living, though some have fallen asleep. ^{7} Then he appeared to James, then to all the apostles, ^{8} and last of all he appeared to me also, as to one abnormally born.

Index 1: Contents of Each Parallel Set

Set	Matthew	Mark	Luke	John
1.a Gospel Prologues	1:1	1:1-8	1:1-4	1:1-14
1.b Genealogies	1:1-17		3:23-38	
2.a Announcements	1:18-25		1:26-56	
2.b Nativity	1:24-25, 2:1-12		2:1-21	
2.c Jesus Boyhood	2:13-23		2:39-52	
3.a John the Baptist	3:1-12	1:1-8	1:57-80, 3:1-20	1:6-8, 1:19-28
3.b Jesus & John	11:2-19	1:6-7	7:18-35, 16:16	3:22-33
3.c John's Death	14:6-12	6:17-29	3:19-20	
4.a Baptism of Jesus	3:13-17	1:9-11	3:21-22	1:29-34
4.b Early Ministry	3:12-17	1:14-15	4:14-30	4:1-3, 4:43-45
4.c Wilderness	4:1-11	1:12-13	4:1-13	
5.a First Disciples	4:18-22	1:16-20	5:1-11	1:35-51
5.b Matthew/Levi	9:9-13	2:13-17	5:27-32	
5.c Disciple Names	10:2-4	3:13-19	6:12-16, Acts 1:12-14	1:40-45, 6:70-71, 11:1-3, 14:22, 19:26-27, 20:1-2, 20:24, 21:20-24
5.d Disciples Sent Out	10:5-20, 10:40-42	6:6-13	9:1-6, 10:1-24	15:18-20
5.e Persecution	10:16-33	13:9-13	21:12-19	15:18-27, 16:1-7
5.f Discipleship Costs	8:18-22, 10:34-39, 16:24-27, 19:25-30	8:34-38, 10:26-31	9:23-26, 9:57-62, 12:4-7, 12:11-12, 12:49-53, 14:25-33, 18:26-30	6:60-69, 12:25-26, 15:18-21
5.g Greatest Disciple	18:1-5	9:33-37	9:46-48	13:20
5.h Death of Judas	27:3-10		Acts 1:18-19	
6.a Healings	4:23-25, 8:14-17, 9:35-38, 10:1	1:29-34	4:38-41	6:1-2, 9:1-7
6.b Healing Leper	8:1-4	1:40-45	5:12-16	
6.c Centurion	8:5-13		7:1-10	4:46-53
6.d Pick Up Your Mat	9:1-8	2:1-12	5:17-26	5:1-15
6.e Resuscitations	9:18-26	5:21-43	8:40-56	11:1-4, 11:38-44

Set	Matthew	Mark	Luke	John
6.f Healing the Blind	9:27-31, 20:29-34	10:46-52	18:35-43	9:1-33
6.g Shriveled Hand	12:9-14	3:1-6	6:6-11	5:16-17
6.h Gennesaret	14:34-36	6:53-56		
7.a Demon	4:23-25	1:23-28	4:33-37	
7.b Gerasene Swine	8:28-34	5:1-20	8:26-39	
7.c Demons	9:32-34, 12:22-29	3:20-35	11:14-28	
7.d Girl with Demon	15:21-28	7:24-30	6:17-19	
7.e Boy with Demon	17:14-20	9:14-29	9:37-43	
7.f Other Demons		9:38-41	8:1-3, 9:49-50	
8.a Calms the Storm	8:23-27	4:35-41	8:22-25	
8.b Big Catch of Fish	13:47-50		5:1-11	21:1-14
8.c Feeding 5,000	14:13-21	6:30-44	9:10-17	6:1-15
8.d Walking on Water	14:22-33	6:45-52	8:22-25	6:16-21
8.e Feeding 4,000	15:29-39	8:1-10, 8:19-20		
9.a About Parables	13:10-17, 13:34-35	4:10-12, 4:33-34	8:9-10	10:1-6
9.b The Sower	13:1-9, 13:18-23	4:1-9, 4:13-20	8:4-8, 8:11-15	4:34-38
9.c Mustard Seed	13:31-32	4:30-32	13:18-19, 17:5-6	
9.d Yeast	13:33	8:14-21	13:20-21	6:31-35
9.e Lost Sheep	18:10-14	6:34, 14:27	15:1-7	10:21-30
9.f Two Sons	21:33-46	12:1-12	20:9-19	
9.g Banquet	22:1-14		14:15-24	
9.h Talents	25:14-30		19:11-27	
10.a Beatitudes	5:1-12		6:17-23	
10.b Salt	5:13	9:49-50	14:34-35	
10.c Grievances	5:21-26	11:25	12:57-59	
10.d Temptation	5:27-30, 18:6-9	9:42-48	17:1-3	

Set	Matthew	Mark	Luke	John
10.e Divorce	5:31-32, 19:3-9	10:2-12	16:18	
10.f Love Enemies	5:38-48		6:27-36	
10.g Lord's Prayer	6:9-13		11:1-4	
10.h Forgiveness	6:14-15, 18:21-35	11:25	6:37, 17:3-4	
10.i Treasure	6:19-21	10:21	12:13-21, 12:32-34	
10.j Two Masters	6:24		16:13-15	
10.k Worry	6:25-34		12:22-34	
10.l Do Not Judge	7:1-5	4:24-25	6:37-38, 6:41-42	8:2-11
10.m Prayer	7:7-11, 18:19-20	11:22-25	11:5-13, 18:1-8	16:23-27
10.n Do Unto Others	7:12		6:27-36	
10.o Narrow Gate	7:13-14		13:22-30	10:1-10
10.p Rock	7:24-27		6:46-49	
10.q Fasting	9:14-17	2:18-22	5:33-39	
10.r Defilement	15:1-20	7:1-23	11:37-41	
10.s Sin	18:15-17	11:25	17:3-4	20:23
10.t Children	19:13-15	10:13-16	18:15-17	
10.u Needle's Eye	19:16-26	10:17-27	18:18-27	
10.v Render unto Caesar	22:15-22	12:13-17	20:20-26	
10.w Marriage	22:23-33	12:18-27	20:27-40	
10.x Commandments	22:34-40	12:28-34	10:25-28	
10.y Widow's Mite		12:41-44	21:1-4	
11.a Fruit	7:15-23, 12:33-37		6:43-45	15:1-8
11.b Sign of Jonah	12:38-42, 16:1-4		11:29-32	
11.c Pharisees	16:5-12	8:14-21	12:1-3	
11.d Cleansing Temple	21:12-17	11:15-19	19:45-46	2:13-22
11.e Fig Tree	21:18-22	11:12-14, 11:20-24	13:6-9	

Set	Matthew	Mark	Luke	John
11.f Woe to Pharisees	23:1-36	12:38-40	11:42-54, 18:9-14, 20:45-47	9:40-41, 10:1-6
12.a Father Knows	16:28, 24:34-36	9:1, 13:30-34	9:27, 21:32-33	
12.b Temple	24:1-3	13:1-2	21:5-6	2:18-22
12.c Deception	24:4-8	13:5-8	21:7-11, 21:20-24	
12.d Persecution	24:9-14	13:9-13	21:12-19	
12.e Hurry	24:15-21	13:14-19	17:30-35	
12.f False Messiahs	24:22-25	13:20-23	17:20-25	
12.g Keep Watch	24:26-28, 24:42-44, 25:1-13	13:35-37	21:34-36	
12.h Son of Man	24:29-31	13:24-27	21:25-28	5:24-30
12.i Fig Tree	24:32-33	13:28-29	21:29-31	
12.j Days of Noah	24:37-41		17:26-29	
13.a Fulfillment of Law	4:16-21, 5:17-20		16:16-17, 24:44	
13.b Light	5:14-16, 6:22-23	4:21-23	8:16-18, 11:33-36	1:4-9, 3:19-21, 5:35, 8:12, 9:4-5, 12:35-36, 12:46
13.c Authority	7:28-29	1:21-22	4:31-32	5:16-23, 7:28-29, 14:10
13.d Messiah	11:2-10, 16:15-20, 24:4-5, 26:63-64	8:29-30, 9:41, 13:21-27, 14:61-62	4:41, 9:20-22, 22:67-70, 24:26-27, 24:45-48	10:24-30
13.e Father & Son	11:27	13:32, 14:36	10:22	3:34-36, 7:28-29, 10:14-18, 13:3, 17:1-5, 17:24-26
13.f Lord of Sabbath	12:1-8	2:23-28	6:1-5	5:8-11, 5:16-18, 7:23-24
13.g Isaiah	12:15-21	1:1-3	4:14-21	12:37-41
13.h Unforgiveable Sin	12:30-32	3:28-29	12:8-10	
13.i Giving Signs	12:38-39, 16:1-4	8:11-13, 16:15-18	11:16, 11:29, 23:8-9	2:11, 2:18-19, 2:23, 3:1-2, 4:48-54, 6:1-2, 6:14, 6:26-32, 7:30-31, 9:16, 11:47-48, 12:17-18, 12:37, 20:30
13.j Mothers, Brothers	12:46-50	3:31-35	8:19-21	
13.k Home Town	13:53-58	6:1-6	4:14-30	4:43-45
13.l Who Do You Say?	16:13-20	8:27-30	9:18-21	4:9-26, 6:35-46
13.m Transfiguration	17:1-13	9:2-13	9:28-36	

Set	Matthew	Mark	Luke	John
13.n Came to Serve	20:20-28	10:35-45	22:24-30	12:26
13.o Authority	21:23-27	11:27-33	20:1-8	2:18-25
13.p David's Son	22:41-46	12:35-37	20:41-44	7:40-44
14.a Death Predictions	9:22-23, 16:21-23, 20:17-19	8:31-33, 9:30-32, 10:32-34	9:22, 9:43-45, 18:31-34	10:14-18, 12:7-8, 12:20-36
14.b Jerusalem Entry	21:1-11	11:1-11	19:28-44	2:13, 12:12-19
14.c Lament	23:37-39		13:31-35	
14.d Plotting	26:1-5	14:1-2	19:47-48, 22:1-6	11:45-54
14.e Anointed	26:6-13	14:3-9	7:36-50	12:1-8
14.f Judas	26:14-16	14:10-11	22:1-6	6:70-71, 13:2, 13:21-30
14.g What Day?	26:17-20, 27:62-64	14:12-17, 15:42-47	22:7-16, 23:50-54	19:13-14, 19:30-31, 19:38-42
14.h Last Supper	26:17-30	14:12-26	22:7-23	6:47-59, 13:1-38, 14:1-31
14.i Predicting Denials	26:31-35	14:27-31	22:31-34	13:36-38
14.j Gethsemane	26:36-46	14:32-42	22:39-46	18:1-3
14.k Arrested	26:47-56	14:43-52	22:35-37, 22:47-53	18:1-14
14.l Sanhedrin Trial	26:57-68	14:53-65	22:54, 22:63-71	18:12-14, 18:19-24
14.m Peter's Denials	26:69-75	14:66-72	22:54-62	18:15-18, 18:25-27
14.n Before Pilate	27:1-2, 27:11-26	15:1-15	23:1-25	18:28-40, 19:1-16
14.o Crucifixion	27:27-44	15:16-32	23:26-43	19:16-27
14.p Death	27:45-56	15:33-41	23:44-49	19:28-37
14.q Burial	27:57-66	15:42-47	23:50-56	19:38-42
14.r Empty Tomb	28:1-15	16:1-8	24:1-12	20:1-10
14.s Post-Resurrection	28:16-20	16:9-20	24:13-53, Acts 1:1-11	20:11-31, 21:1-25

Index 2: Individual Passages

Matthew	Set	Matthew	Set	Matthew	Set	Matthew	Set
1:1	1.a	8:18-22	5.f	14:6-12	3.c	22:34-40	10.x
1:1-17	1.b	8:23-27	8.a	14:13-21	8.c	22:41-46	13.p
1:18-25	2.a	8:28-34	7.b	14:22-33	8.d	23:1-36	11.f
1:24-25	2.b	9:1-8	6.d	14:34-36	6.h	23:37-39	14.c
2:1-12	2.b	9:9-13	5.b	15:1-20	10.r	24:1-3	12.b
2:13-23	2.c	9:14-17	10.q	15:21-28	7.d	24:4-5	13.d
3:1-12	3.a	9:18-26	6.e	15:29-39	8.e	24:4-8	12.c
3:12-17	4.b	9:22-23	14.a	16:1-4	11.b, 13.i	24:9-14	12.d
3:13-17	4.a	9:27-31	6.f	16:5-12	11.c	24:15-21	12.e
4:1-11	4.c	9:32-34	7.c	16:13-20	13.l	24:22-25	12.f
4:16-21	13.a	9:35-38	6.a	16:15-20	13.d	24:26-28	12.g
4:18-22	5.a	10:1	6.a	16:21-23	14.a	24:29-31	12.h
4:23-25	6.a, 7.a	10:2-4	5.c	16:24-27	5.f	24:32-33	12.i
5:1-12	10.a	10:5-20	5.d	16:28	12.a	24:34-36	12.a
5:13	10.b	10:16-33	5.e	17:1-13	13.m	24:37-41	12.j
5:14-16	13.b	10:34-39	5.f	17:14-20	7.e	24:42-44	12.g
5:17-20	13.a	10:40-42	5.d	18:1-5	5.g	25:1-13	12.g
5:21-26	10.c	11:2-10	13.d	18:6-9	10.d	25:14-30	9.h
5:27-30	10.d	11:2-19	3.b	18:10-14	9.e	26:1-5	14.d
5:31-32	10.e	11:27	13.e	18:15-17	10.s	26:6-13	14.e
5:38-48	10.f	12:1-8	13.f	18:19-20	10.m	26:14-16	14.f
6:9-13	10.g	12:9-14	6.g	18:21-35	10.h	26:17-20	14.g
6:14-15	10.h	12:15-21	13.g	19:3-9	10.e	26:17-30	14.h
6:19-21	10.i	12:22-29	7.c	19:13-15	10.t	26:31-35	14.i
6:22-23	13.b	12:30-32	13.h	19:16-26	10.u	26:36-46	14.j
6:24	10.j	12:33-37	11.a	19:25-30	5.f	26:47-56	14.k
6:25-34	10.k	12:38-39	13.i	20:17-19	14.a	26:57-68	14.l
7:1-5	10.l	12:38-42	11.b	20:20-28	13.n	26:63-64	13.d
7:7-11	10.m	12:46-50	13.j	20:29-34	6.f	26:69-75	14.m
7:12	10.n	13:1-9	9.b	21:1-11	14.b	27:1-2	14.n
7:13-14	10.o	13:10-17	9.a	21:12-17	11.d	27:3-10	5.h
7:15-23	11.a	13:18-23	9.b	21:18-22	11.e	27:11-26	14.n
7:24-27	10.p	13:31-32	9.c	21:23-27	13.o	27:27-44	14.o
7:28-29	13.c	13:33	9.d	21:33-46	9.f	27:45-56	14.p
8:1-4	6.b	13:34-35	9.a	22:1-14	9.g	27:57-66	14.q
8:5-13	6.c	13:47-50	8.b	22:15-22	10.v	27:62-64	14.g
8:14-17	6.a	13:53-58	13.k	22:23-33	10.w	28:1-15	14.r
						28:16-20	14.s

Mark	Set	Mark	Set	Mark	Set	Mark	Set
1:1-3	13.g	6:53-56	6.h	12:13-17	10.v	16:15-18	13.i
1:1-8	1.a, 3.a	7:1-23	10.r	12:18-27	10.w		
1:6-7	3.b	7:24-30	7.d	12:28-34	10.x		
1:9-11	4.a	8:1-10	8.e	12:35-37	13.p		
1:12-13	4.c	8:11-13	13.i	12:38-40	11.f		
1:14-15	4.b	8:14-21	9.d, 11.c	12:41-44	10.y		
1:16-20	5.a	8:19-20	8.e	13:1-2	12.b		
1:21-22	13.c	8:27-30	13.l	13:5-8	12.c		
1:23-28	7.a	8:29-30	13.d	13:9-13	5.e, 12.d		
1:29-34	6.a	8:31-33	14.a	13:14-19	12.e		
1:40-45	6.b	8:34-38	5.f	13:20-23	12.f		
2:1-12	6.d	9:1	12.a	13:21-27	13.d		
2:13-17	5.b	9:2-13	13.m	13:24-27	12.h		
2:18-22	10.q	9:14-29	7.e	13:28-29	12.i		
2:23-28	13.f	9:30-32	14.a	13:30-34	12.a		
3:1-6	6.g	9:33-37	5.g	13:32	13.e		
3:13-19	5.c	9:38-41	7.f	13:35-37	12.g		
3:20-35	7.c	9:41	13.d	14:1-2	14.d		
3:28-29	13.h	9:42-48	10.d	14:3-9	14.e		
3:31-35	13.j	9:49-50	10.b	14:10-11	14.f		
4:1-9	9.b	10:2-12	10.e	14:12-17	14.g		
4:10-12	9.a	10:13-16	10.t	14:12-26	14.h		
4:13-20	9.b	10:17-27	10.u	14:27	9.e		
4:21-23	13.b	10:21	10.i	14:27-31	14.i		
4:24-25	10.l	10:26-31	5.f	14:32-42	14.j		
4:30-32	9.c	10:32-34	14.a	14:36	13.e		
4:33-34	9.a	10:35-45	13.n	14:43-52	14.k		
4:35-41	8.a	10:46-52	6.f	14:53-65	14.l		
5:1-20	7.b	11:1-11	14.b	14:61-62	13.d		
5:21-43	6.e	11:12-14	11.e	14:66-72	14.m		
6:1-6	13.k	11:15-19	11.d	15:1-15	14.n		
6:6-13	5.d	11:20-24	11.e	15:16-32	14.o		
6:17-29	3.c	11:22-25	10.m	15:33-41	14.p		
6:30-44	8.c	11:25	10.c, h, s	15:42-47	14.g, q		
6:34	9.e	11:27-33	13.o	16:1-8	14.r		
6:45-52	8.d	12:1-12	9.f	16:9-20	14.s		

Luke	Set	Luke	Set	Luke	Set	Luke	Set
1:1-4	1.a	8:9-10	9.a	12:22-34	10.k	20:27-40	10.w
1:26-56	2.a	8:11-15	9.b	12:32-34	10.i	20:41-44	13.p
1:57-80	3.a	8:16-18	13.b	12:49-53	5.f	20:45-47	11.f
2:1-21	2.b	8:19-21	13.j	12:57-59	10.c	21:1-4	10.y
2:39-52	2.c	8:22-25	8.a, d	13:6-9	11.e	21:5-6	12.b
3:1-20	3.a	8:26-39	7.b	13:18-19	9.c	21:7-11	12.c
3:19-20	3.c	8:40-56	6.e	13:20-21	9.d	21:12-19	5.e, 12.d
3:21-22	4.a	9:1-6	5.d	13:22-30	10.o	21:20-24	12.c
3:23-38	1.b	9:10-17	8.c	13:31-35	14.c	21:25-28	12.h
4:1-13	4.c	9:18-21	13.l	14:15-24	9.g	21:29-31	12.i
4:14-21	13.g	9:20-22	13.d	14:25-33	5.f	21:32-33	12.a
4:14-30	4.b, 13.k	9:22	14.a	14:34-35	10.b	21:34-36	12.g
4:31-32	13.c	9:23-26	5.f	15:1-7	9.e	22:1-6	14.d, f
4:33-37	7.a	9:27	12.a	16:13-15	10.j	22:7-16	14.g
4:38-41	6.a	9:28-36	13.m	16:16	3.b	22:7-23	14.h
4:41	13.d	9:37-43	7.e	16:16-17	13.a	22:24-30	13.n
5:1-11	5.a, 8.b	9:43-45	14.a	16:18	10.e	22:31-34	14.i
5:12-16	6.b	9:46-48	5.g	17:1-3	10.d	22:35-37	14.k
5:17-26	6.d	9:49-50	7.f	17:3-4	10.h, s	22:39-46	14.j
5:27-32	5.b	9:57-62	5.f	17:5-6	9.c	22:47-53	14.k
5:33-39	10.q	10:1-24	5.d	17:20-25	12.f	22:54	14.l
6:1-5	13.f	10:22	13.e	17:26-29	12.j	22:54-62	14.m
6:6-11	6.g	10:25-28	10.x	17:30-35	12.e	22:63-71	14.l
6:12-16	5.c	11:1-4	10.g	18:1-8	10.m	22:67-70	13.d
6:17-19	7.d, 13.g	11:5-13	10.m	18:9-14	11.f	23:1-25	14.n
6:17-23	10.a	11:14-28	7.c	18:15-17	10.t	23:8-9	13.i
6:27-36	10.f, n	11:16	13.i	18:18-27	10.u	23:26-43	14.o
6:37	10.h	11:29	13.i	18:26-30	5.f	23:44-49	14.p
6:37-38	10.l	11:29-32	11.b	18:31-34	14.a	23:50-54	14.g
6:41-42	10.l	11:33-36	13.b	18:35-43	6.f	23:50-56	14.q
6:43-45	11.a	11:37-41	10.r	19:11-27	9.h	24:1-12	14.r
6:46-49	10.p	11:42-54	11.f	19:28-44	14.b	24:13-53	14.s
7:1-10	6.c	12:1-3	11.c	19:45-46	11.d	24:26-27	13.d
7:18-35	3.b	12:4-7	5.f	19:47-48	14.d	24:44	13.a
7:36-50	14.e	12:8-10	13.h	20:1-8	13.o	24:45-48	13.d
8:1-3	7.f	12:11-12	5.f	20:9-19	9.f	Acts 1:1-11	14.s
8:4-8	9.b	12:13-21	10.i	20:20-26	10.v	Acts 1:12-14	5.c
						Acts 1:18-19	5.h

John	Set	John	Set	John	Set	John	Set
1:1-14	1.a	5:16-18	13.f	10:21-30	9.e	15:18-21	5.f
1:4-9	13.b	5:16-23	13.c	10:24-30	13.d	15:18-27	5.e
1:6-8	3.a	5:24-30	12.h	11:1-3	5.c	16:1-7	5.e
1:15-18	4.a	5:35	13.b	11:1-4	6.e	16:23-27	10.m
1:19-28	3.a	6:1-2	6.a, 13.i	11:38-44	6.e	17:1-5	13.e
1:29-34	4.a	6:1-15	8.c	11:45-54	14.d	17:24-26	13.e
1:35-51	5.a	6:14	13.i	11:47-48	13.i	18:1-3	14.j
1:40-45	5.c	6:16-21	8.d	12:1-8	14.e	18:1-14	14.k
2:11	13.i	6:26-32	13.i	12:7-8	14.a	18:12-14	14.l
2:13	14.b	6:31-35	9.d	12:12-19	14.b	18:15-18	14.m
2:13-22	11.d	6:35-46	13.l	12:17-18	13.i	18:19-24	14.l
2:18-19	13.i	6:47-59	14.h	12:20-36	14.a	18:25-27	14.m
2:18-22	12.b	6:60-69	5.f	12:25-26	5.f	18:28-40	14.n
2:18-25	13.o	6:70-71	5.c, 14.f	12:26	13.n	19:1-16	14.n
2:23	13.i	7:23-24	13.f	12:35-36	13.b	19:13-14	14.g
3:1-2	13.i	7:28-29	13.c, e	12:37	13.i	19:16-27	14.o
3:19-21	13.b	7:30-31	13.i	12:37-41	13.g	19:26-27	5.c
3:22-33	3.b	7:40-44	13.p	12:46	13.b	19:28-37	14.p
3:34-36	13.e	8:2-11	10.l	13:1-38	14.h	19:30-31	14.g
4:1-3	4.b	8:12	13.b	13:2	14.f	19:38-42	14.g, q
4:9-26	13.l	9:1-7	6.a	13:3	13.e	20:1-2	5.c
4:34-38	9.b	9:1-33	6.f	13:20	5.g	20:1-10	14.r
4:43-45	4.b, 13.k	9:4-5	13.b	13:21-30	14.f	20:11-31	14.s
4:46-53	6.c	9:16	13.i	13:36-38	14.i	20:23	10.s
4:48-54	13.i	9:40-41	11.f	14:1-31	14.h	20:24	5.c
5:1-15	6.d	10:1-6	9.a, 11.f	14:10	13.c	20:30	13.i
5:8-11	13.f	10:1-10	10.o	14:22	5.c	21:1-14	8.b
5:16-17	6.g	10:14-18	13.e, 14.a	15:1-8	11.a	21:1-25	14.s
				15:18-20	5.d	21:20-24	5.c

About the Editor

David G. Muller, Jr. is an experienced Bible study leader. Educated at Dartmouth College, Stanford University, and the University of Michigan, he is a published Bible historian. He and his wife are retired and live in the Shenandoah Valley of Virginia.

Made in the USA
Charleston, SC
29 October 2016